TE KAUAE TUKU IHO|
INHERITING THE SACRED JAWBONE

Indigenous knowledge holders
re-imagine education

TE KAUAE TUKU IHO|
INHERITING THE SACRED JAWBONE

Indigenous knowledge holders
re-imagine education

Maia Hetaraka

NZCER PRESS

NZCER PRESS
Te Pakokori
Level 4, 10 Brandon St,
Wellington

www.nzcer.org.nz

© Maia Hetaraka, 2024

ISBN 978-1-99-004095-5

No part of the publication may be copied, stored, or communicated in any form by any means (paper or digital), including recording or storing in an electronic retrieval system, without the written permission of the publisher.
Education institutions that hold a current licence with Copyright Licensing New Zealand may copy from this book in strict accordance with the terms of the CLNZ Licence.

A catalogue record for this book is available from the National Library of New Zealand.

Designed by Smartwork Creative

Cover artwork: The fish hook design 'Matau a Maui' depicts the moment Mauī threw his fish hook into the ocean covered with his own blood, representing the optimism, challenges, and giving of self in the pursuit of new knowledge.
© Poutama Hetaraka
Images on p xiii supplied by the author.

Contents

Preface	vii
Acknowledgements	xi
He kaumātua	xiii
Papakupu | Glossary	xiv
Chapter 1 Introduction	**1**
The research premise of Te Kauae Tuku Iho	2
Tēnei au: Writing myself in	8
Chapter 2 Research design	**13**
Te kāhui kaumātua: The participants	15
Tikanga and methods	17
Titiro ki te taumata o te moana: Tauparapara as a tool for analysis	19
Chapter 3 Mā ngā rangatira kia kore koe e whakarerea	**29**
Rangatira will ensure we are not scattered in the wind	29
He Whakaputanga and Te Tiriti o Waitangi: Transformative Te Tai Tokerau narratives	33
Chapter 4 Te tohunga	**43**
Te pūkōrero ō Te Warihi Hetaraka	43
Connecting deeply to mātauranga Māori	60
Te kauae runga: Knowledge that is earned	62
Te kauae raro: Knowledge all have the right to	70
The importance of early economic relationships	75
Knowledge: A highly prized commodity	76
Mātauranga Māori meets print literacy	79
Ma te Atua tātu e manaāki: May God guide and protect us	84
Chapter 5 He toa, he toa!	**91**
Te pūkōrero ō Hori Parata	91
Legislating education for Māori	110
Māori and British law	111
The Education Ordinance Act 1847	114
Collapse of the church boarding schools system	117
Day schools—an opportunity missed	120
Advancing the colonial agenda through education legislation	122
Land alienation through education legislation	123
Dual (but not equal) schooling	124
Tohunga Suppression Act 1907	128

Chapter 6 Te amorangi	**131**
Te pūkōrero ō Te Aupouri Whautere	131
The philosophical underpinnings of modern New Zealand education	140
Classic liberal education philosophy	142
Liberal-progressive education philosophy	144
Sylvia's powerful imagery	149
Continued Māori resistance and a revolving door of policy change	155
Te Herenga	162
Chapter 7 Te māreikura	**165**
Te pūkōrero ō Janet Hetaraka	165
"Mā wai e kawea taku kauae ki tāwhiti?"	178
Tuakiritanga: Identity	179
Legislating Māori identities	181
A response to the discourse of ethnic politics	183
Chapter 8 Kaumātua re-imagine education in Aotearoa	**192**
Reconsidering relationships in education	193
Relationships with education systems and structures	196
Mātauranga Māori in education—fragility and potential	198
Whānau–education relationships	203
Kaumātua address "success as Māori"	205
Valuing individuality	206
Fostering positive cultural identities	208
A perspective shift on role of educators in enabling success as Māori	210
Know who you are, where you are, and why you are	212
Chapter 9 Te Kauae Tuku Iho	**216**
Rejecting cultural competence, re-imagining education	216
An education strategy targeting Indigenous education	220
Divergent goals and purposes for Western education	221
Te Kauae Tuatahi: Systemic transformation	223
Te Kauae Tuarua: Relational transformation	225
Te Kauae Tuatoru: Transformational knowledge	226
He kōrero whakamutunga	228
References	**231**
Index	**242**

Preface

The foundation of this book is my doctoral thesis (Hetaraka, 2020), which interrogated an education policy designed to support teachers to enable Māori students to experience education success, as Māori. The genesis for that project was my own experiences, and the experiences of my ancestors and my descendants within New Zealand's socio-political and education systems. At the beginning of my doctoral journey, I had an impression that my project would be a herenga, a binding together of numerous information sets to make singular sense of my topic. Indeed, one logical outcome of embarking on a journey is to arrive at a point, a place in space. In learning contexts, arriving at a definitive understanding, an intellectual place in space, is a familiar and reassuring measure of "success". What I have come to realise is that the process I undertook was the exact opposite of a binding together—it was instead an un-winding, an un-tangling of ideas to provide a multitude of changing perspectives that are coloured by their contexts and abstractions.

I have come to appreciate this approach of untangling as an essential te ao Māori perspective—colonial thinking has attempted to convince us of the rightness and superiority of the certain and singular, whereas Māori have always thrived in multiplicity. We never have one story, we expect divergence and variation, we accept that some information might be "more right" than others but rather than silence the "less right" we allow space, we show humility, which enables connection. Knowing this then makes understanding the scope of this work a little easier. I have tried to pinpoint the intended audience for this book—the difficulty of that task now makes sense to me. This book is for researchers. This book is for education professionals, new and experienced. This book is for people with an historical bent. It is also for those who want to contribute to future-facing possibilities. This book is to honour my ancestors, my elders, my children, and my grandchildren. This book speaks of experiences of being Māori and being colonised. It is a book about courage, power, and wisdom.

This book is about people, but it began with policy. As such, the current political landscape is an important contextual feature. Since the research conversations in this book took place, New Zealand has had three changes in government. When this project began, a Labour-led coalition formed the Government. This was followed by a Labour Government that implemented significant policy changes, particularly in education and health, which included a Māori health authority, and a refreshed national education curriculum that included Aotearoa New Zealand Histories along with big shifts in the way the curriculum was to be delivered. Under the Labour Government led by Jacinda Ardern, it appeared that New Zealand was on the brink of a level of maturity that would allow us to realise the aspirations of generations of Māori—to learn the histories of our country and therefore come to understand each other and ourselves more deeply.

The potential for change was unprecedented and there was a feeling in education of excitement, trepidation, and resolve to do better. It felt like we were braced to jump—exhilarating but also a little scary. The 2023 election saw the drawn-out formation of a right-wing, National-led coalition with ACT and New Zealand First, who took 6 weeks to form a Government and barely 2 weeks to repeal some of the most transformational and world-leading laws established by Labour. The first of the education policies to be scrapped were sex and sexuality education from the Health and Physical Education curriculum. We currently wait for the education manifesto from the new Education Minister, but reverting to narrow, assessment-focused, one-size-fits-all-type approaches to education seem eminent. Survival of the history-making Aotearoa New Zealand Histories Curriculum seems slim.

It felt as though we were on the brink of real change, we were poised to educate the next generations of New Zealanders about themselves, their places, their identities, and their excellence. This was to be the generation that would leave the battle of injustice based on racism in the past, they were to be a generation who would not have to fight so hard to be valued, they were to put their energies and efforts into solving new and exciting challenges. Instead, we prepare yet another generation of our children to march. The difference is that we now have allies who refused to be ruled by illogical reasoning and imagined fear. I hope one day that we have matured enough as a nation to make this work irrelevant, that it will simply be a record of aspects of our complex and sometimes troubled relationships. For now, though, it is as relevant to our current context as it was to our tūpuna who led the way in envisioning and navigating toward a mutually beneficial and shared future as a diverse and unified nation.

Acknowledgements

Māia e te tipua. Māia e te tawhito. Māia e te kāhui o ngā Ariki!

To my kāhui kaumātua, Te Warihi Hetaraka, Hori Parata, Te Aupouri Whautere, and Janet Hetaraka. You have been present throughout this journey to advise, challenge, and support me. I have said many times that I have little to give you in return for the wealth of knowledge you have willingly entrusted to me. I only hope that I have represented in my words your dignity and integrity, without removing your humanity. We have so much to learn not only from your wisdom, but also from your pain and frustration. It has been important to me to ensure that the essence of your whakaaro is reflected here. Through you I have felt the guidance of our tūpuna and I have done my best to listen.

To Professor Katie Fitzpatrick and Professor Melinda Webber. Your encouragement and enthusiasm to see my thesis made into a book means the insight of kaumātua will be accessible and useful to a wider audience. I respect the wisdom each of you so generously share with me and so many others, I appreciate your friendship, and trust you wholeheartedly. I am beyond grateful for having both of you on my team. E mihi kau ana ki a kōrua.

My extraordinary family have been my drivers, my number one supporters and more often than not my sounding boards. You have spent hours babysitting so I could study/read/write, and you've quietly accepted having to put fun times on hold. Mum and Dad, Gary and Sandra, so much in our lives wouldn't happen without you—kore he kupu, engari ko te aroha mutunga kore. Our whānau wānanga, my awesome siblings and sisters-in-law, Dan and Rach who brought us all back together, and all of our amazing babies. You will see my takes on lots of our wānanga topics woven throughout this work, thank you for the rich discussions, and the food!

Boydie, always you are there with your smile, your support, and a high five. You've kept our household ticking, the kids fed, me fed, everything clean, and you always keep us warm. My beautiful girls, Justice-Te Amorangi, Aorangi Te Haua, and Pounamu-Maurea. You have been caught up in this journey with me for much of your lives, and (while you complain about lots of things!) never have you complained about my work. Even in the summer when I ignored you and didn't leave the kitchen table, you didn't complain. Even when slime tricks, and sunset selfies, and dance-offs were put on hold, you still didn't complain. I hope you know you are my motivation. I am immensely proud of the way you all take on life, with your heads high and your lights shining bright. This work is for you and for my mokopuna, Kahikatea and Kokowai.

Ki a Sandra raua ko Uncle Buster, nā kōrua i okioki ki te ao wairua, ki te whakaminenga o ngā tūpuna, haere mai, haere. Ki a koutou taku whānau, aroha mutunga kore. Tēnei au e tū whakaiti ana i mua i a koutou. Hara mai te toki a Haumi e, hui e, tāiki e!

He kaumātua

Janet and
Te Warihi Hetaraka

Hori Parata

Te Aupouri "Buster" Whautere

Papakupu | Glossary

Note: Where a Māori concept is explained in text it may not appear in the Glossary. Where a translation is given in brackets immediately following a Māori word it will not appear in the Glossary.

aho	thread, cord, string
aho tapu	sacred thread, sacred cord
amorangi	priest, leader
Aotearoa–New Zealand	Aotearoa is often used as a noun throughout the book, whereas New Zealand is often used as an adjective (for example: New Zealand society)
ariki	highest ranking person/group in traditional Māori society
aruhe	fern root
hapū	sub-tribe, pregnancy, pregnant
Hawaiki	name of our ancestral homeland
Hine Ahuone	First Woman
hinengaro	human intelligence
Hine-Nui-Te-Pō	Great Woman of the Darkness (formerly Hine Tītama)
Hine Tītama	Dawn Maiden (daughter of Tane and Hine Ahuone)
hongi	greeting by pressing noses
hui	a gathering, a meeting, a discussion
ira wāhine	female essence
iwi	people, tribe
kanohi ki te kanohi	face-to-face
karakia	prayers, incantations
kare-ā-roto	object of affection, emotions, inner feelings

kaumātua	plural: oldest living generation; singular: elder, old man
kaupapa	foundation, surface
kawa	shortened form of kauae runga, esoteric/spiritual knowledge
kāwanatanga	governance
kōrero	to speak, talk
mana	prestige
mana i te whenua	territorial authority/rights, power from the land, power of the land
mana Māori	Māori autonomy, Māori rights, Māori authority
mana tuku iho	inherited prestige
Māori	Indigenous person/people of New Zealand
mataāpuna	highest ranked tohunga
mātauranga	knowledge
mātauranga-a-iwi	knowledge specific to a tribe
Māui	Polynesian ancestor
mokopuna	grandchildren, grandchild
noa	without restraint
No hea koe?	Where are you from?
Pākehā	New Zealander of European ancestry
pōrangi	crazy
poupoua	to establish, to entrench, to embed
pūkōrero	narrative, research conversation
rangatira	chief, chiefs
rangatiratanga	sovereignty, self-determination
Te Tai Tokerau/Tai Tokerau	Northland, New Zealand.
tamariki	children
Tane-Nui-ā-Rangi	name of an ancient ancestor
tāngata whenua	Indigenous people
tangata whenua	Indigenous person
tapu	sacred

tauparapara	proverb with hidden meaning left for future generations
tawhito	ancient
te ao Māori	the Māori world, including Māori worldview
te iwi Māori	the Māori people
Te Moananui-a-Kiwa	the Pacific Ocean
tika	correct
tikanga	set of values and beliefs that guide/govern what we do
titiro	to watch, look, observe
tohunga	medium between divine and human knowledge
tūpuna	ancestors
tupuna	ancestor
tūrangawaewae	place of origin, ancestral home
unaunahi	carving design of Ngāti Wai, fish scales
uri	descendant/s
wairua	spirit, soul
wairuatanga	spirituality
whakairo	to carve, carving
whakaiti	humble, humility
whakapapa	genealogy
whakapono	faith (not necessarily religious faith)
whakarongo	listen
whakatau	process of welcoming, to settle
whakatauākī/ whakataukī	proverb, proverbial saying
whakawhanaungatanga	process of relationship building
whakawhiti kōrero	discuss, consult
whānau	family, including extended family
whanaungatanga	relationships
whenua	land, placenta

Chapter 1

Introduction

According to Meyer (2008), "we must develop new theories from ancient agency so we can accurately respond to what is right before our eyes" (p. 217). Te Kauae Tuku Iho refers to knowledge inherited from tūpuna. As knowledge flows over the jawbone, it passes from one generation to the next. This knowledge, ancient and changing, developed over generations, forms the foundations of the material for this book. Although contemporary environments and circumstances are vastly different from those of our ancestors, the same conceptual frameworks and knowledges can still be employed to inform research, by critically engaging with the theories left to us by our ancestors. Linda Tuhiwai Smith (2005) explains that marginalised communities, such as Māori, are utilising new research approaches and come with new challenges to research. I venture that the foundational worldview of this book is not new; it is an ancient conceptual framework applied to modern contexts and issues.

With a very broad sweep I will venture that there are many differences between non-Māori teachers and Māori people. One area where I do see a similarity is the sometimes suspicious way both groups view research. A critical theorist (Gibson, 1986) warns that, for many, the word "theory" implies a disconnect from the real world. I've wondered if this is a cause of suspicion for many. If so, this book is designed to convince those who see a disconnect between theory and the real world that the leap between the two is not so great. Many ancient Māori oral accounts illustrate the inherent connection between theory and the real world that my tūpuna understood long before the advent of what is known today as critical theory. Traditionally, the theory of the Māori academy, evident in oral and symbolic representations, was integral to the everyday practicalities of life, and the environments in which Māori lived.

The research premise of Te Kauae Tuku Iho

This book is the product of research that relied on the perceptions of my elders and ancestors in order to challenge the Western worldviews that have controlled academic discourse, maintained power relationships, and fragmented Indigenous knowledges (McKinley & Smith, 2019). The conceptual framework of the research project is inherently Indigenous, it utilises Indigenous knowledge systems that encompass science, philosophy, and knowledge production (Dei, 2011), validating their power and pertinence in addressing modern challenges facing Indigenous peoples. Engaging Indigenous elders who hold specific Indigenous knowledge and perspectives has become essential to the overall framework, and to the findings presented in this book.

The research project investigated select Ministry of Education policies intended to enable Māori to experience education success, as Māori, in English-medium contexts, with a focus on the initiative *Tātaiako: Cultural Competencies for Teachers of Māori Learners* (Education Council New Zealand, 2011). *Tātaiako* is a document specifically for teachers of Māori learners across English-medium early childhood, primary, and secondary education. *Tātaiako* is a resource intended to support relationships and interactions between education professionals, students, and whānau. I had a strong sense that the Māori cultural competencies reflected in this document appeared to silence a range of social, political, and educational challenges inherent in modern New Zealand. *Tātaiako* provided a catalyst for me to investigate what achieving Māori cultural competence involves in a practical sense, especially within the context of New Zealand's history of colonisation. This study, therefore, rejected the idea that education professionals can use Māori cultural competence to support Māori education success, as Māori, without first embarking on a critique of New Zealand's socio-political and historical injustices.

Central to the cultural competencies is the notion that Māori achieve education success "as Māori". Even brief initial discussions with kaumātua and whānau highlighted discrepancies in alignment between Crown-led notions of cultural competence and the thoughts, beliefs, and, importantly, the knowledge of Māori who strongly and positively identify as Māori. While *Tātaiako* is a document that provided a starting point for this project, Māori voices and experiences provide the central focus. The research project was not solely interested in policy; rather, it was concerned with the ecology in which education policies reside, and the effectiveness of that structural framework to enable genuine, positive, educational advancement for all students, and particularly for Māori students.

Shields et al. (2005) argued that pathologising practices in education—such as deficit theorising—remove individual teacher accountability for cultural deficiencies, and assign blame to schools, and students, without an examination of the role of the social environment. The research project sought then to thoroughly examine the impact that social, historical, and political environments have on education policy, practice, and teacher perspectives. A key argument is that the New Zealand education system in its past and current manifestations is severely deficient in its ability to deliver on its own objectives to ensure Māori experience education success, as Māori (Education Council New Zealand, 2011; Ministry of Education, 2013a).

The research assumed the New Zealand English-medium education system continues to be biased toward Pākehā knowledges that prevent Māori from participating equitably in all aspects of society (Bishop & Glynn, 1999). I argued that these biases prevent the lives of all students, not just Māori, in English-medium education to be enriched by Māori knowledge. The research project therefore aimed to contribute to English-medium understandings of Māori cultural competencies with the intention of strengthening education experiences for all students, which is also the intention for this book.

In 2009, the New Zealand Ministry of Education, in conjunction with the then Teachers' Council of New Zealand (TCNZ), developed an education strategy intended to enable Māori to experience success, as Māori, in New Zealand education. The overarching Māori education strategy began with phase one, *Ka Hikitia—Managing for Success: The*

Māori Education Strategy 2008–2012 (Ministry of Education, 2009), out of which fell *Tātaiako: Cultural Competencies for Teachers of Māori Learners* (Education Council New Zealand, 2011). The Ministry of Education saw this strategy as necessary in "... lifting the performance of the education system ..." (Ministry of Education, 2009, p. 4) for Māori learners. However, it is unclear how the Ministry, through the strategy, is enabling educators to examine the causes of the systemic failure they have identified. The Ministry continues to grapple with system shifts across the education sector to enable success for Māori, evident in the continued work stream *Ka Hikitia—Ka Hāpaitia* (Ministy of Education, 2023).

An analysis of *Tātaiako* (M. Hetaraka, 2019) raises questions such as whether the strategy had the capability to enable education professionals to challenge an education system that has historically privileged all things Pākehā at the expense of Māori achievement, identity, and mana (Bishop & Glynn, 1999). Central to this is the deep and located knowledge of kaumātua. The role of those who hold and protect profound cultural knowledge is fundamental to this book, and to breathing life into the aspiration of Māori learning as Māori, as these knowledge holders are people who live "as Māori". They understand and live Māori cultural values and practices and therefore have important insights to add to the notion of Māori cultural competence. This book is one tool to support aims that education students, professionals, policy makers, and school communities may have to understand the hopes and dreams of kaumātua for education in Aotearoa. The intention of this book is to also strengthen understandings about how Indigenous knowledge keepers perceive the education system, and the future of education for Māori, as Māori, within an English-medium education system.

The alignment between the educational aspirations of those who live as Māori and an education system established, designed for, and delivered through European worldviews, has been a long-standing interest of mine as someone who has experienced both te ao Māori and Western forms of education and frameworks. The perspectives of Indigenous knowledge holders from Te Tai Tokerau are a focus of this book, and I pay particular attention to the responsibility the New Zealand education system has to fulfil Māori educational and cultural aspirations as a Te Tiriti o Waitangi[1] obligation. Accordingly, the research that informs this book engaged kaupapa Māori, Indigenous critical pedagogy, and decolonising methodologies in order to effectively draw on the deep narratives of kaumātua to further our understandings about the complexities of Māori educational aspirations and realities. This work is intended to contribute to the development of more cohesive relationships between those who live as Māori, and the education system.

A central theme in this book is my interest in what Henare (2010) describes as the rangatira-to-rangatira relationship between rangatira Māori and the Crown. While Māori have been undermined and marginalised by prejudicial laws, policies, and social "norms" (Walker, 2004), I have never personally felt the subordination of somebody shattered by colonisation. I have felt anger and overwhelming grief at the injustice my people have suffered and which they continue to suffer. I have witnessed and experienced the de-humanising power of negative statistics. But I am not subordinate. I descend from ariki and rangatira. I also descend from Pākehā convicts, seafarers, and entrepreneurs. I am in the fortunate position of never having felt a sense of confusion or shame about who I am or from whom I descend. My tūpuna Māori were powerful beyond question; my non-Māori tūpuna were brave and tenacious. This is my inheritance.

Te ao Māori in contemporary society, whether it be tikanga, reo, or mātauranga, will always be contextual and complicated. By way of explanation, my experience of being Māori is simultaneously simple and complicated. I grew up on ancestral lands throughout Te Tai Tokerau amongst local and national hapū and iwi leaders. While we did not have much money, as children we lived a happy, rural life. My parents used their access to the resources of the land and the sea, combined with the practical resources so often evident amongst women with very little money, to sustain us. While I can empathise with and imagine

---

1 The te reo Māori treaty is referred to throughout as "Te Tiriti o Waitangi" or "Te Tiriti"; the English language draft is refered to as "the Treaty of Waitangi" or "the Treaty"; when neither is specified "the treaty" is used. These differentiations are not applied to references or quotes.

what others' experiences might be, my experience of being Māori is not only positive, but also empowering.

However, I belong to a culture that has been colonised, so there are also competing tensions and complexities. I was brought up, and continue to live, in a society founded on colonisation. I grew up on ancestral lands that my parents either rented from Pākehā or squatted on. We survived financial poverty because my parents were resourceful. They engaged in an age-old barter system utilising resources from the environment and their own skills. In our current political and social circumstances, it is now virtually impossible to sustain a financially poor family in this way. Under today's fishing laws (in particular the Fisheries Act 1996), which criminalise aspects of the traditional Māori barter system, my father would more than likely have criminal convictions for taking part in what we call manaakitanga, and for providing for his family. I grew up around people who were engaged in the all-consuming task of demanding an end to injustice at the hands of our colonisers. These were not people broken by colonisation. These were powerful, confident leaders. While I live in a colonised society, mine has never been a mental or spiritual colonisation (Thiong'o, 1986). This is but one of the complex realities of living as Māori in a contemporary nation state.

I did not grow up in two worlds, nor have I grown up on the margins of society (Smith, 2005), even though being Māori and poor in this country might be perceived as such. I grew up in one world where there was often injustice, misrepresentation, and a lack of alignment between my culture and the laws, policies, and education structures of New Zealand society (Pihama & Lee-Morgan, 2019). This is the space where the tethers of colonisation (Western laws, policies, governments, philosophies) come face-to-face with unwavering mana Māori. This space is complex. The complexity in itself points not to conflicting Māori–Pākehā ideals locked in a binary opposition of two separate worlds, but rather to the existence of nuanced relationships. The nucleus of this book stems from a conceptualisation of a complex relationship, rather than the existence of two separate worlds. This book is also concerned with the social, historical, and political space in which the relationship is enacted.

Experience as an initial teacher educator delivering programmes to both Māori- and English-medium students has fuelled my interest in researching, theorising, and educating about this complexity. Over the years, a range of questions have been raised by me, and by students, about the connections between culture and colonisation, and their impacts on education (Pihama & Lee-Morgan, 2019). Many of my Māori university students have expressed concerns that their English-medium colleagues have not been given the same opportunities they have to explore the history of our country, and to challenge injustices and inequalities that exist between Māori and Pākehā. Some university students in the English-medium pathway have also noticed this and have expressed their desire to learn about wider socio-political issues. There is therefore an opportunity for all initial teacher education students to better understand their position in relation to this complex space, and to be able to safely explore how they might work effectively within it.

There is considerable resistance to the study of injustice in this country. Not all non-Māori resist, however; in my experience, it is more likely to be non-Māori who do. I suspect this opposition is born of a lack of knowledge and understanding of te ao Māori. Deeper education would ameliorate the discomfort some people feel when faced with the realities of our history. My experience as an educator of adult students pursuing a career in education has at times shocked me; for example, for many students, the whakatau at the beginning of the academic year is their first experience of being in a Māori context. It is perplexing that an adult can go through their entire education in a country apparently founded on Māori–Pākehā biculturalism, and yet never experience a Māori context such as this. This has caused me to seriously question the nature of our education, social, and political systems.

My positionality in the research project underpinning this book deviates from and resists the traditional Western research practice of pretending neutrality and objectivity in order to achieve perceived validity (L. Smith, 2012). Jones (1980) argued that responsible education research can be achieved when researchers acknowledge the impact of their own assumptions and values on the research subject.

Tēnei au: Writing myself in

Elabour-Idemudia (2011) describes positionality as the identity of the researcher in relation to the group being researched. I believe it is important to clearly present my position in relation to research for two reasons. First, identifying "no hea koe" (where you are from) is an inherent part of tikanga Māori. Establishing the history, tūpuna, and environment one is bound to helps to clarify one's perspective—literally and conceptually. Once this has been ascertained, lines of communication and understanding can begin to be established between parties. The second is that, in proclaiming my position, I am attempting to resist Eurocentric research practices that have historically claimed objectivity and universality to "prove" that Māori are inferior (Cram, 2001).

Gibson (1986) questions claims that conventional scientific research is value-free and factual. Such claims are problematic in the study of the nature of humanity when, as Gibson further argued, no social fact can be value-free. Writing myself into research and into this book is a statement that this research is located in my cultural perspective, is influenced by my political motivations, and is coloured by the realities of my lived experiences and the experiences of those who have gone before me. In this sense, exposing my values connects to tikanga Māori that considers an introduction of self not as a descriptive profile, but rather as a clear exposition of whakapapa, presenting genealogical lineage as well as aspects of the socio-political history of that lineage. The systematic consideration and reflection on my experiences and analyses of the experiences of others provides a culturally located and informed view of the topic.

My whakapapa links me to many iwi throughout Aotearoa. I also have Jewish, Scottish, and French genealogy. All my grandparents were born at the dawn of the 20th century. My Jewish–Māori maternal grandfather, George Simōn, left school at the age of 12. My Māori paternal grandfather, Wiki Te Pirihi (Wiki) Hetaraka, exited the Western education system at 6 years old after barely 1 year of schooling. My Scottish maternal grandmother, Edna Simōn (nee Veitch), was my only grandparent to attend high school. She left school as a 15-year-old to nurse her dying mother, and to serve tea to the professors of Otago University. Despite having not been particularly well served by the education system, all my grandparents were intelligent, literate by both narrow and broad definitions (M. Hetaraka et al., 2023), and all worked every day of their lives to raise and educate their large families in both te ao Māori and in the swiftly encroaching Pākehā world.

The Western education system they experienced was a smaller imitation of the British education system. Certainly, for Wiki, the idea of Western schooling was an optional novelty—a curiosity of the Pākehā that had little to do with the realities of his rural and very Māori life. The legends of early Western education in Whangaruru, the rural Northland settlement that is my tūrangawaewae, tell of Pākehā teachers who were perceived by local Māori to be limited in intelligence, but a great source of entertainment. Even the acts of cruelty perpetrated by these early educators of the Pākehā system are remembered with mirth, partly because their teachings and pedagogical practices were so far removed from the realities of the students they sought to "educate" that my people can do nothing but laugh at their patronising ways. Yet, in a way I suspect is repeated in many other small Māori communities, these educators were still treated with kindness and manaakitanga by the families who struggled to see the logic in the processes and practices of schooling.

In front of me I see a system that put a dunce hat on my father's head and taught him to sing racially charged and demeaning songs. I see a system that made it compulsory for my mother to learn Latin, and only allowed her to access her own culture as a history topic on "the Maoris", as though we were already extinct. I see a system that allowed a school to shatter my enthusiasm and excitement for education as a 6-year-old by actively discouraging my uniqueness and identity as Māori. Like many other young Māori children, school was not a place I enjoyed, even though I was considered by their standards a high achiever and (after the school I attended as a 6-year-old) had excellent teachers whom I loved. The obstacles I faced in education were not the relationships I had with my teachers or my own abilities, it was the relationship I had with the education system. Even as a small child I intuitively knew that something was amiss with school. I had a sense that school didn't like me very much. I believe that most days my parents understood this, so I spent more time in my father's carving shed than I did at school.

Behind me I have my eldest daughter who has already completed her formal education, having graduated from university with conjoint Bachelor of Laws and Bachelor of Arts degrees, with my two younger daughters engaged successfully in the education system at primary and tertiary levels. My daughters are proudly Māori and are achieving "as Māori". But my daughters are also instinctively aware of a faultline that is present in education and in wider New Zealand society. They have not always been able to name the forces, but they are aware that, as Māori in New Zealand society, they face experiences that are not always equal or equitable to those of their non-Māori peers. For me, Western education or schooling for Māori is not a "topic" I can study theoretically from a safe and objective distance. It has impacted on my grandparents, my parents, on me, and now I watch my children navigate their way through it. It is my greatest hope that the challenges my grandchildren will face in education won't include racial and cultural discrimination.

While I position myself in the marginalised group that formed the basis of the research project underpinning this book, I must also acknowledge my relative privilege within that group (L. Smith, 2012). I have negotiated and survived the education system, and now work in the same system that continues to marginalise many of my people. I also acknowledge that my whakapapa on both sides of my family remains intact and accessible, which also privileges me. Webber et al.

(2013) maintain that in terms of racial-ethnic identity, biological division continues to be common, and powerful in its consequences. For many Māori, biological connections through whakapapa are a cornerstone identity marker. On my mother's side, my whakapapa goes back to Takitimu, who travelled from Hawaiki carrying a cargo of tohunga (Ihimaera, 1986) charged with ensuring the continuation of the ancient academy of Hawaiki in Aotearoa.[2] My Pākehā whakapapa travels back to Europe and also tells of long journeys on sailing vessels carrying old traditions along with hopes and dreams to be pursued in a new world. My father's whakapapa can be traced to Māui, the common ancestor of the people of Te Moananui ā Kiwa. The line from Māui can then be followed to the inception of the universe. My father's whakapapa disrupts the colonial myth that would have us believe no "full-blooded" Māori remain, therefore justifying aggressive assimilation processes. His very existence poses a powerful challenge to the rationalisation of ethnic domination on the grounds of biology (Webber et al., 2013).

I am in the privileged position of walking into the future with an uninterrupted chain of whakapapa at my shoulder. As an Indigenous person who lives in a colonised society, I have a suspicion that this sense of identity is an exception, rather than the rule. I believe this grounding in whakapapa, reo, and tikanga, along with the sense of self-worth and purpose that this knowledge breeds, has contributed as much, if not more, to the education of my family than the Western education system we have all endured.

I am a descendent of many iwi, with particular links to Ngāti Wai, Ngā Puhi, Ngāti Paoa, Ngāi Tai, and Tainui in the north, and Ngāi Tahu and Ngāti Māmoe to the south. I also include myself in the group referred to here as "Māori". With this in mind, it is important to clarify that I acknowledge the diversity of tāngata whenua and value the multiplicity our culture engenders. I also maintain that, as a diverse group, we have experienced the effects of colonisation in similar ways, and

---

[2] For many iwi Māori, the waka their people travelled to New Zealand in is part of their genealogy an d history. Specific waka transported specific people and goods. A waka used to carry people of rank (tohunga, ariki, rangatira) did not transport any other goods; they had a support waka to carry supplies and other people. Takitimu was a waka used only to transport tohunga and ariki.

we may have similar goals and aspirations for the future of our culture. Some of the information I have relied on for this project has come directly from my own tūpuna, and from those responsible for the protection and transmission of the knowledge of my hapū and iwi. I refer to Māori in this book to denote tāngata whenua, not with the intention of assuming homogeneity.

Chapter 2
Research design

The New Zealand education system has successfully maintained and reinforced hegemonic beliefs that Māori bodies of knowledge are subordinate, partially through the use of a predominant positivist discourse (Bishop & Glynn, 1999; M. Hetaraka, 2008). The key research question shaping this project focuses on the implications and application of a specific education policy. However, the social and political educational space in which the policy is located is vital to a deeper understanding of the learnings from this research. The purpose of this approach is to question, challenge, and resist an education system that has taken for granted Pākehā perspectives (Penetito, 2011) at the expense of Māori through racist academic discourse. The sociopolitical and historical analysis in this research demonstrates the racism that positioned Māori as intellectually and socially inferior, a position so prevalent in education as to hinder potential understanding by the education system, and educators, of Māori knowledge and knowledge transmission. Challenging these perspectives must take place at multiple levels within education—social, political, curriculum, and policy spaces. This cannot be achieved by employing the same traditional, Western methodologies and methods that have used research as an instrument of colonisation.

As discussed in Chapter 1, this project grew in part out of an interest in the document *Tātaiako* (Education Council New Zealand, 2011). However, issues of culture, identity, politics, social justice, and power relationships are also central to this inquiry. To investigate these aspects, and to clearly identify how they interact with and impact each other, the research project had two defined parts. The first provided an overview of the *Tātaiako* document in order to establish what the document intends to achieve. It also utilised a kaupapa Māori document analysis approach that applied te reo Māori and tikanga Māori to critique *Tātaiako* (M. Hetaraka, 2019). Providing a kaupapa Māori analysis problematises the document, as well as the notion of Māori cultural competencies, because it illustrates some vast differences in cultural understandings. The kaupapa Māori document analysis also questions how education has arrived at cultural competence as a strategy to empower Māori to experience education success as Māori. Presenting a kaupapa Māori document analysis provides a platform from which to investigate wider socio-political, historical, and educational issues impacting the document.

The second part of the research, and the focus of this book, centralises the voices of Indigenous knowledge keepers, the kāhui kaumātua participants. In order to maintain the integrity of kaumātua voices, each pūkōrero is represented separately as a research conversation, followed by analyses linked to key themes within each pūkōrero. The analyses following the pūkōrero help to contextualise the educational space that *Tātaiako* occupies. Individually, the pūkōrero of kaumātua examine issues of identity, politics, culture, social justice, and power relationships. A brief explanation of the research design is provided here for context.

Key research question:

Kaumātua are holders of mātauranga and expertise in te ao Māori. How do their perspectives, expectations, and aspirations for the education of their children and mokopuna align with English-medium education concepts of cultural competence and education success for Māori, as Māori?

Three related aims of the project:

1. To explore the perspectives of key informants recognised as holders of mātauranga, tikanga, reo, and tirohanga Māori in order to consider their views of issues relating to Māori cultural competencies.
2. To investigate the history of education for Māori to contextualise the policy document *Tātaiako* (Education Council New Zealand, 2011) and better understand how education has arrived at aspiring for Māori cultural competence.

3. To explore the relationship between Māori cultural understandings and English-medium education to progress current thinking about achieving education success, as Māori.

Te kāhui kaumātua: The participants

Engaging kaumātua in this and many other contemporary projects is a way to begin healing some of the damage Māori have experienced in Western education by privileging and taking for granted the validity of Māori voices (L. Smith, 2012). There is a focus in education on understanding the relationships, perspectives, and connections between students, teachers/schools, and whānau (Bishop & Berryman, 2006) in order to enable education success for Māori students. This has provided the education space with valuable insights. However, when considering the issue of education success for Māori, as Māori, it is vital to engage with those members of our communities who have already succeeded, as Māori. The views of people who use and protect immeasurable cultural knowledge must specifically be included in conversations about the challenges and possibilities of activating Māori cultural identity in education. This work centralises the voices of kaumātua, with the purpose of reversing some of the mistrust we have of our cultural knowledge and the wisdom of our elders, a mistrust taught to us by Western education (Battiste, 2008).

The kāhui kaumātua for this project are Te Warihi Hetaraka (Ngāti Wai, Tainui, Ngāi Tai, Ngāti Paoa, Ngā Puhi), tohunga whakairo and my father; Hori Parata (Ngāti Korora, Ngāti Wai), prominent kaumātua, long-serving iwi member, and my uncle; Te Aupouri Whautere (Ngā Puhi), another esteemed kaumātua, iwi member who has served in education for many years, and my uncle; and Janet Hetaraka (Ngāi Tahu, Ngāti Māmoe), journalist, mediator, and my mother. My choice to include in my thesis participants who are related to me had to be fully justified and explained to the University of Auckland Human Participants Ethics Committee, who questioned my relationships to the participants. All of these people have served their iwi and hapū tirelessly for many years across political, social, environmental, and education sectors. They are people who identify as Māori, who operate within Māori frameworks, they have the reo and tikanga of our people, and each of them holds specific knowledge and perspectives of great value to this and many other projects.

Personal relationships have given me privileged access to those whose advice is sought constantly—locally, nationally, and internationally—as Indigenous leaders with mātauranga tuku iho. My long-standing personal relationships with these people ensured that I was able to gain access to them, but also meant that I bore additional responsibility for accurately reflecting their views, while not exploiting these relationships and therefore contributing to the practice of cultural knowledge mining (Battiste, 2008). The participation of this group has enriched this study, as well as the body of knowledge around Māori epistemologies, identity, and the relationship between Māori and Western education.

A wider kāhui kaumātua had been consulted at the inception of this project in an advisory role. They agreed verbally to form an advisory panel for the project, and subsequently those who became kaumātua participants also gave informed written consent to be research participants. They were also consulted to offer names of other potential kaumātua participants; however, time and resources put limitations on the involvement of all suggested potential participants. It is important to note that the term "kaumātua" is used in the traditional, non-gender-specific sense of "kau" being no or to negate, and "mātua" parents; so, a group of people whose status is defined by their having no parents, they are the eldest living generation. This definition includes both men and women (women elders are also defined as "kuia"). This particular kāhui kaumātua consists of three men and one woman; the ratio of men to women is due completely to happenstance, not design.

Meyer (2008) argues knowledge is "... the by-product of slow and deliberate dialogue with an idea, with others' knowing, or with one's own experience with the world" (p. 221). Choosing kaumātua as key informants in this project was a purposeful design decision. As the oldest living generation, they have experiences beyond the rest of society since they have lived through many of the issues we continue to face. They also hold a depth of cultural knowledge, yet they are often not specifically targeted in education research. To develop deep understandings around the topic it was essential to investigate knowledge developed over a long period of time by kaumātua.

The specific targeting of kaumātua to progress understandings around the topic and aims of this project is related to the holistic nature of the research problems, and, therefore, the holistic solutions we must search for. This is succinctly defined by Battiste (2013) who argues, "Aboriginal and Indigenous elders are also aware of the eroding environment and land base that will require new ways of thinking and interacting with the earth and each other" (p. 24). Kaumātua participants in this project have long experiences in interacting with environments and people within Māori frames. Their perspectives and solutions are derived from their living as Māori, they understand the crisis we live in as Indigenous peoples, they feel the urgency for reform (Battiste, 2013). Their contributions impact our physical, spiritual, and cultural wellbeing, as much as they do our intellectual endeavours. The solutions kaumātua perceive are based on ancient ways of knowing and interacting with the universe. In contemporary times, these may appear new, simply because many of us have been disconnected from our ancient knowledge.

Tikanga and methods

The involvement of kaumātua in the research project impacted on the methods I relied on to gather information, and on ways I dealt with ethical considerations. I drew on tikanga Māori to inform my qualitative research approach, which ensured the safety of the knowledge being shared and generated, as well as the people involved. More about tikanga Māori as a qualitative approach can be found in the chapter "Tikanga Māori as research methods" (M. Hetaraka, 2023).

I chose to use the word "pūkōrero" to describe the research conversations with kaumātua. The use of pūrākau as a method in Māori research is strong (Lee, 2008), as it is an innovative approach "... where Māori voices and narratives are articulated through a uniquely Māori approach" (Pihama, 2016, p. 109). While kaumātua shared their stories through pūrākau, in presenting the research conversations I wanted to keep the words of the kaumātua as they spoke them, and found it difficult to present their words as pūrākau in narrative form. My biggest dilemma was that, in my use of pūrākau, I felt I was applying my own assumptions and changing the words of kaumātua. Having consulted with the kaumātua, I settled on using the word "pūkōrero"—"pū" being the original source, "kōrero" discussion. By using pūkōrero I could present their stories as much as possible in their own voices, then analyse their words and behaviours, whilst also making their stories "… available for interpretive analysis by others" (Kovach, 2009, p. 132).

During the research process, participants and I (in numerous configurations—myself and all participants, myself and some participants, and participants on their own) had many hui to continue discussions, to clarify specific aspects of mātauranga, and as advisory sessions. Ongoing consultation with the kāhui kaumātua is an essential part of the process in allowing them to have control over their intellectual property, and to ensure my safety in the research space.

Listening and observation are also used as a method to generate research material, as well as a protection mechanism. Meyer (2008) argued that, "I am empirically configured by my past, and my senses and body were the tools and recording devices through which I retrieved and stored data" (p. 220). This describes the use of listening and observation as a method in this project. The long whanaungatanga relationships I have with participants allowed me to listen to and observe them in many cultural contexts, over many years. Activating what I have recorded over the years allows the pūkōrero to be contextualised and not fragmented, because they are conversations located within a broader context of experience (Kovach, 2009).

Potts and Brown (2005) challenge researchers to strive to be perceptive, "… to pay attention to what we are in the midst of" (p. 255) in order to recognise and respond to opportunities as they arise. Deep listening, observation, and paying attention have been utilised as methods to generate research material to help me moderate my own interpretations, as a way of "checking in" with the information. As Kovach (2009) highlights, participants share their stories in relation to questions in direct, and indirect ways. Observation, listening, and paying attention facilitated my interpretations and analyses of direct and indirect stories, as well as of texts.

Kovach (2005) argued "dreams have long been a source of knowledge in Indigenous writing" (p. 31). Another method, and analysis tool that was used in this project is wairuatanga, in the form of intuition, listening to higher energies, dreams, and kōrero of tūpuna. Listening and observing have been discussed here as essential to developing contextualised stories. For Māori, and other peoples, listening occurs not only on a physical plane, but some of our most important lessons also come from listening to higher energies, listening to our dreams, listening to our environments, and hearing the voices of our tūpuna. Often when I have sought advice from the kāhui they have responded by literally asking me what my gut says. Wairua intervened on many instances during this process, the message was not always immediately clear, but, when wairua intervenes I am learning to listen. This is not always easy in an environment that tends to rely heavily on the mind and intellect. However, when I listen and feel, my perception eventually becomes clearer.

Titiro ki te taumata o te moana: Tauparapara as a tool for analysis

> **Te Oati o Kawiti**
>
> *E te whānau, i te pakanga ahau ki te Atua i te po, heoi kīhai ahau i mate.*
>
> *Nā reira, takahia te riri ki raro i o koutou waewae.*
>
> *Kia ū ki te whakapono, he poai Pākehā koutou i muri nei.*
>
> *Waiho kia kakati te namu i te wharangi o te pukapuka, hei konei ka tāhuri atu ai.*
>
> *Kei takahia e koutou, ngā papa pounamu a o koutou tūpuna e takoto nei.*
>
> *Titiro ki te taumata o te moana.*

> **The Oath of Kawiti**
>
> *My illustrious warriors and people, I had war with the Gods during the night, but I survived.*
>
> *Therefore, I call upon you to suppress war under foot.*
>
> *Hold fast to the faith, for the day will come when you will become like a Pākehā boy.*
>
> *Await therefore until the sandfly nips the pages of the book,*
>
> *Then, and only then, shall you rise and oppose.*
>
> *Do not desecrate the sacred covenant endorsed by your forebears.*
>
> *Look beyond the sea, to the transfiguration of the future.*

(Kawiti at Pukepoto after the battle of Ruapekapeka, 1846)[3]

Te Ruki Kawiti (c. 1770–1854) was an influential rangatira of Ngāti Hine and Ngā Puhi during the 19th century. As a renowned fighting chief and brilliant military tactician, he led his people in at least a dozen military campaigns against both the British and other iwi Māori (Hirschfeld, 2017). The "book" in his oath refers to Te Tiriti o Waitangi, which, only 6 years post-signing, Kawiti believed had been severely breached by the Crown (Kawiti's first campaign—related directly to his opposition to Crown breaches of Te Tiriti o Waitangi—was the Battle of Ōhaeawae, 1845). This oath was given to allies of Kawiti at the Ngāti Wai pā of Pukepoto immediately following the battle of Ruapekapeka, giving clear instruction to uphold the mana of Te Tiriti, even under immense pressure. The following discussion is my interpretation of the messages hidden in the tauparapara. Some of this interpretation has been developed as a result of wānanga and research but is not a universal "truth" amongst the iwi of Tai Tokerau. I first acknowledge that there may be other equally valid interpretations of the tauparapara.

---

3   English translation by Erima Henare.

The war with the gods Kawiti had in the night refers to the decision he and other Tai Tokerau chiefs of Te Wakaminenga[4] had made to embrace the Pākehā gods through Christianity. The British had taught Māori that Sunday was a day of tapu. Yet, as Kawiti and his people observed the Sabbath, Ruapekapeka Pā was taken by the British. Kawiti's incomprehension of a people who disregard the teachings of their own gods can be heard in his anguished cry "i te pakanga ahau ki te Atua i te po". His battle with the gods must also have been a battle with his decision to convert to Christianity, a faith that, following this battle, must have appeared to Kawiti to have gods weaker than men. Te Wakaminenga made the political decision to make Christianity the whakapono tuku iho (inherited religion) in 1835 as a way of encouraging an alliance with Pākehā based on one of the most powerful forces in the Māori context, wairuatanga. Kawiti survived his battle with his new Christian gods, not always an achievable feat when dealing with atua Māori. He woke with great clarity about what the future would hold for his people under the regime of colonisation at the hands of a people who disrespected the power of their own gods.

Following the battle of Ruapekapeka in 1846, Te Ruki Kawiti foresaw that, through force, Māori would become poai Pākehā, like a Pākehā boy. Opposing colonial physical, spiritual, and mental force quickly became the burden of the northern tribes (Hirschfeld, 2017). As Kawiti predicted, Crown military forces rapidly wrested resources from Māori, British laws and social norms would desecrate Māori social and spiritual structures, and Western education would invalidate an education system that had served Māori for centuries.

Poai Pākehā is a term unique to Tai Tokerau, referring, on one hand, to the devastating processes and effects of colonisation on Māori. It suggests that, through colonisation, we would not become Pākehā, but Pākehā boys—child-like versions of the "father". Poai Pākehā is a succinct Tai Tokerau way to describe many of the power relationships and

---

4   Te Wakaminenga/Te Whakaminenga/Te Wakaminenga o Nu Tireni is known in English as the Confederation of United Tribes of New Zealand, a group of powerful rangatira Māori responsible for many of the early political interactions and decisions between Māori and Pākehā during the 19th century. Te Wakaminenga is discussed more fully in Chapter 3.

dynamics forced on Māori through colonisation. However, poai Pākehā also refers to Māori resistance and resilience in our relationship with the British Crown. From this perspective, poai Pākehā is a term used as a challenge to colonial forces, and a reminder that the young learn and then, as Kawiti predicted, they rise up, they oppose. Kawiti intricately makes poai Pākehā as much about patience and maintaining rangatiratanga, as it appears on the surface to speak of forced subordination.

My understanding of Te Oati o Kawiti does not come from an analysis of history books, it is part of my lived experience. Histories such as this were discussed often throughout my childhood, they were kept alive by iwi and hapū, they are the histories of kaumātua who have participated in this project. Te Oati o Kawiti is used to frame the analysis of pūkōrero in this project for two significant reasons. First, for the content of the oath. Each kaumātua participant drew in some way or another on the wairua of Kawiti's oath during our conversations. Te Tiriti o Waitangi was present in each discussion. So too was colonisation. The most important presence was the strength and power of Kawiti's instructions. For this reason, the pūkōrero of kaumātua are prefaced by an investigation of He Whakaputanga and Te Tiriti o Waitangi.

The second reason for using Te Oati o Kawiti is the example it provides of the function tauparapara have as an analytical tool. Since 1846, Te Oati has served as a marker of an important time in our history, and the metaphoric language used by Kawiti has allowed it to be prophetic and aspirational. Tauparapara, karakia, whakataukī often feature in contemporary writing as a modern use of an ancient cultural practice to invoke the spirit and wisdom of the past to inform both the contemporary and the future. This is a way that Māori have for centuries drawn on "the vitality of Indigenous knowledge and its dynamic capacities to solve contemporary problems" (Battiste, 2013, p. 97); this is how taupaparapara can be utilised as an analysis tool.

Throughout the research project, several takutaku and tauparapara were drawn on with the intention of providing a framework to sections of work (in places the words "takutaku" and "tauparapara" have been used interchangeably). Each was selected because of its specific relationship to particular arguments that were made. In this way, the messages of individual tauparapara are significant. However, takutaku and tauparapara have also revealed themselves to be significant in this study as a process, an analytical tool, and a conceptual framework, which is a broad overarching perspective of tauparapara.

As with many Māori words and their related concepts, tauparapara, whakatauākī, whakataukī, and, more recently, karakia have become synonymous with simplistic translations such as prayers, incantations, and proverbs. While each of these words represents different concepts and encompasses meanings in the Pākehā translations, they also represent complex concepts and meanings not easily translatable. In discussing the complexity of transferring the meaning of the word "karakia" into one English equivalent, Te Rangi Hīroa (1982) settles on the word "incantations" as best to describe the vast meanings of the word. Karakia have become known as prayers or incantations and, while karakia are different from tauparapara, there are similarities, one being the limited ability of the English language to describe its meaning satisfactorily.

The word "takutaku" is an ancient form of what many now refer to as "karakia". Tauparapara and takutaku are older concepts that speak to pre-colonial times when Māori theories and epistemologies were taken for granted. The complexities and various levels of information and meaning presented by tauparapara provide a platform from which to utilise ancient concepts, rather than adhering to more recent versions for ease of understanding. I do not intend to provide a succinct definition or translation of the word "takutaku". To do so would only serve to reinforce the perception that understandings between cultures can only be built by contorting one set of cultural meanings to fit another. Such thinking must be disrupted in order to progress the empowering potential of culture in education. What I would rather illustrate is the analytical framework presented by takutaku and tauparapara through an interpretation of their purposes.

Many tauparapara that have traversed and survived the epochs began as premonitions of tohunga, often during times of turmoil. We have examples of ancient tauparapara that precede our arrival in

Aotearoa. Many tauparapara used today are also premonitions revealed during the 1800s. The increase of premonitions during this time evidences the immense social, cultural, and political upheaval faced by Māori. Literally, tauparapara is to cover or camouflage. Tauparapara can be understood as incantations that tell a story in what Hīroa (1982) describes as "double language" (p. 471). They are often prophetic, the meaning hidden until the time it is needed. There is an understanding that those who need the message will be able to decipher it. Importantly, tauparapara continue to survive through time and space because the meanings maintain significance depending on contexts and situations of the people using them.

Takutaku provide an expression of epistemology, Māori worldview, and spiritual connectedness to the universe. They harness the ebbs and flows in energy that sustain life, growth, and progress. Tauparapara also tell stories that can reinforce epistemologies. They are prophetic and often have hidden meanings. In this way, tauparapa provided an approach to analysing information in this project. The stories that each kaumātua shared for this project were given with the intention that I would use the information in some way. By treating the pūkōrero of kaumātua similarly to tauparapara I have been able to make meaning of their stories in holistic and respectful ways over a long period of time.

Kovach (2009) argues that "individuals with the training and experience to inductively analyse patterns were the knowledge-keepers and were highly esteemed" (p. 131). Tohunga had a role in both revealing prophetic tauparapara and interpreting ancient ones. Reverend Māori Marsden (2003) explains that the definition of "tohunga" is not an expert as many translate the word in contemporary times. He argues that the word derives from the root word "tohu" (sign), and refers to somebody chosen by the gods to divine signs. While I am not attempting to elevate myself to the role of tohunga, I am utilising their example of analysing patterns, words, and behaviours in order to make meaning. In this way, using tauparapara as a tool for analysis is an interpretive method, with a level of thematic analysis.

Methods in Indigenous research should allow for interpretive and thematic analysis (Kovach, 2009). Utilising the spirit of tauparapara allows for meaning to be made through interpretation, and by developing themes within broader contexts. By treating pūkōrero like tauparapara I have been able to contextualise kaumātua stories within wider contexts by listening to the words, but also looking for meaning in the wairua of their words. Te Warihi Hetaraka's pūkōrero, for example, carried underlying messages regarding mātauranga Māori and mātauranga tuku iho. His role as tohunga helped me to find that meaning. The pūkōrero of Hori Parata was used in order to contextualise the impact of law-making on Māori education. His background as a soldier and a powerful Māori advocate for justice came through in his pūkōrero and I was able to interpret meaning from this. Te Aupouri Whautere has great concern and care for the individual child within the education system, which allowed me to investigate what it is about modern education that perhaps causes a lack of care and consideration for Māori. The wairua of Janet Hetaraka's pūkōrero was identity, and the role of identity in enabling success for Māori, so her words contextualised identity-discourse in education. Each pūkōrero chapter first presents the words of participating kaumātua, followed by an in-depth analysis of the various themes raised by each.

Tauparapara as an analytical tool enables inductive analysis in that holistic meanings (Kovach, 2009) can be drawn from pūkōrero and from texts. It also allows for inductive analysis as it encourages the researcher to interpret and present "self-in-relation analysis" (Kovach, 2009, p. 131). Western analysis tools typically cause the researcher to extract meaning from interviews and texts, whereas tauparapara forces the researcher to understand contexts, to understand the position of kōrero in relation to history and to the present, it asks the researcher to position themselves in relation to the kōrero in order to make meaning.

A key element of using tauparapara as an appropriate analytical tool is that it allowed me to address issues of power in terms of who gets to make sense of the information (Potts & Brown, 2005). Analysis of information is connected to issues of power and of protection. Applying positivistic analysis tools has the potential to remove power from the people who have given the information, re-package it, then return it in an unrecognisable form. Through tauparapara, kaumātua speak for themselves as individuals and the work is presented as much as possible in their own voice (Kovach, 2009). As a researcher, I interpret or uncover what they have shared in relation to this project. Therefore, as an analysis strategy, I amalgamated participant words and thoughts around questions or ideas they had each addressed as individuals, rather than look for central themes.

Utilising tauparapara as an analysis tool enables me to give kaumātua and their knowledge the respect they are due. Making meaning through listening, interpreting, and feeling the wairua of their messages respectfully, and within broad contexts, has made me consider how they are represented as well as the expectations they have of me as a researcher (Potts & Brown, 2005). Importantly, tauparapara allows me to make meaning of information as it relates to this project, but it also leaves information open to be interpreted by others, such as the kaumātua and their uri, who may also benefit from their own uncovering of hidden meanings.

Under the rules of the Western academy implemented in New Zealand, culture and education have been treated as separate entities. Centralising the voices, aspirations, experiences, and knowledge of kaumātua forms the nucleus of this project, as it has the potential to reimagine education. Kaumātua who agreed to take part in this project have mastered the art of what many Māori refer to as "walking in two worlds". From my perspective, these kaumātua simply walk as whole people in a world that they have experienced, articulated, and theorised according to the knowledge they have of our tūpuna. Coming to understand and utilise their ability to de-compartmentalise culture and education could transform our approach to education in this country.

The modern, conventional education system has taught Indigenous peoples to mistrust not only the wisdom of our ancestors, but also to mistrust our own instincts, inspirations, and creativity (Battiste, 2008). By reclaiming aspects of tikanga to guide ethical interactions, employing whanaungatanga and pūkōrero as qualitative methods, and tauparapara as an analytical tool, I hope to contribute to the transformation of hegemonic power structures within research and education. I also have faith that my own instincts, creativity, and cultural identity can contribute positively to the interpretation and knowledge generation in this project.

A key purpose of decolonising methodologies is objecting to the silencing of Indigenous voices that has transpired through positivist research practices (Denzin et al., 2008; L. Smith, 2012; Thiong'o, 1986). This project addresses issues in education policy and challenges the framework in which the policy is carried out. The inquiry confronts social and educational injustices and the institutional racism that continues to impact on Māori education success, as Māori. Accordingly, the design of this project responded to all of these issues by privileging Māori knowledges. Decolonising methodologies have also been utilised in this research project to challenge Eurocentric biases (Battiste, 2008) that continue to shape education policy and practice.

The design of this research project sought to repair the spiritual, emotional, and physical damage that has been suffered by Indigenous peoples through practices of colonisation (Dei, 2011). It attempts to do so by asking questions that have the potential to challenge the Eurocentric education framework, by emphasising rangatiratanga through the utilisation of mātauranga and tikanga, by validating Māori epistemologies, and ensuring that they inform all aspects of the research process. Absolon and Willett (2005) maintain that "[r]esistance to colonizing research methods involves envisioning and utilizing research methods that better reflect Indigenous world views" (p. 122).

This book centres the voices of the kāhui kaumātua, and much of the discussion draws specifically on Tai Tokerau perspectives, including of the role of rangatira in early political relationships between Māori and Pākehā. What will become evident is the foresight and determination of rangatira Māori to maintain mana i te whenua rights and responsibilities whilst establishing a specific relationship with the British Crown. Tūpuna rangatira gave powerful examples that have been taken up by the kāhui kaumātua in this study, and throughout

Te Tai Tokerau. The Tai Tokerau perspective presented in the following chapter has the potential to provide a foundation for more effective, genuine, and thoughtful bicultural interactions which are as relevant and as urgently needed today as they were 184 years ago. The role of rangatira and the impact of their relationships are also an important pretext to the arguments presented by the pūkōrero of the kāhui kaumātua because it highlights the stark differences between what many Māori believed we were entering into in our relationship with the British Crown, and what eventuated through colonisation as defined by the narratives of kaumātua.

Chapter 3
Mā ngā rangatira kia kore koe e whakarerea

Rangatira will ensure we are not scattered in the wind

A basic definition of the composition of the rangatira "class" in traditional Māori society is ariki (highest of the rangatira rank), rangatira, and tohunga—who were experts in their fields and mediators between the physical and spiritual (Walker, 2004). Terms used to describe this collective are kāhui rangatira or kāhui ariki; they held political power, their obligation was to ensure the unity of their people for purposes of prosperity, as highlighted by the whakataukī in the chapter title. This was a system of governance very different from the democratic system so highly prized in Western societies and therefore difficult to understand if democracy has been held up as correct and superior. Māori are sometimes described as, and sometimes consider ourselves to be, a people of consensus; we certainly do take every opportunity to discuss issues of importance. However, Tai Tokerau elders have defined the governance of kāhui rangatira over lands and people as an authority bestowed upon them by hapū. They were duty-bound to protect the interests of hapū, they had the power over life and death, and their hapū were confident in their authority (Te Kawariki & Network Waitangi, 2012).

Under this form of governance, it was dangerous for hapū members outside of the kāhui rangatira to question political decisions made by rangatira. It was also unreasonable to expect rangatira to engage in consultation with hapū about high-level decisions. These conditions meant we were not a people of consensus, but nor are these conditions indicative of an autocracy; it was a carefully negotiated relationship between the "ruling class" and the people. Patu Hohepa captured the complexities of this relationship in this excerpt from *Ngāpuhi Speaks:*

> The most important thing is that the hapū is the leader of the leaders. The mana of a rangatira could be inherited or bestowed, but the new holder had to exercise it appropriately and fully, or they would desert him: 'It's the hapū who are the chiefs of the chiefs.' (Te Kawariki & Network Waitangi, 2012, p. 30)

Colonial forces have distorted the intricacies of traditional Māori social order, so in contemporary times only a semblance of these social structures (and our traditional conceptions of them) remain. We no longer have a kāhui rangatira, nor do we live according to the kawa and tikanga that once served us and bred confidence and trust in such leadership. However, kaumātua were always the knowledge holders and held esteemed positions in Māori society (Walker, 2004). In many ways, kaumātua have now taken on the role of rangatira, especially in terms of mediating between Māori and Pākehā cultural frameworks for the success and prosperity of hapū and iwi. The wisdom of kaumātua will ensure our cultural identities are not scattered in the wind.

All kaumātua involved in this study argued emphatically that the key to success for Māori students is the positive reinforcement of their cultural identity. However, they also all agree that reinforcing positive Māori identity within the context of colonisation is problematic. The kāhui kaumātua all evoked, and were driven by, their belief in the power of He Whakaputanga and Te Tiriti o Waitangi as essential to contextually understanding colonisation and knowing, as Hori Parata puts it, who we are, where we are, and why we are. The context they operate from is markedly different from the framework of colonisation in which the education policies and practices of this country have been developed (Bishop & Glynn, 1999). Alarmingly, the political discourse of New Zealand's National-led coalition Government disputes the role cultural identity, including language, plays in academic success, with little evidence to support their proposed policy changes or to dispute the large body of national and international evidence that substantiates the perspectives of the kāhui kaumātua involved in this study.

Key to the contexts of this kāhui kaumātua are their perspectives and experiences of colonisation, and the strength inherited from their tūpuna. Tai Tokerau narratives of colonisation contextualise and provide a foundation from which to discuss the potential of Māori cultural competence in English-medium education settings. This chapter will establish the foundations of the Tai Tokerau context as well as define the position of the kāhui kaumātua involved in this project. The position and shape of Māori cultural competencies is impacted by three realities: New Zealand's colonial history; Māori–Pākehā relationships initiated prior to Te Tiriti; and Māori–Crown relationships post-1840. Aspects of each of these will also be analysed in this chapter in order to raise questions about the implications and implementation of Māori cultural competencies against the backdrop of our history of colonisation.

Conceptualising Māori–Pākehā relationships as a binary opposition, featuring a superior Western civilisation contrasted against a subordinate, uncivilised Māori culture, does not provide a base from which to find solutions to current educational, economic, and social crises faced by Māori. What might be helpful is recognising the valiant, forward-thinking, purposeful actions and courage of our tūpuna in their interactions with one of the most powerful nations on Earth during a period of unprecedented social change. The horrific injustices of our subsequent colonisation are inadmissible. However, recognising and evoking the power and intelligence of our tūpuna could potentially hold the key to recapturing our pre-colonial mana to determine and control our futures. The legacy of strength and courage left to us by our tūpuna is an inspiring narrative to inform our current and future interactions.

By investigating new metaphors for relationships at all levels of education, Bishop and Glynn (1999) advocate using the Treaty of Waitangi, and the metaphors inherent in the dual texts. The context presented in this study progresses that thinking away from metaphor and the problematic focus on dual texts (Burns et al., 2024), toward an exploration of the rangatira-to-rangatira relationship (Henare, 2010) between Māori and Pākehā pre-colonisation, which was particularly evident in Te Tai Tokerau. Greater understanding of this relationship may transform perceptions that Māori–Pākehā relationships are built on the foundation of subordinate Māori and dominant Pākehā identities. This chapter emphasises Tai Tokerau perspectives of colonisation, and particularly the expectation held by many northern rangatira that they were entering into a political relationship based on equal mana between parties. This chapter will highlight that colonisation was not necessarily a process that "happened to" Māori as though we were submissive bystanders, but that many Māori were agentic and politically involved, not in our own colonisation, but in attempting to establish relationships that would preserve our rangatiratanga in a swiftly changing social climate.

A great deal of evidence was produced by hundreds of claimants in the Ngā Puhi Nui Tonu claim to the Waitangi Tribunal.[5] Much of this evidence has been collated in an independent report, *Ngāpuhi Speaks*, by Te Kawariki and Network Waitangi, commissioned by kaumātua and kuia of Te Tai Tokerau. This chapter relies heavily on *Ngāpuhi Speaks* (Te Kawariki & Network Waitangi, 2012) because it presents the arguments and perspectives of many elders and leaders of Tai Tokerau, including members of the kāhui kaumātua involved in this research. While referencing conventions have prevented me from referencing individuals throughout this chapter, it is important to know that a Te Kawariki and Network Waitangi reference is representative of a range of northern elders and/or leaders. My analyses of these narratives highlight that the Māori–Crown political relationship in Te Tai Tokerau pivots around three critical points in history:

- the rangatira-to-rangatira relationship northern Māori sought with the Crown
- He Whakaputanga
- Te Tiriti o Waitangi.

These moments are crucial because they contribute to the spirit that the kāhui kaumātua operated from throughout this study and have implications for conclusions to this project.

---

5   Wai 1040 is also known as Te Paparahi o Te Raki, and the He Wakaputanga/He Whakaputanga claim.

Ritskes (2011) highlights the transformative power of Indigenous knowledges and history. Employing historical realism principles, which are inherent in kaupapa Māori research, but also in Māori and Indigenous ontologies, are a means by which the present can be informed—not by positivist truths, but by lived and embodied Indigenous experiences—to transform the present and to project into the future. The transformative power of Māori naming and resisting colonial forces is evident in present day contexts. The following discussion identifies specific and purposeful actions of our tūpuna in their interactions with Pākehā during the earliest contact in our shared history as a nation. It is intended that transformative power be drawn from the examples left to us by tūpuna in their exertion of rangatiratanga and political sovereignty over our own people, knowledge bases, resources, and economic power.

He Whakaputanga and Te Tiriti o Waitangi: Transformative Te Tai Tokerau narratives

In terms of trade, politics, religion, and Western education, northern Māori have had a long relationship with Pākehā. According to the tribes to which I whakapapa in the north, this relationship, from its infancy, was intended by our chiefs to be a rangatira-to-rangatira relationship. Since the time of Hongi Hika (c. 1780–1828), our relationship was with the English sovereign (Henare, 2010) not with settlers, or a settler government. Even in contemporary times, many iwi and hapū in Tai Tokerau conceptualise the Māori–Crown relationship as being one between our people and the Royal family, tracing back to the relationship forged between Hongi Hika and King George IV (1762–1830) (Te Kawariki & Network Waitangi, 2012). The relationship was forged in the physical meeting of two rangatira and is therefore personal, implying that it is far deeper than a symbolic, "on paper" type relationship. The benefits of such a relationship are greater due to the reciprocation of mana; however, the involvement of personal mana in any relationship also means wounds are much deeper and retribution more complex if betrayal occurs.

In his pūkōrero, Hori Parata shares some of the history of his tupuna Mahanga, sometimes referred to in history books as Moehanga.

Mahanga was the first known Māori to travel to London in 1805, and on his return was renowned for talking endlessly to any interested party about the fantastic things he had witnessed in the land of the Pākehā King (Jones & Kaa Jenkins, 2017). The Māori perspective, which Hori Parata shares, is that Mahanga, on his return to Aotearoa, became an informant to tohunga and rangatira such as Hongi Hika.

Both Thomas Kendall (1778–1832), one of the first missionaries in New Zealand between 1814 and 1822, and John Nicholas (1784–1868), a young adventurer and prolific writer who accompanied Anglican missionary Reverend Samuel Marsden (1765–1838) on his evangelic mission to New Zealand in 1814 (Nicholas, 1817), have been recorded as being in awe of Hongi's mechanical genius (Cloher, 2003). They were especially impressed in Hongi's art of stocking guns—a very new technology for Māori—with no prior training (Cloher, 2003). What early Pākehā were probably unaware of was that rangatira and tohunga had been informing themselves of European practices and arts through young men such as Mahanga. Māori international travellers during the 19th century became a source of information, which helped to quickly build Māori understandings of the workings of Pākehā (O'Malley, 2015).

By 1820, Hongi Hika was one of the most powerful chiefs in Te Tai Tokerau. As a disciple of the war god Tūmatauenga, Hongi was a military genius possessing both an intelligent mind and, ironically for a man of war, a gentle nature. Cloher (2003) gives a thorough sketch of Hongi's character, including a record of British military officer, Richard Cruise, who documents his impression of Hongi when he came on board the *Dromedary* in 1820 as a "... fine looking man ... one of the most powerful chiefs in the Bay of Islands, and its bravest and most enterprising warrior, he was by far the least assuming of those who had been permitted to come on board ..." (Cloher, 2003, p. 78). What is less well documented in written historical accounts are the motivations and resolve of rangatira such as Hongi in their dealings with Pākehā.

Our chiefs had been collecting information about Pākehā since the early encounters of the 1700s. By 1820, they had also obtained nearly 20 years' worth of research about important British political and social structures through adventurous men such as Mahanga.

The alliance that Hongi intended to make with King George IV when he set out on his expedition in 1820 was informed by insights from young international travellers. Hongi was interested in establishing a political alliance with the King and the King alone because, according to his analysis of the information at hand, King George was the only member of British society holding a rank equal to his own (Te Kawariki & Network Waitangi, 2012).

Hongi and George were perceived by Māori as rangatira of equal standing who, because of Hongi's actions, had a personal relationship. This relationship was perceived to be so powerful to the people of Te Tai Tokerau that it formed the basis for the development and signing of He Whakaputanga and it carried them through to the signing of Te Tiriti o Waitangi. It even caused the people of Te Tai Tokerau to declare war on Germany in 1914 before the New Zealand Government, because "Ngā Puhi would hold to its covenant to the King of England" (Te Kawariki & Network Waitangi, 2012, p. 77). According to rangatira, the covenant obliged Tai Tokerau to provide support to our partner Britain in their time of need. Even as recently as 2024 Ngāti Kahu evoked this relationship in their request to King Charles III to intervene over what they describe as violent attacks on Te Tiriti o Waitangi (McCaull, 2024). Hongi and George's direct relationship is key to the narrative of colonisation for Te Tai Tokerau and, to this day, continues to fuel an insistence on the honouring and continuation of our rangatira-to-rangatira relationship.

He Whakaputanga of 1835 was a document produced by rangatira Māori (in the form of Te Wakaminenga) as the first written representation of the tatau pounamu (sacred covenant), established between Hongi Hika and King George IV (Te Kawariki & Network Waitangi, 2012). In many hapū "tatau pounamu" is a person, often a female, responsible for ensuring the amalgamation of two hapū or iwi according to agreed terms. It is significant that He Whakaputanga and Te Tiriti o Waitangi are recognised as a tatau pounamu, as they are written documents given high-ranked human status by hapū and iwi. The words and thoughts of rangatira were recorded in He Whakaputanga by Eruera Pare Hongi (c. 1815–1836), a nephew of Hongi Hika chosen by his elders to learn to read and write in both Māori and English (Te Kawariki & Network Waitangi, 2012). The purposeful choosing of young people, including Eruera Pare Hongi, Tuai (c. 1797–1824), and Hone Heke (c. 1807–1850), to take part in Western literacy learning, was carried out in the same way elders chose students for whare wānanga. It was the foresight of our tūpuna who, by providing an education for young people from two cultural contexts, were hoping to ensure that iwi would be positioned strongly to take advantage of the changing social circumstances they faced.

He Whakaputanga signalled internationally that New Zealand remained in the sovereign possession of the rangatira of New Zealand represented by Te Wakaminenga, who declared absolute "… Rangatiratanga o to matou wenua a ka meatia ka wakaputaia e matou he Wenua Rangatira …" (para. 1) ["authority and leadership of our country and declare them to be prosperous economy and chiefly country"].[6] Te Wakaminenga also declared their interest in developing an alliance specifically with the British Crown by sending a copy of the declaration to the King of England along with "… to matou aroha …" (para. 4) ["our love"] in order to show "… ka atawai matou, ka tiaki i nga pakeha e noho nei …" (para. 4) ["our friendship and care for Pākehā who live on our shores"]. He Whakaputanga confirmed our rangatiratanga to the world. The document stated that Māori retained political control in New Zealand, to which the British sovereign agreed, and nobody ever challenged its legitimacy (Te Kawariki & Network Waitangi, 2012).

He Whakaputanga confirmed the mana and sovereignty of rangatira and was the basis on which many rangatira in Tai Tokerau later signed Te Tiriti o Waitangi. Without a question of a doubt, they would retain their rangatiratanga, as well as their rangatira-to-rangatira relationship with the Crown (Te Kawariki & Network Waitangi, 2012) in the signing of Te Tiriti o Waitangi. It is also crucial to note that rangatira agreed to the terms of Te Tiriti o Waitangi, not to the terms of the Treaty of Waitangi. My elders rarely use the terms "Te Tiriti" and "the Treaty" interchangeably as is often done in New Zealand society. In the first instance, it is highly unlikely that any rangatira at the time

---

6   Translations based on that of Dr Mānuka Hēnare https://nzhistory.govt.nz/media/interactive/the-declaration-of-independence

were at all cognisant of the English draft now known as the Treaty of Waitangi—they were presented only with Te Tiriti, they understood Te Tiriti, and it was this document they agreed to. The notion of "versions" and the subsequent confusion they caused is a modern-day invention that only serves to attempt to justify unjustifiable acts (Burns et al., 2024). According to rangatira signatories there was one version; they debated the merits and challenges of the proposal, but they were not confused about what they agreed to in their signing of Te Tiriti. The betrayal that quickly followed was not caused by confusion or difference in text—it was quite simply an horrific duplicity by agents of the Crown.

Many of our elders do make a clear definition between the two because the Treaty ceded sovereignty of New Zealand to Queen Victoria, a clause that evidence suggests did not exist on 6 February 1840 (Fletcher, 2022), or if it did, was certainly not made clear to chiefs at the time. On the other hand, Henare (2010) maintains that rangatira believed Te Tiriti represented a mutually beneficial relationship between Māori and the Crown. Henare (2010) argues that had rangatira had the slightest suspicion that they were ceding their mana and sovereignty to the Queen through Te Tiriti, the consequences for all Pākehā in Aotearoa at the time would have been violent and swift.

Many Māori have long been politicised and conscientised to our situation under Pākehā rule, due largely to the scrupulous government of rangatira, who worked to maintain mana i te whenua and our mana tāngata amidst huge structural upheaval. The 1840 signing of Te Tiriti o Waitangi is a history somewhat known by New Zealanders. I am hesitant to describe it as a "well-known" history due to the non-Māori records of events that continue to dominate understandings of the history of our country. Much work is being done by many people from diverse backgrounds to balance the historical landscape of early contact in this country. However, the relationships, thinking, and politics of Māori pre- and post-Waitangi is history still largely unknown in this country.

The Treaty of Waitangi, and in some social groupings Te Tiriti o Waitangi, are known as New Zealand's founding documents. For many, the signing is the nucleus of the political relationship between Māori and the Crown. However, for Tai Tokerau iwi, this alliance began in the early 1800s under the astute political foresight of rangatira. The awareness of strong political leadership informed by observations of Pākehā concepts and behaviours is illustrated by the existence of Te Wakaminenga in Tai Tokerau as early as 1808 (Te Kawariki & Network Waitangi, 2012). This group consisted of rangatira and tohunga from within Tai Tokerau who were concerned with the welfare of their iwi amid the growing number of ungoverned and unruly Pākehā settlers. Te Wakaminenga had been in consultation and action as an organised political body since the early 19th century.

The existence of a systematised political group made up of rangatira and tohunga from a number of influential Tai Tokerau hapū during this period is central to this study. It provides a specifically Tai Tokerau context of our colonial history which foregrounds the power and responsibility of rangatira. The kaumātua participants in this project, along with many other kaumātua in the region, continue to draw on that strength to guide their current work. It is also important because this history has the potential to transform the way we understand current issues and relationships. It is this narrative, which centralises Māori intelligence and knowledge, which can provide useful pathways forward in education. Recalling the rangatira-to-rangatira relationship our tūpuna insisted on establishing with the Crown, not with settlers or a settler government, should form the basis of current resistance to regressive National-led coalition policies—the likes of which Aotearoa has not seen for almost a generation.

The histories of the group, Te Wakaminenga, and the document He Whakaputanga are powerful Te Tai Tokerau narratives that have driven the lives of many of my people. These narratives are emphasised in the pūkōrero of the kaumātua who have participated in this work. These narratives reinforce the intelligence, strength, and foresight of our tūpuna rangatira and provide the context in which Te Tiriti o Waitangi was subsequently signed. To atomise Te Tiriti o Waitangi and to view it as a document disconnected from He Whakaputanga is to negate both its meaning and the conditions under which rangatira agreed to sign it.

For many years, the history of Te Wakaminenga and He Whakaputanga has been overshadowed by records that contribute its establishment and the declaration to the foresight of the British Resident[7] to New Zealand, James Busby (1802–1871). The dominant historical perspective is that the declaration of Te Wakaminenga was designed by Busby as an attempt to thwart other international interests, mainly French and American, in the colonisation of New Zealand (Orange, 1987). Non-Māori histories centre James Busby and he is represented as the convener of the gathering of chiefs on 28 October 1835 when He Whakaputanga was signed (Orange, 1987). This cements the incorrect belief that both He Wakaminenga and He Whakaputanga were Pākehā initiatives established, on a whim, by the British Resident concerned with protecting the unsuspecting "Natives" from international threats to their sovereignty.

The Māori historical record of the signing of the He Whakaputanga contrasts sharply with the dominant (Pākehā) narrative. Many northern Māori view He Whakaputanga not as an isolated event driven by British urgency to obstruct other imperial powers from securing a foothold in New Zealand in 1835, but within a broader context over a longer period of time. Te Kawariki and Network Waitangi (2012) position Te Wakaminenga as an active political force as early as 1808, and as being responsible for the Proclamation of New Zealand of the same year. The Proclamation is extraordinary in that it saw Ngā Puhi chiefs Hongi Hika and Ruatara (1787–1815), working alongside their traditional Ngare Raumati opponent, Korokoro, as well as with Pākehā (Jones & Kaa Jenkins, 2017). The 1808 Proclamation of New Zealand provides an example of an early model of pan-tribal, Māori–Pākehā, shared rangatiratanga—in contemporary terms, the Proclamation of New Zealand 1808 is the first example of co-governance. The Māori history of Te Wakaminenga also attributes them with the establishment of an alliance with the British Crown, with Busby's appointment as British

---

7   British Residencies were political offices representing the British Crown prior to a country being formally annexed.

Resident in New Zealand, and with the development of a flag (known as Te Kara) as a sign of a sovereign nation (Te Kawariki & Network Waitangi, 2012). All these events took place before the signing of He Whakaputanga in 1835.

For northern Māori, the mana of He Whakaputanga is immense. Erima Henare argues that it was "... constructed from the thoughts and intellect of each and every chief" (Te Kawariki & Network Waitangi, 2012, p. 98). It is considered to be truly a rangatira proclamation, containing in its language the depth of Māori thought. The power of He Whakaputanga is still relied on and evoked by contemporary rangatira in Tai Tokerau because of its status as a Māori document to protect Māori interests.

This version of history centres Māori as conscious proactive participants in the development of relationships with international forces. Divergent histories of Te Wakaminenga and He Whakaputanga have had a dual effect on history records. On the one hand, Pākehā versions of events removes the power and control of the shaping of our country from rangatira Māori. It puts us in the background and reinforces the perception that we never were political decision makers in the Māori–Crown relationship. On the other hand, northern Māori have always taken ownership of He Whakaputanga and the context in which it was fostered. It signifies the intentions and actions of our tūpuna to maintain control over a developing alliance with Britain (Te Kawariki & Network Waitangi, 2012). While He Whakaputanga belongs to all Māori,[8] it also reflects experiences unique to Tai Tokerau, and the intentions of our tūpuna with the Crown from the beginning. The Treaty came from agents of the Crown and has, in many ways, come to reflect the poor communication that has marred Māori–Crown relationships.

Both Māori and Pākehā live daily with the consequences of our colonisation. However, the inception story for Te Tai Tokerau is one of strength, of integrity, of courage, and an intense intergenerational belief in the power of chiefly relationships. My earlier tūpuna, and my rangatira of today, were willing allies with their treaty partners, Great

---

8 The signing of high chiefs Te Whero Whero and Te Hāpuku from outside of Tai Tokerau, alongside their northern counterparts, makes this so.

Britain, right up until the Vietnam War. Iwi narratives tell us that the 28th Māori Battalion[9] was named for the 28th day of October 1835, the day the first representation of the covenant between kings—He Whakaputanga—was signed. Māori communities sacrificed many of their strongest members to the war effort, to be recognised in our own country as equal citizens (Ngata, 1943), and in the case of many A Company soldiers from Tai Tokerau, to honour the relationship between the British monarchy and Ngā Hapū o Tai Tokerau, first forged by Hongi Hika and King George IV (Te Kawariki & Network Waitangi, 2012).

During the 1960s and 1970s there was confusion for many Māori about the role, relevance, and distinction between Te Tiriti and the Treaty. First, the Treaty was labelled a fraud. Then there were debates about having the Treaty ratified in order to force the Crown to meet their responsibilities. At a meeting of the Māori Council in Waitangi in 1979, Janet Hetaraka, then a journalist, recorded esteemed Ngā Puhi rangatira Tā Himi Henare warning the Council that any law could be repealed, which would pose an irreversible threat to Te Tiriti, and subsequently to Māori rights according to our agreement with the Crown. Tā Himi reminded the Māori Council that Te Tiriti o Waitangi was an honourable document signed between two peoples. One group of people had honoured their side of the agreement and were waiting for their partner to reciprocate. Tā Himi led the country in a new cry, to honour Te Tiriti. His prudence and knowledge of Pākehā law ensured that Te Tiriti o Waitangi remained outside of New Zealand legislation so as not to be repealed or amended. His son, Erima Henare, movingly told the Crown: "Every cemetery here [in the Tai Tokerau region] has kaumātua and kuia with gravestones. They went to their graves waiting for you to come. And they all say, 'Honour Te Tiriti o Waitangi'" (Te Kawariki & Network Waitangi, 2012, p. 77).

In his covering letter to the Constitutional Advisory Panel (2013), Erima Henare reminds us that:

---

9   The 28th Māori Battalion (also known as Te Hokowhitu a Tū) was formed in 1940 as an infantry battalion of the New Zealand Army. The Māori Battalion was made up of five companies based on tribal regions throughout New Zealand.

> ... Te Tiriti o Waitangi was never intended as an instrument for the alleviation of grievances. Rather, its purpose was more forward looking, guaranteeing and entrenching certain rights to those representing tino rangatiratanga ... and establishing new rights for those representing kawanatanga ... Te Tiriti o Waitangi is about the past, but has also always been about the future. (p. 2)

To wrest back some of the innovative intent of Te Tiriti o Waitangi, perhaps Māori could reclaim the Māori–Crown relationship established almost 180 years ago. This is the context from which the kaumātua in this project, and many others, operate. They have fanned the embers of He Whakaputanga and Te Tiriti o Waitangi that have been inherited through generations, stubbornly refusing to extinguish the powerful actions of our ancestors. First and foremost, a central message from this kāhui kaumātua is that enabling all New Zealanders to understand and operate from this context has the potential to transform social, political, and educational frameworks in Aotearoa New Zealand.

The following chapters first provide the pūkōrero of kaumātua before presenting an analysis of their words and issues they raise. Across the pūkōrero, an argument is developed that the current education strategy for Māori has a particular history located in Pākehā dominance, which has perpetuated unequal achievement for Māori, differential treatment, and Pākehā privilege. The pūkōrero of kaumātua and the associated analyses will argue that arriving at Māori cultural competence is a result of an education system that has swiftly and relentlessly worked at actively removing the cultural structure and mātauranga of our people. The kāhui kaumātua raise questions about the validity of a strategy that calls for educators with varying degrees of Māori cultural knowledge to enable education success for Māori, as Māori, in an environment that has actively sought to fracture Māori identities. Tracking the whakapapa that emerged in each pūkōrero is essential in understanding how education has arrived at cultural competence as a solution to continued systemic problems in education.

Chapter 4

Te tohunga

Te pūkōrero ō Te Warihi Hetaraka

At the heart of what has become known as the Hīhīaua Precinct is "The Shed". Hīhīaua is a small peninsula deep inside the Whangārei Harbour. The land known today as Hīhīaua is reclaimed; however, the awa and the original site of Hīhīaua has had great cultural significance to local hapū through generations since the time of the ancient tribe Ngāti Manaia. A large, unkempt former boat-building shed is now Te Warihi's carving shed. At the time our conversation takes place, every inch of the dusty, old building is filled with carvings, waka, logs, whalebones, and countless artefacts from our rohe that have been entrusted into Te Warihi's care. The shed is messy, almost shambolic, but it has become a magnet to schools, to researchers, to a multitude of organisations, to people on personal journeys of discovery. All are drawn to the energy of the place, and of the people, particularly to the energy of this man, who was cloaked as tohunga by the final traditional rangatira of Te Tai Tokerau, Tā Himi Henare, before I was born.

A few hundred metres past the shed is an award-winning stone sculpture carved by Te Warihi and internationally renowned stone sculptor Chris Booth. The piece was produced to herald in the new millennium. Te Warihi chose the location at the end of the Hīhīaua Peninsula amidst scoffs from the public that nobody would ever see it, as at the time the peninsula was unused wasteland. He insisted that the historically important location would once again become important to the people of Whangārei. Today, the Hīhīaua Peninsula is alive once again with people, art, education, and the living stories of our ancestors. The Waka and Wave sculpture is important to this story as it depicts a stone waka being almost engulfed by a wave. The waka represents Māori. The wave is the wave of colonisation that has attempted to overwhelm the waka. However, the waka remains intact. The prow of the waka pierces through the crest of the wave, symbolic of Māori abilities to overcome the negative effects of colonisation.

Many people mistakenly describe Te Warihi as an artist. His own definition of his work is that of an historian. The Waka and Wave sculpture is part of the recording of our contemporary history. The energy and message of the sculpture that returned people to Hīhīaua can be felt as I nervously prepare to commence what has begun to feel like a very formal interview with my father, the tohunga. Instinctively, I know he wants to give me answers that he hopes will add value to my project. What I am hoping for is the spontaneous wisdom that comes when he just talks. I have had thousands of these conversations with my father. He often speaks in metaphor with layers of meaning; when a particular meaning is needed, it suddenly becomes clear—this is what I hope will come from this discussion.

He begins by reciting a karakia to focus us both and put us into a space that will facilitate an exchange of knowledge. My first question is about his mokopuna. The sense of emotion I feel as I ask what he considers education success for his mokopuna takes me by surprise. I realise I have never specifically asked what he wants for his grandchildren, who include my children, and the gravity of this stirs a love that aches in my chest.

His response corresponds with his actions and treatment of his mokopuna and reflects the tikanga by which he was raised. He was named after the last, pre-Iron-Age tohunga whakairo of Ngāti Wai. He was then given specific educational experiences and networks that enhanced his inherent talents. His individual excellence was recognised from a young age and was then carefully nurtured by a wide network of elders. With this in mind, his desires for his grandchildren are not entirely surprising:

> I think education success for my mokopuna will depend entirely on their individuality, on their aspirations, and not on our aspirations ... for me, the value that they gain from their education through the system is that they take with them their whakaaro Māori, their

tikanga Māori ... if they did that then I think it will enhance their education. For me success is doing it to the best of their ability, rather than the expectations of others.

While his focus on the individual child doesn't come as a surprise to me, it does spark an interest in his thought around the concept of the "group" that dominate many contemporary beliefs about Māori, particularly in relation to the idea of education success "as Māori" that is encouraged by the Ministry of Education. I ask if he believes that education success "as Māori" is the same as being a successful Māori. The first part of his response refers to the confusion caused by the break in cultural understandings many Māori have experienced in contemporary New Zealand:

... the word 'Māori' ... even around 'Māori culture' has changed drastically from the time even when I was being raised ... Families these days live by a different standard to Māori raised in the village ... although it's changed, they still have a semblance of their Māori whakaaro with them, except they can't identify it as being that, that's in my view. For example ... many of them that we meet do things instinctively and they are not sure why they do things that way. Then when I explain the principles of our culture ... they can relate to that concept ... but initially they couldn't identify why they did things that way.

The second part of his answer pinpoints the complexity many Māori face in reconciling education success with Māori cultural understandings, which often appear to be at odds with each other:

... I think for them to succeed through the system, then we are going to ... need our learners to be able to understand where they are coming from in order to nurture them through to their ... appropriate outcomes ... what their aspirations are.

He then goes on to explain the role education has played in preparing students for jobs that may not meet the needs of the learner, or that may not even exist, because their education has focused on a forecasted outcome, rather than on the skills, talents, and aspirations of the individual:

> *Education leads our students to an outcome that is over-saturated. If the outcome of education is that our students are able to get jobs ... that they are able to find meaningful employment, according to the system ... what I mean ... is that it's in that area it reaches a saturation point with over training. So, we have students who ... come out at the end ... and there's no employment to go into.*

Te Warihi was educated during a time in New Zealand where students' employment potential was pre-empted by the perspective of educators. As a young rural Māori male, he would not have been considered for an academic future, he would have been educated in preparation for a trade, as all his brothers had been. The tikanga by which he was raised saw his pathway altered by his elders who had focused on his individuality, rather than leaving him to be educated by a system that did not see him. The response above indicates that, while there have been many changes in terms of choice in education, governmental forecasting focused on the national economy essentially produces the same outcomes as the old practice of syphoning students toward either a future in the trades, or in the professions.

Te Warihi then goes on to discuss the importance of carefully analysing potential future needs to ensure success for all students. His response here also clearly indicates that success for Māori in education must have an endpoint of meaningful employment as a means of economically sustaining ourselves:

> *... success for our students ... and that goes right across the board, is that we identify ... the areas ... growing rapidly ... and ... re-establishing the concept of our culture within our education system in order for them to be directed towards that field of work, whatever that may be.*

This idea of re-establishing Māori cultural concepts within education speaks directly to the problem central to this project and I hope Te Warihi will elaborate on this point. I ask if he thinks Māori cultural concepts should be developed within education. My question is clumsy and does not actually ask what I mean, which is: "Is the system the most appropriate place for these concepts to be developed?" Fortunately, his intuition, and perhaps his deep understanding of me, helps him to decipher my meaning. He discusses what is essentially a task in rangatiratanga and power sharing in terms of finding a solution to the complex problem of re-establishing space for Māori cultural understandings in education:

> ... allowing the appropriate Māori organisations that are established, to carry out that role ... what I mean by Māori organisations, Māori groups, not necessarily coming under any framework of the institutions, be allowed to carry out that function in regards to education of our kids ...

Te Warihi explains one of the ways colonisation has disrupted education for Māori "as Māori" is by removing the role of parents in educating children in their culture:

> The days are gone where ... we used to learn everything about our culture from the way we were bought up by our parents ... the parents of today haven't had the same upbringing ... [students] are not getting [cultural education] at home. The education they get is ... entirely from another culture's perspective, not necessarily ours ...

He then goes on to highlight the role of schools in constricting learning for Māori students by segregating learning into boxes. He refers to my first teaching job in Cambridge where I was charged, as a beginning teacher, to establish a bilingual unit:

> You identified that that project wasn't going to work ... if it was just you focusing on developing it ... for it to succeed the whole staff had to take ownership of it. So that concept of segregating learning within an institution ... needs to change, and it should be compulsory that ... if kaupapa Māori is taught, that everybody comes under that kaupapa Māori programme in order that those tutors receive the appropriate mātauranga or knowledge to reach Māori students. They know they won't be only reaching Māori students but they'll be reaching across to our Pākehā students, Chinese students, Japanese students, and then everybody becomes confident.

The message here is clear. Māori cultural understandings will benefit all students in New Zealand schools, and it is the responsibility of all educators to take part in kaupapa Māori initiatives, not just the responsibility of Māori, or bilingual units, or those interested in Māori education. He further illustrates the detrimental effects caused by segregating learning into "Māori education" and "education":

> ... at the moment it is them and us and we gotta get rid of that. Even the way these schools are set up, these decile schools ... you got what we called a white flight. You know what happened when I was teaching at Bay [of Islands] College, as soon as the Māori numbers came in, you got Māori kids coming from all the schools, then all of the White kids took off to Keri Keri ... and yet we've got the cheek to call ourselves bicultural, what the hell is that about?

The frustration is deep and longstanding. Te Warihi taught at Bay of Islands College in the late 1970s and has seen little change in real, shared responsibility being taken for the education of Māori students since that time. The lack of value placed on Māori understandings in education is also evident in the next part of our discussion:

> It has to be shared across the board ... Education is supposed to touch all aspects of what we do in society. We can't reach it if we are only half trained, we've gotta look at the holistic approach, which includes all forms of mātauranga. You know ... it doesn't take a rocket scientist to figure out that if there was a large pot of gold at the end of Māori education, everybody would be racing for that, they'd be wanting to learn it. But because the pot of gold is at the door ... of the Chinese, the Japanese, the United States, everybody is breaking their necks to learn about those cultures as quickly as they can ... you know everything about all the other places in the world, but you don't know your own country.

We share a laugh over how ridiculous it is that some New Zealanders don't know where Taupō is, let alone how to pronounce it correctly. But the seriousness of knowing our own culture and our own history is ever present. As with many conversations I have had with Te Warihi, Te Tiriti o Waitangi soon makes itself felt:

> Knowing our own. Knowing our own culture, and our [New Zealand] culture is based on the signing of Te Tiriti o Waitangi. That's the foundation of who we are [as New Zealanders], and it's between us [Māori] and the people that we agreed to sign the Treaty

with, and everybody else who comes into this country comes under that kaupapa.

This short paragraph holds profound meaning. Te Warihi uses the words "the people that we agreed to sign the treaty with" indicating agency, critical thought, and deliberate action on the part of our tūpuna. I am yet again reminded of the strength of my ancestors, and the foresight they had to want to protect the interests of their descendants as best they could with the information they had at hand. At this point, I also have to admire my father's diplomacy. Anybody who knows him will testify to his love of unity. But this must not be mistaken as a sign of a "yes" man willing to sacrifice the rights of his people in the name of unity. In his last sentence he clearly puts a pou in the ground. He values the contribution all people make but, in this country, there is a sacred agreement between two people; everybody else comes under the protection of that partnership. A point raised by this kōrero, and often missed by Pākehā-centred commentary about the Treaty, is that Te Tiriti gives non-Indigenous people the right to call Aotearoa home.

This triggers me to ponder the depth of knowledge many New Zealanders have about our own history, and I think about the lack of education many of our teachers have about our history. I ask Te Warihi what skills he thinks teachers might need to adequately educate his mokopuna. I did have a preconceived idea of what his response to this might be, but in true Te Warihi style he first takes a path I hadn't expected, highlighting the significant role of parents in the education of children:

> *... Unfortunately, with the way the system is set up, it focuses only on one aspect of our learning ... it doesn't include the parents. I think with the ... revival of our reo is the realisation that it's no good just teaching te reo at school, it needs to be spoken in the home as well in order for that child to succeed. So that concept needs to go right across the board, right across all of the other subjects as well. In other words, bringing the parents on board so the parents are up to speed with what the children are being taught ...*

This statement reminds us that, as educators, we need to broaden our focus. For children to be educated, we need educated parents. I then point to the problem many schools have in engaging parents. I am aware of many schools working hard to bring parents on board, with varying levels of success. I'm interested to know what Te Warihi thinks might help schools to engage parents better:

> *For Māori I think [it] is gaining their trust, the trust of the parents ... I remember when you were going to school, I was reluctant going into that school situation cos I had a bad time at school. You know, we weren't allowed to speak our reo and I ... put up an invisible wall between myself and that system ... you fullas were lucky that Mum didn't have that problem ... she was raised in the Pākehā world and understood it quite well. So, success in regards to you fullas then, was the balance between what I was taught and what your mum was raised with.*

A lack of trust of schools is still an issue for many Māori families. In my own family circumstances, we had a parent who wasn't afraid of Pākehā systems and had no trouble volunteering for active involvement in school governance or confronting issues in the school environment. Many Māori families have not been as fortunate and are, therefore, now experiencing intergenerational lack of trust of the very education system that has given them a "bad time".

Te Warihi then goes on to explain that, in addition to a lack of trust, many Māori families are disengaged because of the circumstances in which they live:

> *Most of our Māori families these days are tied up with all the negative aspects of the culture we've adopted—or that was forced on us. I'm talking about alcohol, drugs and all those sorts of things that are adversely affecting our people. So those are those social issues that need to be resolved ... and that's beyond education ... simple, it means that we need to go back to the village concept, where everybody becomes responsible, where everybody in that village becomes responsible for the ... outcomes of education and the wellbeing of society itself.*

The notion of the village raising children resurfaces again and I begin to wonder if this is a theme that will recur throughout the interview. I ask how we might strike a balance in providing support for whānau, parents, communities, schools, and teachers, and where whānau who are living in difficult circumstances might get support for their tamariki in schools:

> *Look, for example, at the child being educated by the village ... being raised by a village. Every child goes through that village system ... the only way they can succeed is ... if everybody is on board with the concept. Everybody.*

He proceeds to lay a challenge down for the various organisations in our community to work together more for the benefit of families:

> *... look at the government organisations in this community—we've got social welfare, we've got the police, we've got [Oranga Tamariki], we've got the education system, we've got health. We've got all of these systems, and at the moment they are opposing each other, everybody is scrapping over the funds in order to keep their systems in place. Imagine what'll happen if those bodies united around the wellbeing of a family.*

There had been a commitment from the Labour-led coalition Government and the subsequent Labour Government 2017–23 (elected after this research conversation took place) to work across sectors more to achieve the type of united approach Te Warihi discusses here. The idea of making connections between organisations leads me to think about mātauranga Māori and the connectedness found there. For me, I feel a deep sense of connection to mātauranga, tikanga, and te ao Māori, but I am also very aware that many people, including teachers of Māori students, do not. I ask Te Warihi who he thinks should support teachers in learning about things Māori. I also discuss with him the practice many schools have of employing a "Māori" teacher who takes on the responsibility of leading everything Māori in the school, and the problem of schools with limited knowledge about things Māori in finding appropriate people to provide them with appropriate guidance and advice. As longstanding and connected members of our community we have seen many organisations, including schools, be misguided because they have not asked the right questions of the right people. Te Warihi points out that accessing appropriate people and resources is part of the responsibility of schools:

> *That's all part of knowing the village that you are in … once you get to know it, you'll identify key people who hold certain information or knowledge pertaining to our culture. They are there … they've [schools/teachers] got to come to know that.*

Te Warihi and I discuss the induction practices that some organisations have involving a noho marae with experts in the given area who inform inductees of the relationship between Māori culture and the sector in which they work. This is a practice I have experienced. Unfortunately, once the induction is over, everybody tends to go about their business with little thought to the cultural experiences and people they have been introduced to. I raise the Ministry of Education objective of "productive partnerships" between schools and Māori, which call for an exchange of knowledge and understanding:

> *A lot of that realistic understanding of the exchanging of knowledge, when it comes to Māori, it's normally one way from my point of view … They come, take, and leave … and leave me with nothing.*

As a key figure in the community, Te Warihi has had a huge amount of experience in this process that many organisations like to think of as "partnerships". It doesn't take a lot of inspection to see the flaw—a relationship that leaves one party with nothing cannot be regarded as a partnership. Nor is such a relationship productive. A feeling of guilt finds its way under my skin. I have to reflect on my own role in this plunder of knowledge—I have little to offer in return for the thousands of hours I've sat at my elders' feet taking in their conversations and wisdom. I hope that the work I do will give them something in return. It seems the tohunga picks up on my reflective thoughts as he states with a small smile:

> *If you were not my daughter, I'd be very reluctant to sit here and talk to you.*

This is true. I think this is also true of the other kaumātua who have agreed to share their stories with me. If I was not Te Warihi and Janet's daughter, I believe they might also be reluctant to talk to me. This speaks of an understanding of the interlinked nature of knowledge sharing and relationships. The knowledge that will be shared, the quality and depth, is utterly dependant on the relationship between those involved in the process. I comment on an attitude both Te Warihi and I have seen where people expect that, if they ask for certain information, it will be given to them to do with as they wish. Te Warihi's response is profound in terms of how our perspectives and attitudes toward knowledge and information sharing have changed in modern contexts:

> ... that's coming to understand, getting to know your village and the people within your village ... there is no trade off in regards to knowledge sharing in that situation. Because, from my point of view, the way I was taught, you had to earn the right, and a lot of it comes through whakapapa, to learn what you learn. You have to earn the right. And what you learn is considered tapu, or sacred. The difficulty I have is when people come to me like that, they expect that, without having gone through the processes that I've gone through to respect that knowledge that they are seeking.

I tell Te Warihi that this is a challenge I have been trying to think through that, on the one hand, we have many teachers who have little knowledge of their own cultures, let alone te ao Māori. On the other, we have people, like him, who have a wealth of knowledge; meanwhile, a non-Māori entity is saying that the solution is to "share" knowledge. Te Warihi has already pointed out that "sharing" in this case means one side giving, the other taking. But he has also highlighted another complexity: that one side has not actually earned the right to access the knowledge they seek. I ask then, should it be given regardless? As he begins to reply, the sounds of a haka being practised at the nearby kura drifts into the shed:

> The only way we can share something is if we have something of equal importance. What I mean by that is that from the time of colonisation, both of us, the Pākehā and the Māori, lost their identity. So, we've now reached a stage where we have Pākehā who say they don't have a culture, we have Māori who say 'Yeah, we have a culture but I don't know what it is.' So, it's a loss of our identity. But there are groups within that arena who do hold the knowledge, that knowledge was passed down to. So, then it becomes lopsided. We have ... academia who say you have to go through their process in order for them to give that knowledge freely to me. I'm saying, you

> have to come through my training to deserve that knowledge I have to give you.

I ask then if we are at an impasse:

> It comes back to that trust thing. We've got to be able to trust each other ... We've seen in the past, information given over, and then that information that we refer to as sacred ... [is] takahia-ed on. So, it builds up a distrust in us that they are not going to treat the information that we give with the respect that it deserves ... all knowledge is sacred, it is just the value we connect to it that is different. One is focused on crass materialism, the other is focused on wairua and the wellbeing of the soul.

I hear snippets of the haka the students are performing; these children are talking about colonisation, about their ancestors, about injustice, and also about cultural pride. What I hear gives me hope that te ao Māori and education is not in a complete deadlock. However, this is a Kura Hourua (now Special Character School) based on the kaupapa of tūpuna Māori, specifically tūpuna of the 28th Māori Battalion. I ask if English-medium education as it stands is capable of building trust with Māori, of coming to know its village, of producing Māori children who will lead successful lives:

> We have to get together the right people. There may be the right people in place now that could find a solution to this. There could be. But I think that just looking at all of our people who acquire doctorates and degrees, some of them are degree-ed up to the hilt, and kore au kite hoki te hua o rātou mahi. Ā, wēnei te kōrero o tāku nei matua: tēnā mahi pēnā hoki ki te mahi ngutu, ko te mahi ngutu anake tēnā. Koinā hoki te kōrero o te Pākehā.

Mahi ngutu has a particular meaning in the context of my hapū. Mahi Ngutu is the name of a pā in Mokau, given to it after an attack by a Hauraki tribe just before it was opened. The Hauraki tribe timed their attack to commence while our men were out hunting in preparation for the opening, leaving the women and old people to defend the newly built pā. The only entry point was a narrow opening at the summit of a hill. The women, alerted to the imminent attack, simply sat concealed at this entrance to the pā dispatching warriors with their aruhe beaters. It wasn't until the creek at the base of the pā ran red with blood that the Hauraki chief realised he had lost his war party. The pā was well planned, engineered and built with precision, in an excellent strategic position, and proved to serve its purpose of protecting the people well. However, because blood had been spilt on the pā before it was opened, it became unusable.

Out of respect for the rank of the attacking chief, his body was hung in a tree ready for his people to collect and return to his home. The bones of the Hauraki ope taua eventually became the responsibility of my great-grandmother, then my family, to protect. We continue to teach our children to re-bury the human remains that find their way to the surface of the sand banks at Mokau. So, mahi ngutu could be understood as lip service, words unsubstantiated by actions. It can also be understood within the context of this story, as hopes, dreams, planning, hard work, and aspirations that are never fulfilled because of transgression of people and place. Te Warihi again returns to the idea of the village in terms of ensuring that good intentions actually come to fruition by changing the force that motivates and drives us:

> *We've got to come back to that village concept. I think the expertise we have out there only focus[es] on aspects of it—so long as those aspects have a pot of gold at the end of them. Whereas we need to … look at the health and wellbeing of the entire community before we even look at that pot of gold. Because being a well community means we are looking after our environment.*

I know that Te Warihi is talking about wellness according to a mātauranga Māori perspective, so I ask him if he believes there is a place for mātauranga Māori in English-medium education settings. The question comes out rather bluntly; if he were somebody else, perhaps I would have phrased it a little more subtly. However, I think we both can feel that we are getting to the crux of our discussion. What is interesting is that, while Te Warihi tells me he thinks English-medium education is not ready for mātauranga Māori, he talks about "this stage of our development", again reinforcing the idea that education is not in a hopeless place when it comes to its relationship with te ao Māori. Te Warihi states:

> At this stage ... of our development, I'd say they're not ready for it, cos anything Māori, any mātauranga we give them, they slap it straight into a little box and give it back to us in a way that is foreign to us. So, at this stage ... that's not the ideal forum to be delivering our mātauranga Māori. That needs to stay with the appropriate people within Māori communities to nurture, look after, and pass on to our tamariki.

As a teacher who has always been proactive about using te reo and mātauranga in the classroom—including English-medium classrooms—the notion of English-medium education contexts being inappropriate for mātauranga Māori perplexes me. I consider myself to be somebody who knows enough about te ao Māori to know I know barely anything at all, and I hold very few credentials to allow me to take that knowledge into a classroom setting. So, from this standpoint I would agree. Yet I am also aware I know more than some and, as a teacher who is proudly Māori, I consider it my duty to bring te ao Māori into English-medium settings to try to educate and build understanding for Māori and non-Māori. I uncertainly check with Te Warihi if he is saying that mātauranga Māori should not be available to teachers to use in their classrooms. He is quick to correct me:

> I was answering it [the previous question] from the point of view that our entire mātauranga be placed in that forum. I don't have any issue about them passing on parts.

He also makes very clear a point I have heard him refer to many times over the years, that "we" need to choose the parts of te ao Māori and mātauranga Māori that we wish to share:

> We need to identify those parts of our culture that will benefit our students.

Of course, the enigmatic "we" captures me and draws me into the complex terrain of identity. I ask him who needs to identify those parts of our culture. He laughingly tells me that the "we" will be the forum I will develop. When I continue to probe him and attempt to tie him to naming the group of people referred to as "we", he moves instead to identifying areas in which a range of people have particular skills and expertise. The "we", therefore, moves away from a specific group of people, and toward skill sets and mātauranga:

> *We have expertise in health ... in whakairo, we have expertise in philosophy, we have expertise in ... science. In other words, we have a perspective on every topic that exists within the system ... and that's without having to go through the [Pākehā] system to learn it.*

His thoughts then return to the concept of the village in terms of knowledge sharing and dissemination:

> *So, part of that village thing ... we still have to come to that ... stage in our relationship where we trust entirely that they'll treat our mātauranga with the respect that it deserves.*

Te Warihi then offers a perspective on the current education system and its relationship with mātauranga Māori:

> *... part of that is not sticking to their concept of education, of how it should be taught to our people.*

For someone like me, who has been educated entirely through the current Pākehā education system, the concept of thinking outside of the contemporary education box is both exciting and somewhat daunting. It also involves a level of trusting in ourselves, and our ability to teach our concepts our way. Te Warihi also points out that the process of decision making is a shared process, again reinforcing the importance of equality in the relationship between Māori and Pākehā:

> *So, that group I'm talking about is having experts within Māoridom and ... on the Pākehā side as well, to work out how we can ... utilise that information for the benefit of our young ones coming through ... It's got to be different to how it is being done at the moment ... it's finding ... the right approach.*

The vision Te Warihi shares excites me for its immense possibilities and potential for real change in the way education is presented in Aotearoa. I ask how Te Warihi would describe teachers who were capable of teaching in a way that would satisfy both Māori and Pākehā education aspirations. His response is simple, and yet speaks to potentially educating all New Zealand children in a way that will cause them to have a greater understanding of who they are and the history of the country in which they live:

> *That's a well-rounded teacher ... [it] doesn't matter the colour of the skin. It depends how those individuals take it on board. With Māori it is their responsibility and I expect them to do that, and for Pākehā it's a good way of getting the message across to Pākehā students. It's working both ways you see.*

He then uses the teaching of Christianity to the Romans as an example of how education between two different peoples can be achieved:

> *... when Christianity was first taught ... Jesus Christ ... chose Peter as the rock of his faith ... he passed his mana to Peter, and yet it wasn't Peter who spread it around the world. It was the Christian Slayer, his name was Saul, [who] became Paul ... he was raised by the Romans, he was raised and brought up, educated by the Romans. He understood the whakaaro ... the psyche of Romans ... in regards to taking on different ideas. So, he was able to ... interpret the Christianity that was left to Peter to teach, he was able to interpret it and sell it to the Romans, the way that the Romans could understand it ... So it's going to take both of us, both sides, to do this, to work this issue out is what I'm saying.*

I ask him if he believes the type of teaching he is describing could be considered as "culturally competent":

> *For me it's cultural understanding ... it's as simple as that. It's cultural understanding. Because from understanding comes respect ... For me just coming to understand a culture is what's important.*

Te Warihi begins to think about people he has known who came to understand both Māori and Pākehā cultures and reflects on their success as people of capacity:

> *... we have Māori figures ... that walked equally in both worlds. So, we look at people like Sir James Henare and Dame Mira Szaszy ... they were raised in the Māori community, ka haere ratou kia whai hoki te mātauranga o te Pākehā and they took that on board ... they to me were the complete New Zealander ... It is people like them who have earned the right to call themselves New Zealanders. Because they understood the Pākehā world completely, all the way through the West, way out to Westminster. [They understood] concepts that come out of*

Westminster [and they understood] their mātauranga Māori that comes from Te Kore.

I am acutely aware that, for many today, the goal of becoming a "complete New Zealander" such as these rangatira may never be attainable due to our saturation in the Pākehā world; many concepts from our own culture have become coloured by the impacts of colonisation. Many of those who walked equally in both te ao Māori and the Pākehā world were raised in a time when their parents could not even begin to comprehend the loss of language and identity that subsequently occurred. I am interested to know if Te Warihi thinks this may be possible within the context of colonisation in which we now live. His response clearly indicates two points—that to achieve an equal balance, Pākehā people need to take up the Māori cause, and that the systems that govern society in this country need to change:

> *I've known a lot of Pākehā old people who were brought up with us, spoke the reo fluently, just like us. Tō rātou nei mita, tino reka hoki te taringa te rongo hoki tō rātou nei reo. So, they became very competent in our culture, but you can't say that's the case ... with the 'system'. We ... talking about the system becoming competent ... We can have individuals within it becoming competent ... but the system needs to become competent, because that's where our problem starts—all the way from Wellington. The system needs to become competent. Otherwise, the individuals that are in it ... will struggle ... Because the system is killing us.*

Visitors knock on the door of the shed, which indicates to both Te Warihi and I that our conversation must be coming to an end. He asks me to go away and think about the things we have talked about. His final comments are in regard to cultural difference, to the need for systemic change in order for positive transformation to happen, and also for systemic support of the hard work of individuals within education:

> *... this is the conflict we have with each other, us, we hold on to the wairua. They say to us 'I can't see it, I can't feel it, so it means nothing.' I'm saying the same thing of the system—'I can't see it, I can't feel it, it means nothing to me.' And that's what we have to come to terms with ... It's hurting all of us. Those two bodies need*

to come together. It's almost like science and religion needing to come together ...

Connecting deeply to mātauranga Māori

A key theme that recurred during Te Warihi's pūkōrero was the concept of the village raising each child. An underlying message of this is that success—in whatever shape or form that might take for each individual—relies not on teachers developing cultural competence, but rather on shared responsibility for our children, our communities, our future and, importantly, shared understandings about knowledge. A message that was inherent in his pūkōrero was that for communities to be fully conscious we must come to know our history, our environments, each other, ourselves, and develop understandings about our relationships and how they have been formed over many generations. Te Warihi's assertions are reflective of arguments Penetito (2009) makes for Place-Based Education.

Repeated throughout all the research conversations was an insistence on developing education based on shared responsibility, influenced by Māori perspectives, just and critical historical understandings, and more effective personal and environmental relationships. This connects to the argument presented by Meyer (2008) that racism, colonisation, power, hegemony, and oppression are all symptoms of acts of denial, and are an unawareness. Te Warihi and the other kaumātua argue (as becomes apparent in the following chapters) that knowledge is the key to combating the unawareness bred and encouraged by colonial structures.

Te Warihi's notion of the village requires conscious connectedness between people, environments, concepts, and times in order for children to succeed, for teachers to teach effectively, for families to overcome the many hardships they face, for communities to be well. Te Warihi presented a perspective here that the disconnect from culture and wairua, which many Māori over several generations have experienced, is negatively impacting on education. To reconcile this, the village must again become responsible. The following analysis links directly to the connection Te Warihi made to the role that knowledge has in not only the education of a village, but also in the overall health and wellbeing of that village. The analysis will also consider the distinction Te Warihi referred to between the knowledge we need to know, and the knowledge we "earn the right to know".

Within the New Zealand context of colonisation, education has always been highly political. Education, according to this study, cannot be viewed in isolation from the ever-present political intentions and policies of New Zealand Governments. To understand the disruption caused by longstanding assimilationist and colonisation policies on Māori epistemology and society, we first must have an idea about what mātauranga Māori is. If educators can develop a sense of the depth of mātauranga that once existed within Māori education and society, they may be able to gain a greater understanding of why the system of education imposed on Māori has been and continues to be problematic for so many.

The way in which education prior to colonisation is conceptualised in this project is a key aspect in centralising mana Māori and reimagining contemporary education. Education did not arrive with Pākehā, it is an inherent building block in the foundations of our culture. Education was carefully nurtured and expanded as our tūpuna traversed the Pacific, ensuring the spiritual and physical needs of the people were met on the ocean, and in new lands. In the thesis that underpins this book, I made the strategic decision to include mātauranga Māori in my methodology and methods to demonstrate that mātauranga Māori and Māori pedagogical practices drive this entire project and are relevant to scholarly endeavours. I do not intend to present Māori education in a passing comment about, for example, the historical form and function of whare wānanga (the ancient site of higher academic learning), or as a backdrop to the introduced form of Māori education at the hands of our colonisers. Mātauranga Māori is taken for granted here as a robust and valid education system that collided with an equally robust knowledge system. The education system that was imposed on us has now become status quo as "Māori education".

Te Warihi is tohunga, though he may not refer to himself as such, it is the role bestowed on him by our rangatira and acknowledged by all those who know him. One role of tohunga is to understand and disseminate knowledge. Theirs is the realm of mātauranga—physical and practical, esoteric and spiritual. The following analysis of mātauranga is linked to the pūkōrero of Te Warihi because of the assertions he makes in his narrative, but also because of his role as tohunga. His kōrero as well as his role has allowed me to analyse mātauranga Māori, its position, shape, and survival in modern contexts. Te Warihi has discussed mātauranga in this project with two very clear distinctions—mātauranga from the kauae runga, and mātauranga from the kauae raro, and the intricate link between the two. In the following chapters, it becomes clear that other kaumātua in this project also define mātauranga in this way.

In the next section, I first consider these differentiations to establish a foundational understanding of mātauranga Māori. I will then investigate the ideological nuances between mātauranga Māori and the current Western education system in order to understand how aspects of mātauranga Māori have been both utilised, and silenced, in education. This chapter will assist in developing clarity around the politics of Māori cultural competence. It defines the knowledge that once was secure and taken for granted in Aotearoa, which will highlight the destructive power of colonisation that is examined and critiqued in the following chapters. Te Warihi is steeped in mātauranga Māori; it can be heard in his pūkōrero, it is the foundation of his wisdom, and informs how he operates in modern society.

Te kauae runga: Knowledge that is earned

"Tēnei te Pou, te Pou ka eke, te Pou kai a koe, te Pou o tatou mahi. Tiaho i roto, wānanga i roto, kōrero i roto ..."

This is part of a takutaku (incantation) that tohunga would recite over pia (students) before they entered into wānanga. It was used to release students from the material world so that they could be open to the new learning of the whare wānanga. The takutaku would instil pia with tapu, a prerequisite for learning. The pou is a metaphor for knowledge which is enlightening, knowledge and understandings that quicken and are transformative, knowledge that has the power to consume, knowledge that will provide prosperity in return for effort (Te Warihi Hetaraka, personal communication, 29 March 2014).

The takutaku illustrates a perspective my tūpuna had of knowledge. That is—knowledge is tapu, it has the power to quicken, to be transformative and illuminating, education has the power to consume us in both positive and negative ways. A Māori perspective, as illustrated by this takutaku, is that knowledge of all kinds must be critically analysed and considered in order to be of value to humanity. Mead (2012) explains that the Māori religious system forms the philosophical underpinnings of traditional mātauranga Māori and, therefore, provides ethical rules about notions of tapu and noa. On this foundation, Māori identity, culture, language, social structures, politics, and norms were developed.

The perspective that all knowledge is tapu formed the basis of the first iteration of formal Māori education in Aotearoa. It is knowledge from the kauae runga, the upper echelons, that formed the curriculum of whare wānanga, and was then used to inform the learning of the kauae raro. A traditional narrative exemplifying these types of knowledges also give us the names "kauae runga" and "kauae raro". In the version of the pūrākau I was taught, Māui is said to rip the jawbone from his grandmother, Murirangawhenua, and later uses it to complete many missions, including fishing up the North Island of New Zealand. To understand how this story relates to knowledge from the kauae runga being used to inform the kauae raro, some analysis is needed.

Māui's grandmother, Murirangawhenua, must have seen Māui as a candidate capable of carrying her ancient knowledge into the future, because, according to the pūrākau, Māui inherited the jawbone of Murirangawhenua in the dark, and alone, a pedagogical practice common in whare wānanga. Her knowledge was ancient and sacred, its origins unknown, but many Māori may argue that it came from a divine source. This was the knowledge of the upper jawbone—te kauae runga. In the narrative, the knowledge of Murirangawhenua is represented by her jawbone. In many examples of traditional learning, only one part of the teacher's body would move—the jaw. When the ancestor Māui sat at his grandmother's knee and inherited her jawbone, he was a student of the kauae runga.

Māui was entrusted with knowledge from Murirangawhenua and used it to navigate across the Pacific to Aotearoa several times, without ever settling here. Māui's journey was not extraordinary for people who, even during Māui's time,[10] must have been spectacular navigators. What is exceptional is Murirangawhenua's knowledge from the kauae runga. Murirangawhenua was an old, in some accounts blind, woman. How did she know the location of islands far to the south that had never felt human footfall? How could she know the constellations to follow that were most likely in a different hemisphere? Murirangawhenua was able to instruct Māui on the best route to travel, on the length of time it would take, and on the best time to travel and return. She knew that, in this land, which had never been seen before, Māui would find resources aplenty to ensure his safe return home.

The island Māui found under his grandmother's direction became known as Te Ika Nui ā Māui (The Great Fish of Māui), yet neither Māui nor any of his descendants for many generations had technology capable of seeing the fish-like shape of the North Island of New Zealand. This narrative provides multiple examples (beyond the examples I have discussed here) of knowledge from the kauae runga. This knowledge is not easily explained, its origins cannot be easily determined. While we may not know where it has come from, often it is accurate, and, increasingly, science is proving the accuracy of many Māori and Indigenous knowledges. Māui took knowledge from the kauae runga for practical use and his feats in doing so became narratives handed down for generations—kauae raro. What has not travelled as freely is the knowledge Māui inherited in the form of his grandmother's jawbone, because through millennia kauae runga continued to be protected information. The Māui narratives have retained kauae raro knowledge through time; the kauae runga knowledge remains, but is often not immediately obvious, usually becoming evident only through analysis of the pūrākau.

---

10 Some hapū and iwi narratives and whakapapa indicate Māui was alive at around the same era as Jesus.

These two distinct forms of knowledge form the wider context of mātauranga Māori. However, it appears that for many, the differences between the two are confused by modern contexts and by competing epistemologies—including traditional Māori, modern Māori, non-Māori, and religious epistemologies. It is important to this project to differentiate between the two forms of mātauranga Māori. First, because the kaumātua involved clearly stated that there are parts of mātauranga, from the kauae runga, that Māori maintain the right to protect and will be selective about what is shared. Second, the systematic dismantling of our mātauranga, which in turn endangered our language and removed our traditional social structures, began by disrupting mātauranga from the kauae runga. That disruption then filtered through to the kauae raro. I will argue that, in English-medium education, aspects of the kauae raro can be seen, but that the imbalance between understandings of raro and runga has left us with an incomplete education.

I recall a discussion between my father and my uncle, Erima Henare (who at his untimely death in 2015 was the Māori Language Commissioner). I remember them discussing three distinct types of reo Māori: everyday language; formal language, such as that of the marae; and the language used to access higher-level concepts, the language of wairua, which appears in ancient takutaku. These three distinctions are reflected in the Ngā Puhi proverb "Tuhi kohuru, tuhi korae, tuhi marae kura. Language of the gods, language of the world, language of every marae." The whakataukī links language distinctions with differential mātauranga Māori. Edwards (2010) explains that "tuhi kohuru" is the language and knowledge of the gods, unknowable to humans, "tuhi korae" is the language and knowledge released by the highest power, Io, to the world, and "tuhi marae kura" is the contextual language and knowledge specific to each region.

In analysing the language in this whakataukī, we are afforded a small glimpse into the world of mātauranga Māori. First, "tuhi" in a modern context means "write". However, this older version of the word is used to encompass "... te reo ... me te mātauranga ..." (Edwards, 2010, p. 58), the language and the knowledge. This older definition of tuhi also aligns to the term Tā Himi Henare made visible in New Zealand society, "te reo me ōna tikanga".

The language and knowledge unattainable by humanity is described as "kohuru", which can be understood as to clothe, or to feather. Kohuru (kōhuru if macrons are used) is also the word for murder, murderer, or to assassinate. I would argue that, in terms of describing the knowledge inaccessible to humanity, my tūpuna purposely employed a word that had dual meaning, which as previously discussed was a common practice. When aligned to only a fragment of the takutaku used at the beginning of this section—" ... te pou ka eke, te pou kai a koe ... knowledge that quickens, knowledge that consumes ..."—a perspective of powerful knowledge that must be respected is formed. I believe "kohuru" is used here to illustrate the power (to both protect, and to harm) and the potential danger of attempting to gain knowledge that we have no right to attain. How our ancestors knew of the existence of this knowledge is a study far beyond the scope of this book and is, perhaps, a test of the link between spiritual and physical in that, in this world, there remain concepts that simply require people to have faith.

"Korae" is the brow. Edwards (2010) describes "tuhi korae" as "... te reo tērā me te mātauranga i tukua e Io Matua te Kore ki te Aotūroa" (p. 58), the language and knowledge released by Io the Parentless into the physical world. Te tuhi korae is the mātauranga that constitutes the kauae runga and formed the curriculum of the ancient whare wānanga. These words provide yet another example of the absolute link between higher-order knowledge and wairua. Meyer (2008) maintains that the link between knowledge and spirit "... allows knowing to be a conscious act ..." (p. 219), just as the movement towards "te ao mārama" can be understood as striving for "full consciousness" through the engagement of all our senses.

The importance of the korae or rae is strongly linked to the practice of tā moko, and specifically to facial tattoo. The facial tattoo was a personal record of the wearer's mana, their whakapapa, and their characteristics. The korae/rae, forehead or brow, is reserved for the depiction of kape tī and kape tā. There is no simple translation of these words; however, in wānanga, Te Warihi has explained that kape tī and kape tā represent the left and right hemispheres of the brain, which is why they are placed on the forehead. Neurological studies (MacNeilage et al., 2009; Sperry, 1975) determine that the frontal lobes of the brain each have specialist functions—the left operating linguistic, mathematical, symbolic, logical, and analytical tasks commonly thought of as our conscious mind. The right hemisphere is the domain of spatial, creative, visual, and unconscious thought. Importantly, contemporary Western education is dominated by activities more commonly associated with left-brain activities such as reading, writing, and maths. While these activities certainly have the potential to be creative, the focus in schools is often on the technical and process aspects of these tasks, rather than their creative potential.

The concepts of kape tī and kape tā are intimately connected to Māori constructs of mātauranga in that full consciousness can only be achieved through complete balance of the conscious and subconscious, between structure and creativity, between the spiritual and physical, between feminine and masculine energies. According to Māori philosophy, a full education requires the equal engagement of both hemispheres of the brain, illustrated by the symmetrical representation in tā moko of kape tī and kape tā on the brow.

Learning in kauae runga took place under tapu in order to preserve the knowledge for longevity. The whare wānanga was the site of higher-order Māori academy, of scholarship, of mātauranga and pedagogical practices restricted to men and women specifically chosen as young children (Hemara, 2000) by tohunga and kaumātua. Higher-order Māori academy has been in existence for generations and yet, in the search to rectify current disadvantages in the education system for Māori learners, nothing of the kauae runga is reflected in the cultural competencies, in the curriculum, or in contemporary pedagogical practice. A possible reason for this is that many Māori did not have access to this level of scholarship, as it took place in isolation from everyday life. Another reason may be that so much of our traditional forms of education in both kauae runga and raro was entrenched in societal structures and ways of living that have been denigrated through colonisation.

The selection process for whare wānanga illustrates mātauranga Māori and pedagogical practice that has been made defunct by Western education. At birth, every child came under the protection of the māreikura in the form of female relatives, whose express duty was to teach children the knowledge of tuhi marae kura, and to closely observe the nature of each child. The māreikura would carefully observe children for individual characteristics, interests, and skills, then give them specific learning experiences that would enhance their natural propensities and prepare them for future roles relevant to the characteristics they exhibited.

Ceremonial hair cutting, usually at around 7 years of age (Jones & Kaa Jenkins, 2017), was symbolic of the severing of a child's ties to their education and protection under the female energies of the māreikura, and a transition to education under the male energies of the whatukura and experts in the field in which they had shown skills. For some, this would be the beginning of their tutelage in the whare wānanga. The process of education from before birth was highly intensive and required extreme observational skills. The disruption of colonisation has meant that, in modern times, many Māori have become so disengaged from our culture that this level of shared dedication to the education of our children, and attention to detail, is no longer common.

Marsden (2003) argues that the Platonic dualistic perspective of the universe that partitions life into secular and spiritual was a position reinforced by Enlightenment scientific philosophies. The isolation of knowledge from spirit is reflected in modern New Zealand education, which is founded on the notion of free, secular, and compulsory education for all (Pākehā) children as prescribed by the Education Act 1877. However, before this Act, from our earliest encounters with Pākehā education, "[t]he unifying thread, the spiritual dimension had been withdrawn" (Marsden, 2003, p. 43) forcefully and purposefully by colonial forces that came to control our education. The epistemic perspective that knowledge is bound to spirit permeates Māori language, and yet "Māori" education ploughs on largely ignoring the broken threads as we continue to compartmentalise and isolate knowledge from wairua.

Sharma (2005) argues that structural practices exist that "... persist in otherising certain minority spiritual ideologies, values and sacredness ..." (p. 154). In the New Zealand context, those structures have been built by forcing underground higher-order mātauranga in Māori communities. The security surrounding the knowledge of the kauae runga perhaps made for an easier othering process because, in a relatively short period of time, tohunga and their teachings became not just othered, but feared, subterraneous, and ridiculed in wider New Zealand society. Meyer (2008) contends that, worldwide, the weight of hegemony and forced assimilation collapsed the higher orders of knowing; for Māori that came from the kauae runga.

Te Warihi illustrates how introduced conceptualisations of knowledge, which remove it from wairua, continue to erode the sacred nature of knowledge from the kauae runga, and impacts those who hold that knowledge:

> ... *from my point of view, the way I was taught, you had to earn the right, and a lot of it comes through whakapapa, to learn what you learn. You have to earn the right, and what you learn is considered tapu, or sacred. The difficulty I have is when people come to me like that, they expect that without having gone through the processes that I've gone through to respect that knowledge that they are seeking.*

Modern education, and literacy, have been viewed as a means of power that can be used to control society and the environment (Jenkins, 1993). By this definition, knowledge is power; it is profitable and can benefit us personally. The view that Te Warihi presents puts a lot more weight on the responsibility attached to attaining knowledge. Knowledge from the kauae runga is earned. While it is tied to whakapapa it is not a birth-right, or a commodity of the elite. The process of attaining this knowledge is difficult, not for the purposes of fostering elitism, but to ensure that the knowledge is respected. Mead (2012) concurs that mātauranga Māori is a specialist field, highly regarded by those who do not have it. In a society that expects instant gratification and access to all knowledge at all times, the notion that one must earn the right to learn some things may be incomprehensible.

Meyer (2008) contends knowledge that endures is driven by spirit, it is a life force connected to all other life forces. This is the power of the wairua of knowledge from the kauae runga. Despite the strength of Western knowledge and culture, some people retain this level of knowledge, and are respected for it (Mead, 2012). However, Māori in general have been left with fragments that we attempt to piece together. The discussion presented here is evidence of the fragmentation caused by the deeply and successfully entrenched structural practices that have othered our spiritual ideologies. I am not imbued with that higher-order knowledge, I do not possess the capacity to function at full consciousness, so all I am able to present is my analysis of words and concepts that I have been lucky enough to have had shared with me. I know that, by the standards of Indigenous knowledge keepers, my analysis is incomplete, it can never express the wholeness of the knowledge of the kauae runga, nor would I want it to in this forum, which is not our own.

Te kauae raro: Knowledge all have the right to

Presenting the mātauranga Māori dimensions of the kauae runga and kauae raro separately is not intended to give the impression that they are entities that operate in isolation from each other. A key feature of the kauae runga and kauae raro is that, whilst the pedagogies and audiences were different, they were interconnected by wairua, and by action. In defining differences between kaupapa Māori theory and mātauranga Māori, Royal (2012) asserts that "Mātauranga Māori ... is used merely to label a body of knowledge. It does not tell us what we might do with this body of knowledge ..." (p. 33). If knowledge from the kauae runga and kauae raro are viewed as separate entities or, conversely, rolled together as one entity without definitive layers, rather than being viewed as essential parts of a broader context, this conclusion is understandable. However, if we understand that each dimension plays a specific role in this overall body of knowledge, then mātauranga begins to look more like theory—kauae runga—and action—kauae raro. In kaupapa Māori theory, G. Smith (2012) describes this as praxis.

Kauae raro can be understood as the knowledges attached to human activity that are accumulated, reflected upon, and adjusted as each generation invents new innovations in the times and environments they face (Mead, 2012). In this way, knowledge from the kauae raro can be seen as "how" we do things, with the "why" embedded in the kauae runga. For example, tikanga—an aspect of kauae raro—deems a new building be constructed by men then opened at dawn, with the first person entering the building being a puhi. Kawa, an aspect of the kauae runga, provides the reasons for doing this, and is a complex acknowledgement of the interaction between the physical and spiritual, and the balance between the sacred roles of both men and women.

For example, the opening of a building is symbolic of childbirth. Women are restricted from the building process because of their sacrosanct role in childbirth. The men's role is to construct, the women's role is to give life to that construction. The opening of a new building must happen at dawn to re-enact the process of passing through the dark birth canal, into the world of light. The ancient takutaku that are recited during the opening rituals tell of Tane Nui ā Rangi travelling to the furthest reaches of the universe, retrieving all conceivable energy forces to imbue them into the heart of the new building. The only person capable of ensuring the building is infused with those energies gathered by Tane, or to give life to the building, is a puhi, the highest-ranking virginal female. This is not to say we believe the building is alive, it is an acknowledgement of the energy in the environment that went into the making of the new structure. It links the physical to deeper spiritual energies of the universe. It is a sign of respect to those things that will continue to protect and give us sustenance.

This is a very abridged version of the "why" of one small aspect of human activity, used simply to demonstrate the link between the kauae runga and the kauae raro. It also serves to illustrate how, in modern times, our "why" is often absent from the "how" because of the degradation of mātauranga Māori. When mātauranga Māori is perceived singularly, absent of layers, devoid of the essential element of analysis that once had its foundations in the kauae runga, the problem is not one of having a label for the body of knowledge with no instructions as to what to do with the knowledge, as Royal (2012) indicates. Conversely, it essentially becomes a body of knowledge that does tell us what to do, but we are not given reasons as to why we are doing it. Our actions become meaningless, and our energies disconnect from the energies of the rest of the universe. Just as Graham Hingangaroa Smith (2012) argues that action without analysis is dangerous to kaupapa Māori theory, I argue here that separating practice in the form of kauae raro, from theory and/or analysis in the form of kauae runga, in understanding mātauranga Māori is also dangerous, and has happened as a result of the education system forced on Māori.

The intertwined nature of these knowledge bases is also demonstrated through the traditional structure of Māori society. Ariki, tohunga, and rangatira were educated through whare wānanga and therefore had access to epistemological and spiritualised understandings of the workings of the universe. Because they had access to te tuhi korae, it was their responsibility to make political decisions informed by wairua that could strengthen the power base of their iwi. Their education contributed to the confidence hapū had in their ability to be scrupulous in their leadership. Members of whānau, hapū, and iwi were then responsible for the tuhi marae kura, the knowledge and language distinct to each region, and for developing and passing on knowledge from the kauae raro.

The differential knowledge bases were in constant dialogue with one another via the differential ranks within traditional society. Academia analysed ancient bodies of knowledge in relation to their current contexts, they interpreted the flow of information, processes, and events of the universe (Marsden, 2003), and they discerned what knowledge would be disseminated more widely, and when. This information continually informed the actions and developments of hapū and iwi, ensuring that all action, whether our modern perspectives perceive them to be good or bad, were informed by an analysis of wairua and the wider universe.

I again reiterate that it may be difficult to understand this form of social order when we have been so conditioned to perceive anything outside of a democratic society as suspect, elitist, and regressive. It is hard to step outside of our conditioning to grasp that this was a completely different social structure which relied absolutely on connected, dynamic, and intricate relationships between people and environments. It also relied to a large extent on trust and trustworthiness. The democratic system under which we live today could be argued to be more suspect, more elitist, more regressive and pose a far more serious threat to people and environments than traditional Māori social structures ever were.

Marsden (2003) argues that the Māori perception of the material world being subordinate to the spiritual continues, in some cases subconsciously, to be reflected in our thinking, and in our language. This links strongly to Te Warihi's experience of people who, "... still have a semblance of their Māori whakaaro with them, except they can't identify it as being that ... when I explain the principles of our culture ... they can relate to that concept ... but initially they couldn't identify why they did things that way." Prior to colonisation, there would have been no confusion as to why things were done in a particular way; our education was whole because our knowledge systems were whole, and our social structures were able to function unmolested.

The kauae raro is the domain of practical and social knowledge and constitutes what Te Warihi referred to in his pūkōrero as the knowledge we need to know in order to function, be productive, be innovative, be successful, and to socialise in the physical world. Meyer (2008) discusses knowledge such as this as having a unifying wisdom, as it is embedded in function, awareness, and usefulness. This is the knowledge that all members of any society are entitled to because it is essential to development, socialisation, sustenance, and cultural reproduction. The cultural milieu of an iwi was instilled in children not through formal schooling but through their living and participating in all aspects of their community, over a long period of time (Marsden, 2003; Rangihau, 2011). I will argue that Pākehā knowledge became included in what Māori perceived as knowledge from the kauae raro, to which they were entitled in order to function effectively in our new social circumstances. I will also illustrate that assimilationist policies and racist attitudes toward Māori were used to prevent us from fully participating in the positive aspects of New Zealand society.

The function of the kauae raro as a means by which to reproduce and modify cultural and social knowledge is the reason the term "mātauranga tuku iho, inherited knowledge" was chosen by Te Wakaminenga in 1835 to describe the cultural knowledge that would be handed down from one generation to the next as Māori experienced greater contact with other cultures (mātauranga-ā-iwi). Mead (2012) describes mātauranga Māori as having a past, present, and future. This concept is reflected in the processes of Te Wakaminenga. They understood that our culture would evolve with ongoing contact with other cultures, and they maintained the power to decide what aspects of our culture would be vital to retain so that Māori could continue to prosper and be proactive within a changing social landscape. Significantly, aspects discussed by Te Wakaminenga to be included as mātauranga tuku iho included new Western knowledge that they had come into contact with, illustrating their intention to broaden our knowledge base to include useful aspects of other cultures. This confirms Mead's (2012) conviction that mātauranga Māori as a pool of knowledge is inclusive and dynamic.

Social and functional knowledges are more readily accessible and visible, even between social groups, so it is aspects of the kauae raro that tend to be seen in contemporary education and society. However, it will be argued that this has caused particular complexities for Māori in our relationship with our Treaty partners, and in our relationship with Western education. Mātauranga Māori, in the broad sense, is made up of two distinct levels of knowledge that constantly communicate with each other and form the basis of Māori culture. This depth of understanding was the context from which Māori engaged with new cultures and technologies. It was against mātauranga Māori that decisions were weighed as rangatira navigated iwi into the future. It was mātauranga Māori that also came to be the target for extermination, first by missionaries then by Crown agents and agencies, with schooling being the tool of choice. Ours is not a narrative of subordinate Natives dominated by the West; rather, it is a history of complicated and nuanced relationships backed by powerful but often competing epistemologies.

The importance of early economic relationships

Māori–Pākehā relationships have come to be defined as one of subordination of Māori through the dominance of our colonial heritage (Bishop, 2003). Māori have indeed found ourselves struggling in a position of forced subordination, under-representation in the positive aspects of society, and over-represented in the negative (Bishop & Glynn, 1999). However, during early contact between cultures, Māori quickly looked for correlations between their own political structures and those of Pākehā. One of these structures was the power rangatira Māori had over life and death (Henare, 2010). Māori seem to have applied this understanding to their perspective of rangatira Pākehā, causing Māori to seek out Pākehā they believed had the same level of power as our own rangatira with whom to foster political alliances. This is illustrated in the distinct relationships that developed in the two main areas of Māori–Pākehā early contact (O'Malley, 2012) with Tai Tokerau in the north, and Murihiku to the far south.

The rich abundance of food and pounamu first drew Māori to Te Wai Pounamu (Evison, 1997). The fertile resources also attracted the likes of sealers then whalers from as early as the late 1700s. O'Malley (2012) describes these resource hunters as largely being from the lowest European social order, looking for little more than escapism and reprieve from the New South Wales penal system. Māori extended manaakitanga to the sealers and whalers, engaged commercially with them, allowed transient camps to be set up, and in later years, as my own whakapapa shows, married them. However, there is no evidence to suggest there were any early attempts by Māori to initiate political relationships beyond mutually beneficial trade arrangements and marriages with these hunters. The peace alliance forged between Ngāi Tahu and Ngāti Māmoe around 1780 (Evison, 1997) remained the sovereign political force in Te Wai Pounamu until the advent of Te Tiriti o Waitangi.

In contrast, Māori–Pākehā interactions in the north were more frequent and therefore more varied. Exchange between the two had been frequent enough by the late 1700s that a familiarity with European vessels, youthful lack of caution, and strong desire for iron, as shown by Tukitāhua and Hurukokoti, may have inadvertently led to their kidnapping from Motukawanui (the Cavalli Islands) by the crew of the *Daedalus* in 1793 (O'Malley, 2012). The subsequent story of Tuki and Huru being forcibly taken to Norfolk Island to educate Lieutenant-Governor Philip King (the first Commandant of the Norfolk Island penal colony) in the dressing of flax cloth (Jones & Jenkins, 2011) is relatively well known in the north.

Also obvious to many northern Māori is the gap in King's cultural knowledge, as women dressed flax, not men, so Tuki and Huru would have only been able to give rudimentary instruction in this practice. The abduction and safe return of Tuki and Huru is a crucial moment in our history—these two young rangatira essentially became teachers of te reo, tikanga, and the geography of Aotearoa to Pākehā. This episode signals a transition from a trade relationship between Māori and Pākehā based on the acquisition of goods, to the trade and acquisition of intellectual property. This, just like the trade in physical resources, was originally a relationship based on reciprocity (Jones & Jenkins, 2011).

Knowledge: A highly prized commodity

Since the early 1800s, a flourishing resource trade between Māori and Pākehā had formed the basis of a tenuous relationship, with both parties eager to benefit from trade deals. Māori were quick to adopt the European custom of barter when trading with Pākehā, which had similarities to the complex lore of manaakitanga. Māori were also fast to reciprocate the "... roguery ... practised to a great extent on the part of Europeans" (Yate, 1835, p. 30). This illustrates cultures influencing and learning from each other. What Māori quickly understood about their earliest trade partners was that sealers and whalers were commoners, and therefore held no political power. This conclusion was also drawn later in contact with ship makers and flax traders.

Māori were, therefore, happy to enter into trade deals with them, but if any political engagement was to be entered into it must occur with rangatira Pākehā. During the early days of first contact, Māori perceived ship captains to be rangatira so chose them to interact with, as they seemed to be the highest ranking amongst the foreigners (Petrie, 2015). However, this was not to suffice for long; Māori saw captains had rank but, in their view, ship captains were not equal to the power of rangatira.

An important chief who was among the first Māori to travel to England was Ruatara (1787–1815). In 1808, Ruatara set off from the Bay of Islands with the purpose of meeting face-to-face with the person rangatira had identified as holding equal rank to themselves, King George III (1738–1820; r. 1760–1819). Ruatara was not to fulfil his goal of discovering the workings of the rangatira Pākehā, as he was severely mistreated by the ship's captain and some sailors. His mission was ridiculed, he was beaten then put on a convict ship destined for New South Wales (Jones & Jenkins, 2011).

Ruatara's fateful attempt to meet King George III and his subsequent arrival in Australia was to become a defining moment in our history in relation to schooling. Also aboard the *Ann* in 1809 was Samuel Marsden. Marsden, a Mihingare (Anglican missionary) had developed a relationship in 1805 with Bay of Islands chief Te Pahi (b. unknown–1810), who had effectively interrogated Marsden about European society (Jones & Jenkins, 2011). Te Pahi had made it clear to Marsden that Māori were only interested in a relationship that would give Māori access to the knowledge and resources of the modern world (Jones & Jenkins, 2011). The relationship rangatira in Tai Tokerau sought to establish with missionaries was based not on Christian teachings, but rather on the potential for economic advancement (Petrie, 2006). Marsden was therefore aware that he would need to preface his evangelical mission to Aotearoa with the infiltration of skilled artisans (Jones & Jenkins, 2011). He also learnt that developing personal relationships with Māori would be beneficial to his mission.

Samuel Marsden's extension of friendship to a dejected Ruatara in 1809 on board the *Ann* was a move that would impact Māori–Pākehā relationships for many years to come.

By the time the *Ann* made port in Port Jackson in 1810, Ruatara and Marsden had developed a warm friendship, which led to Ruatara remaining in Sydney for 2 years with the Marsden family (Jones & Jenkins, 2011). His time in Sydney exposed Ruatara to many new technologies—the industrious rangatira quickly saw the economic advantages that could be gained for his hapū by exporting wheat and extending his existing crops at home in the Bay of Islands. His observation of children being taught to read and write must have had a significant impact on the forward-thinking chief, who specifically asked Marsden to send a teacher to the Bay of Islands before he returned home in 1812 (Jones & Jenkins, 2011). Marsden somewhat urgently sent for Thomas Kendall, not a trained teacher but a missionary (Binney, 1968), to fulfil this role.

Ruatara's request for a teacher illustrates a perspective of the arrival of missionaries to Te Tai Tokerau in a way that contrasts with the dominant narrative of this part of our history. The work of Jones and Kaa Jenkins (2017) is significant in the retelling of our history in ways that align more succinctly with Māori perspectives. Both missionaries and rangatira Māori were working in purposeful ways to advance their separate aspirations and were relying heavily on developing relationships with each other to achieve their goals. Importantly, this perspective offers an alternative to the dominant narrative, in that Marsden and his missionaries did not simply arrive on our shores in 1814 by happenstance, coincidence, or even solely under the force of the missionaries' own determination to Christianise Māori. They were expressly invited by one of the most influential chiefs in Te Tai Tokerau at the time, Ruatara. His goal was to have Māori children taught the Western method of reading and writing in order for Māori to compete economically in the modern world (Henare, 2011). This is the first instance in our history of a common goal between Māori and missionary in education, but for very different purposes. The contrasting goals and views of Māori and missionary have had a substantial impact on the education of Māori and will be discussed further in this chapter.

The meeting and friendship between Ruatara and Marsden taught both Māori and Pākehā several lessons, particularly in terms of engagement and interactions that could be negotiated to secure benefits for both sides. Marsden learnt some Māori language, cosmology, politics, and social structures and came to know the intelligence and industrious capabilities of rangatira (Jones & Jenkins, 2011). He then used this information to plan his approach to the teaching of Christianity in Aotearoa. Ruatara, alongside other Tai Tokerau chiefs, learnt many of the workings of Pākehā technologies and social norms, and saw opportunities for export and economic expansion for hapū. He also came to understand that Pākehā such as Marsden did hold an amount of mana in English society and would therefore be far more useful to Māori than the traders, whalers, and sealers they had been dealing with thus far (Jones & Jenkins, 2011).

Their relationship highlights an increasing need from both parties to access the intellectual property of each other's cultures. Ruatara goes so far as to initiate the acquisition of a new kind of property. He wanted to obtain a high-ranking Pākehā to increase both his mana amongst other iwi (Jones & Kaa Jenkins, 2017) and the ability of his people to navigate and access the economic benefits of the world he knew was fast encroaching. Ruatara chose Marsden. Regardless of their differing, even opposing, intentions and goals, both Ruatara and Marsden found in each other a deep friendship that would allow Marsden to gain unchallenged permission to enter the Bay of Islands. After Ruatara's death, his nephew Hongi Hika continued to honour the alliance with Marsden, offering his protection to the missionaries. Without the protection of Ruatara, then Hongi, it is questionable whether Marsden and his missionaries would have been successful in establishing a foothold in New Zealand at all.

Mātauranga Māori meets print literacy

In the midst of early, more widespread formal Western education in Aotearoa, English print literacy impacted the lives of two young rangatira from Te Tai Tokerau. The work of Jenkins (1993) and Jones and Jenkins (2011, 2017) has traced and made public the stories of Tuai and

Titere, which since their deaths had largely remained within the protection of their hapū and iwi, or buried in historical records. The role of print literacy in the lives of Titere, and specifically of Tuai, a tupuna of mine from Ngare Raumati, are important to this work in terms of this being a significant event in the whakapapa of mātauranga Māori. Their stories provide us with a microcosm of the dilemmas that would face Māori at the interface of two knowledge systems. This was a unique moment in time where young rangatira who had been initiated in whare wānanga were introduced to a completely foreign knowledge system and faced with the daunting, perhaps even exciting, prospect of assessing the suitability of this new knowledge to their own cultural contexts. The history of Tuai and Titere provides a first glimpse into the role literacy learning has had on Māori knowledge bases.

Tuai and Titere were the first generation of Māori to have grown up familiar with foreign ships and their inhabitants (Jones & Kaa Jenkins, 2017). Tuai was also part of the collective of rangatira that included his older brother Korokoro, Ngā Puhi chief Ruatara, and his nephew Hongi Hika, to spend an extended period of time during the early 1800s in Parramatta with missionaries Marsden and Kendall learning English, the tenets of Christianity, and the mechanics of Pākehā society (Jones & Kaa Jenkins, 2017). That Ngare Raumati chiefs Korokoro and Tuai undertook this journey together with their Ngā Puhi rivals Ruatara and Hongi, spoke of the power the chiefs saw in obtaining information regarding the form and function of Pākehā society. At this point in time, it was more valuable to them all than the ongoing, intergenerational rivalry between Ngā Puhi and the iwi of Manaia from the north-eastern coast. These influential chiefs were in a race to garner the most information regarding Pākehā technologies so as to wrest control over its influx into Aotearoa and to advantage the position of their hapū and iwi.

An opportunity arose in 1817 for Tuai and Titere to travel to England from Parramatta to learn English under the Anglican tutelage of the Church Mission Society (CMS) (Binney, 1968). The intention of the CMS was that once these two young men had learnt to read and write in English they would return home and pass on these skills to other iwi

(Jenkins, 1993). The underlying desire for the missionaries to teach Māori written literacy is clear in the words of Tuai himself:

> Mr Eyton ask me, better read the Bible and he give me good book he tell me better learn read Bible and go home to my country, and speak to my countrymen, and learn him to read book. (Jenkins, 1993, p. 8)

However, Tuai's brother Korokoro agreed for this new education to take place not for the purpose of his younger brother becoming a Māori missionary; rather, he saw the potential for an expansion of mana for Ngare Raumati in having a chief able to read and write in English (Jones & Kaa Jenkins, 2017).

Jenkins' (1993) analyses of letters written by Tuai and Titere during their time in England identify their progression in learning English, as well as their internal reflections on their struggles to learn the new skills, their perception of how the teaching programme would be received in Aotearoa, as well as their excitement, loneliness, and contemplation of the power of the missionary gods. Two aspects of Jenkins' work (1993) that relate specifically to this study are, first, the inference missionaries made that Tuai "forgot" all he had learnt in England on his return to Aotearoa, and second, the lessons Marsden and Kendall learnt from the English education of Tuai and Titere, which impacted their belief that they now knew how to relate to Māori.

Missionaries used images to project an impression of Tuai being culturally transformed and superior to his countrymen. Thanks to their work "[h]e has become English. His literacy has transformed him" (Jenkins, 1993, p. 7). The depth of their disappointment must have been palpable when he returned home to have his facial moko completed and to continue living as he always had, undoubtedly giving rise to their assertion that he must have simply forgotten the "civility" taught through English literacy. Jenkins (1993) discounts the assertion that Tuai forgot what he had been taught in England, on the basis that his cultural context had very little relevance to the cultural and material education he had obtained in England. His traditional way of living gave Tuai no reason to pass on the Pākehā education he had been given. I would also venture to add that, as a young rangatira, Tuai would also have been operating from Māori social mores in his decision to not teach his new education to his countrymen.

Tuai was teina (a younger brother) to Korokoro, who was a powerful Ngare Raumati chief with great influence throughout the Bay of Islands. I have no doubt that even those parts of his new education that Tuai did find useful would not have been "taught" to others in the way missionaries had envisioned if it had meant overstepping the rank of his older brother. Indeed, Tuai must certainly have found parts of his new education useful, as he later used his knowledge of Pākehā society and literacy to his great advantage in establishing a strong trade-based economy in the Bay of Islands (Petrie, 2006). However, while he was rangatira, he was also teina with little political influence (Jones & Kaa Jenkins, 2017), and within this context it would have been inappropriate for Tuai to return from England and teach what he had learnt if it was perceived to be transgressing the mana of his older brother.

As already mentioned, on his return to Aotearoa Tuai had his facial moko completed, as was his right as a rangatira initiated in whare wānanga. His actions flew in the face of the hopes missionaries had that he would become one of the "standard-bearers for Christian civility" (Jones & Kaa Jenkins, 2017, p. 157). However, even before making port back in Aotearoa, missionaries were alarmed at Tuai and Titere's seeming antagonism toward them and their Christian teachings (Jones & Kaa Jenkins, 2017). Despite desperate attempts by missionaries to win over Tuai and Titere, which included everything from loving kindness to accusatory guilt trips, both Tuai and Titere were convinced that the intention of the missionaries was to "… possess New Zealand in the same way as they had Australia" (Jones & Kaa Jenkins, 2017, p. 158). This led them to reject the role of becoming Māori missionaries, and they refused to teach other Māori to read the Bible. However, Tuai did use his knowledge of both Māori and English literacy to take on the role of educating Kendall, earning Tuai the station of the first teacher of teachers (Jones & Kaa Jenkins, 2017).

These were the first young Māori men to be fully educated within the academy of their ancestors, as well as in the curriculum of missionaries. Tuai was of a generation that truly had to navigate two very different worlds. His abilities to communicate in English meant he became a translator between Māori and Pākehā—even on behalf of adversary iwi (Jones & Kaa Jenkins, 2017). He wore Pākehā clothing, and he used his knowledge of Pākehā language and society to establish himself as a successful businessman (Petrie, 2006). By completing his facial moko, Tuai very clearly expressed his final stand on what must have been an overwhelming process of analysing and assessing the relevance and place of new knowledge against the knowledge inherited from his tūpuna.

Tuai, in his unique position of having been educated within both Māori and Pākehā education systems, evaluated how to best use this new information for his economic prosperity but maintain his identity as Māori. As a young rangatira, he undertook an important role as Kendall's Māori teacher, but he did not become the Māori teacher of Christianity that had been the hope of the CMS. Ultimately, the knowledge of his tūpuna won. His identity as rangatira Māori could not be overridden by threats of eternal condemnation should he not repent his sinful, uncivilised ways.

The short life of Tuai provided evidence that our tūpuna expected to understand, utilise, and adapt Pākehā knowledge to benefit themselves and their iwi. Tūpuna such as Tuai saw the potential in blending some Pākehā knowledge for its usefulness to Māori society and envisioned unprecedented progress for iwi Māori through the complementary use of Pākehā technologies with mātauranga Māori. However, this was not to be. The first systematic blows to Māori educational structures coincided with the widespread introduction of Christianity. Early missionaries made a deliberate and sustained attack on the belief systems that underpinned all of Māori society—our wairuatanga. The attack also targeted the conveners of this belief system, our tohunga. Binney (1968) argued that the intention of the missionaries was to not only transform Māori social structures, but to eradicate them through their actions and their words.

Ma te Atua tātu e manaāki: May God guide and protect us

Many Māori have a longstanding and deep mistrust of Pākehā education and social structures, as is evidenced by the pūkōrero of kaumātua in this study. The trusting relationship that had been fostered between Ruatara and Marsden disintegrated almost immediately in subsequent dealings of missionaries with Māori. The relationship between Ruatara and Marsden provided the foundation for the entry of missionaries to Aotearoa. Ruatara was motivated to bring British teachers to Aotearoa by what proved in the end to be a misconception—that written language would ensure Māori rangatiratanga authority and the retention of mana in dealings with Pākehā (Jones & Jenkins, 2011). Marsden was operating from a different agenda, to spread the teachings of Christianity, which in practice translated to Western morals and civility. Ruatara and Marsden had forged a genuine friendship that they both hoped would serve their differing aspirations. The relationship between missionaries and Māori that developed from this friendship was a more tenuous one in which the differing aspirations of Ruatara and Marsden became more pronounced. The goals and perspectives of Māori and missionaries deviated relatively soon after the formal arrival of missionaries in New Zealand.

While missionaries have been described as the "advance guard of a civilisation which was to kill so many" (Beaglehole, 1970, p. 25), initially evangelists presented an argument that colonisation was contrary to Māori wellbeing (Petrie, 2015). Their argument was that the colonisation of New Zealand be strictly limited to missionaries, tasked with the improbable responsibility of redressing Britain's past tyranny of Indigenous peoples by spreading the Gospel. However, in order to teach the Gospel, they first needed a grasp of the Indigenous language and customs. Missionaries essentially became the first teachers of formal Western education to Māori, and the first organised group of non-Māori to be educated by Māori.

Marsden's humanitarian objectives for his missionaries were woven into the sometimes supportive, sometimes oppressive relationship between Māori and missionary. By their own reckoning, theirs was a mission of civilisation, enlightenment, and goodwill. They believed their work was positive, despite the destructive impact it was to have on Māori (Binney, 1968). Wesleyan missionary Danderson Coates (Lay Secretary of the Church Mission Society) provides an example of the complicated stance missionaries held in regard to Māori. Coates argued in the House of Lords in 1838 against the colonisation of New Zealand on the basis that the sovereignty of New Zealand had already been acknowledged by Great Britain through He Whakaputanga (Select Committee of the House of Lords, 1838). He went so far as to contend that "... European colonisation, in every instance ... has resulted in the most disastrous consequences to the Aborigines of those countries which have so been colonised" (Select Committee of the House of Lords, 1838, p. 246).

In contrast to this apparent concern for the welfare of Māori, accounts such as those by Anglican minister Reverend William Yate (1802–1877) paint a picture of a beautiful country ripe with rich resources but inhabited by savage people and practices that the good missionaries are doing their utmost to eradicate (Yate, 1835). In the same meeting of the Select Committee on the Islands of New Zealand mentioned above, Coates confirms the image of savagery and adds it to his rationale opposing the colonisation of New Zealand, as New Zealanders are individuals of "... vigorous physical powers and of warlike character, but numerously armed with muskets, and habituated in the use of them" (Select Committee of the House of Lords, 1838, p. 248). This image of Māori was projected in contrast to the perception of gentle-natured Indigenous peoples of Australia, who were in the midst of colonisation.

Another missionary warns the House of Lords that Māori are difficult to trade with due to their trickery, that obtaining land needed for mission stations was marred with unpleasantness from Māori (Select Committee of the House of Lords, 1883). Māori chiefs and tohunga of the time had developed a great mistrust of Pākehā, missionaries underestimated Māori connection to the land, and they misunderstood Māori notions of ownership (Lee, 2006). Māori were simply exercising rangatiratanga rights according to our cultural norms and laws in response to Pākehā who believed they could deal unjustly with Māori, which was perceived as "unpleasantness" as described by Coates (1838).

These examples highlight the complicated perspective missionaries had of Māori. Many missionaries had a paternalistic respect for Māori, due to their observations of industriousness, intelligence, and in many instances, kindness. However, as these examples illustrate, missionaries appeared to be unable to perceive Māori as anything but uncivilised, whose salvation lay in relinquishing their pagan practices for the civil, godly practices of the West. They wanted to protect Māori from the full-blown colonisation that had devastated so many other Indigenous people, yet at the same time they wanted to "rescue" Māori by removing our culture and forcing their religious and social constructs on us. Linda Tuhiwai Smith (2012) argued that even in modern contexts insensitive and offensive subjugation of Indigenous peoples is justified as long as it is for the "good of mankind" (p. 26).

Perhaps the earliest examples of cultural competencies for teaching Māori learners were the qualifications Marsden dictated as essential for missionaries who would settle New Zealand. According to Marsden (Binney, 1968), missionaries must possess the qualities of piety to cater to the welfare of the poor Natives; patience to endure the challenges they would face; industry so they would not fall into temptation; and prudence would be needed to "govern a Savage [m]ind" (p. 9). These competencies echo 19th century humanitarian ideology and illustrate the intentions of the missionaries in their relationship with Māori. Christianity was to be the vehicle of salvation and civilisation for heathens.

Early missionaries introduced perhaps the first version of cultural competencies to New Zealand as a mechanism for teaching the tenets of Christianity. The CMS believed young Māori should be educated in the teachings of the Bible so they could subsequently influence their parents, and that in order to access the "truths" of the Bible, one must learn to read (Beaglehole, 1970). The perceived failure of the curriculum used to educate Tuai in England, which entailed learning to read the Bible in English, had taught Kendall and other missionaries that te reo Māori was essential as the language of instruction for Māori (Jones & Kaa Jenkins, 2017). Therefore, the first iteration of Western education for Māori in New Zealand emphasised the importance of reading in te reo, so that Māori could read the Bible in our own language, and therefore willingly convert to Christianity.

Missionaries believed that the success of converting Māori to Christianity was reliant on te reo Māori, and on Māori teachers (Lee, 2008). From 1813, before the opening of the first Mission School in Rangihoua, Marsden was conducting religious education to relatively large numbers of Māori youth from his home in Parramatta, at what became known as Marsden's Seminary (Beaglehole, 1970). Many of these youth were tūpuna from tribes I whakapapa to in Tai Tokerau, who returned home to become teachers and cultural intermediaries as Māori and Pākehā intersected more frequently.

Missionaries such as Kendall were enthusiastic to learn te reo in order to spread the teachings of Christ (Binney, 1968). Missionaries understood that to teach Māori learners they would need an understanding of te reo. Tūpuna such as Tuai understood this also; as discussed, he was keen to obtain Pākehā technologies for economic progression, and so was motivated to take on the role of teacher to Kendall. Kendall, motivated by the desire to teach the Gospel to Māori, immersed himself in both reo and tikanga Māori (Beaglehole, 1970) under the tutelage of Tuai.

Kendall found himself in the fortunate position of being under the protection of chiefs such as Tuai, and therefore gained access to many rituals and tikanga. His admission to observe our cultural practices was unique and could have given Kendall great insight in to the deep-rooted spiritual and epistemic beliefs of our culture. However, his prejudices distorted the intentions and significance of the customs he was privy to (Binney, 2005). His commitment to te reo and tikanga Māori as a teacher could serve as a lesson for teachers of today. His distorted perspective of Māori culture and unchanged prejudices unfortunately continue to reflect some of the attitudes that continue to persist in education.

Within the first year of the mission school being opened under Kendall's leadership, attendance grew from 33 Māori students to 70 by April 1817 (Beaglehole, 1970). The school at Rangihoua was a day school, as were the early mission schools throughout the country. At this point in our schooling history, the purpose of Western education was to convert Māori to Christianity, therefore the aim was to enable Māori to access print literacy so we would be able to read the Bible. For Māori to be educated at a day school whilst living within traditional whānau and hapū structures was, at this point, deemed permissible by missionaries—this would change as colonisation became part of the education agenda. They were reluctant, however, to have their own children educated alongside Māori who were, according to missionaries, in a state of degradation (Beaglehole, 1970).

It also was not long before the inability of missionaries to distinguish between the tenets of Christianity and the conventions of Georgian England saw Kendall, and other missionaries, purposefully interfere with Māori social structures (Binney, 2005). To be Christian was to be English, to be civilised was to be English, to be literate was to be English, and so the work of the missionaries inevitably became a task in preparing Aotearoa for colonisation (Binney, 2005; Jenkins, 1993; Stephenson, 2009). The forward-thinking intention of learning te reo as a teaching tool was perverted by the underlying motivation to "... destroy their [Māori] culture, considered merely indicative of the degradation of its creators" (Binney, 1968, p. 13). Similar sentiments would later infiltrate education laws and policies of future New Zealand Governments.

Despite the initial popularity in mission schooling, growing decline in attendance due to an increasing indifference to religion (McKenzie, 1985) began to vex missionaries. Many Māori of the 19th century still maintained their own religious beliefs; others had become disillusioned with Christianity. Māori motivation to access print was not in the content of the texts, but in text as a useful tool in itself. The provision of print literacy by missionaries marginalised Māori aspirations by restricting literacy access to religious material, and only in te reo. While the initial enthusiasm for missionary education had declined, what had been achieved in the first few decades was the ability of hundreds of Māori to read and write in our own language, and a natural flair and fervour for teaching Pākehā literacy was also evident (Barrington, 1970). Our language and culture would be in a beautiful space if as many Māori could read and write in te reo today.

However, what Māori wanted by the mid-1800s was access to print literacy in English (McKenzie, 1985), which would enable them to protect themselves, their economies, lands, and resources. Missionaries didn't see any need for Māori to have access to English print literacy, or to content outside of the scriptures. Rangatira wanted an opportunity to operate in New Zealand's changing circumstances on equal terms to their Pākehā counterparts (Henare, 2011). Māori wanted to define the Western education accessible to them but were denied that opportunity because of authoritarian views of missionaries.

Western education in the hands of missionaries had disengaged Māori learners through paternalistic attitudes that they knew what was best for Māori. McKenzie (1985) records a missionary's admission that, whilst they had made gains in providing a limited Western education, and arguably converting many Māori to Christianity, they had "... no hold on their children" (p. 30). Missionaries were therefore aware that the education they were providing had disengaged Māori, yet no alternative was offered to the restrictive and minimal education they provided. With whare wānanga also swiftly becoming a subterranean institution, Māori were quickly being forced into a position of being inadequately educated in both Pākehā and Māori institutions.

From the initial stages of Western education in New Zealand, Māori language and culture were exploited as devices to impose a foreign language and culture. This continues to be reflected in the superficial way the contemporary cultural competencies are employed in educational contexts—the underlying intention remains the same, to appropriate the existing culture and perspectives to teach a "better" way of knowing. Many of the problems with the education system of the missionaries in the 1800s are problems that continued to hinder Māori progress in education through to modern times (Beaglehole, 1970). Our tūpuna used their agency then by exiting a system that was not beneficial to them. In recent years, we have seen the development of many initiatives such as the cultural competencies; however, the underlying education system remains unchanged. The reality for many Māori is that the education system still has very little hold over our children.

"Tēnei te pou, te pou kai ā koe."

Chapter 5

He toa, he toa!

Te pūkōrero ō Hori Parata

I set off early for this interview because I was unsure of where Matua Hori's house was. As with all these research hui, I was quite nervous; the responsibility of gaining information from people I hold in high regard is weighty. Matua Hori had not been feeling well so I stopped to get some fresh fruit and lemons. Then I made my way into the neighbourhood I grew up in, and proceeded to drive around in circles, down people's driveways, in and out of private property. Finally, I pulled into the right driveway, and was astounded at the amazing collection of taonga Matua Hori has in and around his home. These are the pou whakamahara of a lifetime spent fighting on a range of fronts for the survival of our people and resources.

Hori grew up in coastal villages around Te Tai Tokerau, largely in Pātaua, but also in Whangaruru with members of his wider whānau. As a young man he enlisted in the New Zealand Army and served on active duty throughout Asia, including Borneo and Malaya. Matua Hori has a background as a soldier; he is also a soldier for the rights of our people, serving on endless committees and kaupapa over many years. His role is that of tohunga and mātanga in the protection of our natural resources. Hori has been a huge contributor to environmental care and management but has had particular impact on national scientific and cultural advances in knowledge of kiore, whales, and kauri. His involvement in dealing with the regeneration of kiore on our tūpuna islands, strandings, and with kauri is guided by our cultural understandings.

Hori has become a national authority on culturally appropriate approaches to strandings of all marine animals and mammals, oil spills, the ancient practice of hauhake (flensing and harvesting), and use and protection of natural resources. It was Hori who insisted that, in terms of environmental and resource management in the north, the Department of Conservation (DoC) had only one responsibility—to control and eradicate the invasive species introduced to our lands and waters. Ngāti Kuri was one of the iwi to take heed of his call. They now have an exemplary working model of co-management of their taonga species, with DoC playing a support role to the iwi. Matua Hori is a straight talker and has dedicated much of his life to challenging and pushing back against injustice at the hands of lawmakers and New Zealand Governments. He is currently the chairman of Ngāti Wai Kāhui Kaumātua.

After karakia, we sit at his kitchen table with our cups of tea, amongst his own PhD study material, to begin our kōrero. The first thing I ask is about a comment I heard him make during a recent hui. He had said, "I have no first language. I went to school and got a hiding for speaking one language, and then came home and got a hiding for speaking another language." Other than being an incredibly painful reality, what captured my interest was that Hori is a fluent, native speaker of te reo Māori, yet he feels as though he has no first language. I was interested to know more about his perspective. His response makes clear the effects of having lived through the confusion and trauma generations of young people face in claiming their identity when they are receiving multiple, often contradictory, messages simultaneously. These contradictions have caused Hori to feel uncomfortable, and unconfident about using both Māori and English languages:

One of my chapters that I'm writing about talks about generational trauma, and it was used, that kōrero as a basis of my own trauma. Is that when we were kids ... most of our kids were Māori kids and yet it was a Pākehā school, which I really hated, and so naturally you've got all your cuzzies and that aye, when you're not at school we're all talking Māori to each other. So, you just forget ... you wanna call out something to one of your relations at school and they would get the strap, go and get the strap. And the other one ... with my parents ... well not too sure which one of them really because they sort of shifted aye, my Mum and Dad, like one time, my Mum, she'd say 'Well, you fullas go and learn English' you know, or next time might be our Dad ... but that's what that was about, you'd be at home and you might say something in Pākehā and slap.

So, our discussion for this project is framed by generational trauma caused by colonisation. In many ways I feel this is fitting because, in my eyes, Hori is a freedom fighter. From the time of my childhood, I've heard his whaikōrero in many settings. He has been somebody who has fought injustices and fought fearlessly with great passion. Hori is also a holder of mātauranga Māori. His approach is what many would describe as "straight up"; that is, he will tell you what he thinks even if it will make you uncomfortable.

Hori is a teller of stories. His responses to all my questions during this discussion are contextualised with pūrākau. Our discussion on this mild morning is one that spirals into itself, everything is related, and we end where we begin. In response to my first question regarding what Hori believes to be education success for Māori, Hori first makes a point to highlight that "education" from a Māori perspective is very different to "education" from a Pākehā perspective:

... our tūpuna's way of educating mokopuna was a lot different to this Pākehā ... thing. The first lesson you learn is: that's your titty, that's where the kai is [our first lessons are at our mothers' breasts] ... and then of course from there, you start learning from there. And you don't stop learning. You learn all your life. Where Pākehā, you get to a certain age, let's say five, and then now you must go to school. And you learn Jack and Jill went up the hill and all sorts of stuff like that, which ... just don't fit with us. Especially with people like Māori, we were dependent on our environment for our survival. Our knowledge of it, our understandings of its behaviour, and things like that, that's where our education came from. And our classroom was either in the garden, or it was up at the mahinga kai, or it was something like that.

With some fundamental differences established, Hori then acknowledges that access to new technologies and a wide range of philosophies has changed education, and that there are many aspects of a modern education that are important for mokopuna. However, maintaining cultural identity is of utmost importance:

> ... we talk about our mokopunas, we talk about all these things we are talking about now, and we say 'well our mokopuna are all doing that now' [looking at screens/devices], and you don't even finish a meeting and what you've been talking about is already on Facebook! ... I think it's still important. That's why I say to my boy Kauri, he's learning political sciences and philosophy. So, he's looking at all of those Pākehā theorists, like Foucault and all of that, and I say 'that's great', I say 'by all means look at all of that stuff and search it out', but I said 'Kaua e wareware koe', look at some of our tūpuna's philosophies as well.
>
> I think that one of the most important things to know is to know who you are, where you are, why you are ... and if you learnt all of this other stuff, without even knowing that well then, as a Māori, you're just another number on the planet.
>
> It's that grounding. And I think that that's probably some of the most important pieces of education for a Māori kid.

I ask Hori who he thinks should be responsible for educating Māori children in the way he has described, which is giving them grounding in Māori identity as well as access to other forms of education. He is clear in defining two different sources and forms of education:

> Well, like I was saying there before, you've got two sides of this story. One is our own, Māori, nearly 170 years of being deprived ... our rightful place in our country. And on the other hand, you have this Western paradigm thing, which is all over the world aye, and outer space.
>
> So, I think that that first education, that one that I was just talking about, about knowing who you are and those sorts of things, I think that's got to come from home. That's got to come from home. And then of course the rest of that education comes from wherever, you know if you want it, it's out there, and you just go and look for it. So ... the first one is at home, with your family, and the other one's out there in the world.

What I find interesting here is that Hori has not specifically mentioned school as a context in which to gain access to either form of education. I probe into this by asking if English-medium education in its current form can deliver the type of education he is referring to:

> *No. No I don't really. Seems like somehow you come upon education by accident, rather than design.*

This sentiment has been a reality for many Māori in the education system. It seems for many Māori, success in schooling is somewhat of a lottery. Hori then goes on to discuss a fundamental shift in Māori thinking regarding education that came about due to colonisation:

> *I remember even when we were kids. Like our parents you know, that were becoming colonised and things like that ... they thought it was their responsibility to make you something ... which was a Pākehā thing. 'Oh, I want my child to be a doctor, oh, I want my child to be a bus driver.' Which our tūpuna never did that. I don't believe anyway.*

Hori then goes on to illustrate the skill Māori once had of observing a child then shaping specific learning experiences, and establishing appropriate networks for each child:

> *I believe that it was about looking at the little mokopuna you can see what he's gonna be, and you give him that time to show it, and then you promote it in them. Like if you, as a child, inside of you if all you going to be is a bus driver well then that's all you gonna be, aye? And so that's what our tūpunas would look at ... you don't interfere with the wairua of that child, you let that child remain in freedom so you can see—oh this child is a real talker, or a studious person, or this one just likes doing things with its hands. So, you look at those sorts of things, and then we say well you know because this kid likes to do certain things, we know someone ... when a child come of a certain age, well then you let the child go across and be with those people, to learn that.*

The crucial role of cultural identity and awareness of time, place, and space in a child's education again comes to the fore. Hori makes it clear that this education must begin at a young age for children:

> ... the first foundation in your education is got to be back home ... with your family, and knowing who and what you are and where you are ... And it didn't matter where you went in your life after that, if you knew how to earth yourself again, if you got lost somewhere.

I am aware that many Māori are disconnected from their Māori cultural identities or through a range of circumstances have a lack of depth in their knowledge of tikanga and reo. I ask if there is a way that this form of education might happen in modern settings given our context of colonisation. Hori first establishes some of the flaws in trying to push Māori education agendas within Pākehā frameworks:

> I think that ... us on our own it won't happen. See because, part of the way that Western paradigm maintains control is by themselves controlling the funding ... And even if they like your proposal a little bit, they'll still continue to try change parts of it. And by the time you do get funded you find that you're not teaching what you wanted to teach in the first place ... So, I think that that is part of the problem for us ... Because somehow you've got to ... go cap in hand to them ... it's belittling. Especially for something as important as educating our mokopuna. It's, it's very belittling, and demoralising too.

One of Hori's fields of expertise in mātauranga Māori is natural resources, which puts him in high demand with a range of government organisations. Part of his responsibility to his people is ensuring that obligations to tāngata whenua are being met by government organisations. This work, and his work on Te Tiriti o Waitangi claims, has given him first-hand experience of the processes that can leave Māori feeling demoralised. However, through the humiliation of being made to jump through hoops, Hori still sees solutions. As with the other kaumātua in this study, his solutions are profound in their simplicity:

> I'm saying, well it seems like only hearts and minds. It's not like anything massive has to change, it's just really in your heart and mind where the change has got to be made.

The need for the hearts and minds of both Māori and Pākehā to change is essential; however, Hori sees that this, while not massive, is problematic:

> ... Pākehās are not prepared to do that, they're scared actually, I think they're very frightened to change from the path that they've been on with us ... There was another neat saying that I found ... it talks about people who started believing that they wanted to go somewhere and then after a while, they get let down here, let down there and ... they sort of stopped. And the saying goes something like this: 'The only way forward is back. But there they stand at the crossroads of idiocy seemingly determined to complete the journey.'
>
> It's a bit like us in this [Waitangi Tribunal] claims process. It's a bit like that. The only way forward is back.

The concept Hori is referring to is much like the ontology of historical reality and is a concept strong in Māori tikanga. We walk into the future facing the past. According to Hori's perspective, this difference in perspective is one of the factors that hinders a change in hearts and minds, and is also a source of extreme frustration:

> ... how many times do we have to tell these blinking [Pākehā] about these things? Cos they got no memory. They have no memory. They don't have institutional memory. Because they know they've done so many blimey things that are hē, that they don't want to really remember any of that.

As with many discussions about cultural injustice in this country, our discussion turns to the relationships tūpuna Māori have had with Pākehā, and thwarted attempts at achieving an effective working relationship from the outset:

> ... [in] a lot of my research ... I'm just running into so much stuff ... right from the beginning our tūpunas tried to say to these Pākehā ... this is the problem, we're prepared to work with you, together with you, to help to fix them up. But those Pākehās they don't do nothing with it ...

The history that Hori shares next is important in terms of contextualising the origins of the political relationship between Māori and the government, and the inherent differences in perspectives in terms of that relationship. Where the rangatira of Te Tai Tokerau, particularly around the Bay of Islands region, believed the British would set up government in a position where they could monitor the situation, the representatives of the Crown had different ideas:

> ... when the Treaty was signed, well by that time already I think it was Gilbert Mair[11] who owned Ōkiato. Ōkiato had wharves and deep water and all of those sorts of things, plus concrete buildings, so Hobson bought those when he signed the Treaty. And our tūpunas were quite happy with that because this fulla's going to set his government up here where we can monitor it. But he ... only stayed in his new dwellings for about nine months, and by that time that was when Tāmaki Makaurau, Ngāti Whātua, invited him to come down there and set his government up there. So, he took off. He took off up to there and took his favourite riff-raff with him, and started building ... stone walls, bringing in soldiers and those sorts of things. And died, and then his favourite riff-raff ... run the ... government for nearly over two years before Fitzroy came.
>
> I'm saying here that as Māori we have to deal with the good, the bad and the ugly of these ... Pākehās ... and so between the three of them, between the good, the bad, the ugly they've been running our government ... they've been governing us ... for 177 years.
>
> And I guess it's those sorts of things, like uara ... our values and principles and things like that, it's not like as if they're the same aye?
>
> So monoculturalism, the imposition of monoculturalism on people like us has been horrendous. It's all but destroyed us really.

Given that there are some teachers in New Zealand schools who do operate from monocultural perspectives, I ask Hori what skills those teachers might need in order to fulfil the Ministry of Education's objectives for teachers to progress in the cultural competencies, and to teach Māori students in ways that will allow them education success as Māori:

---

11 Gilbert Mair Snr was one of the first settlers to exploit the kauri gum industry. He set up a very successful trading station from the Wahapū inlet, where Ōkiato is located, and traded kauri gum to the United States. Mair was an advocate for declaring New Zealand a British colony and was a founding member of the controvertial Kororāreka Association, which attempted settler self-rule (for more, see https://teara.govt.nz/en/biographies/1m4/mair-gilbert).

> *I suppose if I was being truthful, I would say ... that they shouldn't have anything at all to do with our kids at that age. That's just me ... Because that is the part in that child's life where that child's ging to make it or break it.*

Hori refers to school environments that continue to operate largely as monocultural as being unsafe spaces for Māori students. I then ask him what might make schools safe places. He refers back to a shift in the hearts and minds from individual teachers, right through to the overall education framework:

> *Well, it's back in hearts and minds again ... and it's not only the hearts and minds of the teacher, it's the hearts and minds of the system that controls teachers.*

Hori also points out that Māori teachers who have a lack of reo Māori and tikanga also feed into maintaining a monocultural education system, and they too need to shift their perspective and ways of thinking to meet the needs of Māori students. Change, from Hori's perspective, will happen once people let go of fear:

> *... if it's a Māori [teacher], if that Māori does not have the reo, and some understanding of Māori worldview, well then they're no different ...*
>
> *... they're afraid of it. They are very afraid of something that they are not familiar with. And that's one of the reasons why I'm saying they shouldn't have anything to do with our kids at that age.*

Hori returns to the lessons left by our tūpuna to find resolutions for the damage that can be caused by a monocultural education system that can, in his words, take a "healthy minded young child" and "shut them down". His view again emphasises cultural differences in pedagogical practices:

> *... I guess what I'm trying to balance here is how our tūpunas understood learning ... it wasn't something that you jammed into somebody's mind, it sort of went gently in there, you know, like something you liked ... I felt that a lot of the style of teaching ... is kind of like force fed. You take it or else.*

> ... that's the other thing about our tūpunas too, you know you're watching all the time and if you can see that that child is shut down for now, well don't keep trying to jam it in there: Jack and Jill went up the bloody hill. Just let them go and do something else for a little while, and then you can see, you're watching, and they always come back on again, and they're away again.

There are also implications for initial teacher education to mitigate inflicting damage on young children through a monocultural approach to education and pedagogy:

> ... a lot of those ways ... Western teachers and that are taught how to teach is a part of the problem.

> Once your child has reached that intermediate stage, well then they're pretty much ready for the world. But if you damage them on that journey to that point ...

Hori has a strong stance and perspective on education and the negative effects of colonisation. I wonder what his stance is on the role of mātauranga Māori in English-medium schools. I'm interested to know whether teachers having more access to mātauranga Māori may improve teaching practice, or if he believes mātauranga should remain the domain of those who hold the knowledge:

> When we talk about mātauranga, you know, Māori ways of knowing, all of those sorts of things ... that's more like a university level. And just in regards to that, I do believe that mātauranga needs to be protected. But if you allow it to be used down at that kōhanga level—I'm not talking about the kids, I'm talking about the teachers—if you allow it to be used down there it gets contaminated, or it gets interfered with just to make it fit these little kids. There're some bits ... that are very relevant in our mātauranga. But mātauranga per se, to me, is a university knowing. There's another level, a higher level of knowing.

Given that mātauranga Māori is seen here as a higher level of knowing, and that most teachers are not at that level, we discuss the complexity of merging mātauranga Māori into contemporary frameworks such as education. Hori gives me an analogy that illustrates how complex the idea is, but the complexities need to be untangled:

If you like ... what we just talking about now it's like, let's say your fishing line just got all tangled, and it looks hopeless when you look at it, you think 'Wow', and you're trying to make a decision about whether you cut it all off and throw it away, or whether you try and untangle it. A fishing line was too important in our tūpuna's time to just go and cut it. So even those sorts of things, like different karakia, now we talking about things that really do belong in that mātauranga realm, you know, karakia to just help you sort that tangle out.

While Hori believes kaumātua should be the ones who choose the appropriate types of knowledge to share, at the appropriate times, we must be careful about how we use and understand the term "kaumātua". As with so many other aspects of Māori culture, the notion of "kaumātua" has been coloured by external definitions and perspectives. The most common understanding of "kaumātua" is a person who is of a certain age, usually older than 60:

... I know that a lot of our kaumātua ... a lot of them know less than some of our kids know. Let alone that they don't know our reo, they don't even know their whakapapa, or even stories about themselves ... I feel really aroha for them.

... it's like that tangled fishing line thing that I'm talking about. You know, there are some parts of the tangle that are easy, there are other parts that are really difficult, they're almost 'Where's my pocket knife?' stuff. But you imagine back in our tūpuna's time, you don't cut line, well you'll get off the boat and swim home!

So, some of that untangling is 'What is a kaumātua?' Part of the kaupapa that I'm talking to my kaumātuas and that about is that kaumātua they have certain responsibilities. We've got a tangi on down the marae, or there's a serious take going down on the marae and it needs to be handled in a Māori context ... So, what I'm saying in there to my kaumātuas is that you are only a kaumātua if you can perform in a Māori frame.

Along with knowing how to work within a Māori context, Hori also believes that the expertise of kaumātua must be recognised, and that they should be the group to whom Māori institutions such as rūnanga and trust boards are accountable:

> ... we're a different kaumātua to my parents' time. In my parents' time they were just flat out trying to handle being Māori, or just trying to be a person, whereas kaumātua today—this person has been in education, you know worked for the education system all of its life, and now it's a kaumātua, this one here did health, this one here did something else, so we're a different kaumātua to back then. So, what I'm saying in there is that kaumātua will have veto over our legal systems, our trust boards, and rūnangas, and things like that, and that's quite a biggie ... because if you didn't do that, the only line of accountability for those bodies is back to the enemy.

This concept has the potential to impact education in terms of finding ways to move forward with te ao Māori in education that is safe for all involved. However, it will also require an untangling of the way many schools view and engage with kaumātua. Instead of only turning to kaumātua for ceremonial purposes, schools would need to genuinely engage and listen to the advice and wisdom of kaumātua.

Our discussion then leads to a problem that has been addressed in this project—the appropriation and/or use of Māori words and concepts outside of Māori contexts that then take on a new, often very disconnected, meaning from the Māori understanding. Hori is calling for a discontinuation of the use of the word "kaumātua" unless it is used correctly, not simply to denote age:

> ... they don't know what the hell it means, they think they know, but what it does, it belittles kaumātua. There's no doubt about it, this person's 80, but this person has ... married its husband down in Wairoa or somewhere down the line, brought its kids up and everything, and the kids are all left home, and the husband's died, and now this person come home, and say: 'I don't know what you fullas talk about, boy, when you fullas talk Māori. I don't know nothing about our history, of our marae, or even who we damn well are!' But there's no question about it, that person is 80. So, we're

> *saying that that person will not be called kaumātua. That person will be called an elder ... An elder member of the tribe.*
>
> *... it's not their own fault that they can't speak Māori. It's cos ... we were all told it, even in my kid-time: 'Hey, you fullas need to go and learn to speak Pākehā and understand the Pākehā world' ... That's what Kawiti said, you know, go into the institutions ... and find out how they establish their uara.*
>
> *So that's what I'm saying ... therefore, things like mātauranga and that needs to be held in the realm of ... experts in our knowledge. Tohunga.*

There are lessons here for education in terms of utilising kaumātua in more culturally appropriate ways, as holders of particular knowledge, not to plunder, but to seek advice from and to ensure that things Māori in education are carried out correctly. Another implication is that the scope and process of untangling is difficult even for Māori who identify as Māori, so for non-Māori who do not know the nuances and history of the culture, the task could prove insurmountable. Hori believes the solution is for decisions to be made by knowledgeable Māori, not by others.

Hori then discusses "Te Whakaputanga o Te Puea", a document he was involved in developing, which intends to protect Māori rights to natural resources and intellectual property and is directly linked to the WAI 262[12] claim. He points out in particular the "Morality Clause" attached to that document:

> *... they made a description of morality being something that you do over a long period of time and it becomes customary, traditional, but at the end of the day ... it helps you to understand what is right and wrong about something. Now that was really important ... because we'd been saying for some time that the Crown were wrong in the way that they were doing stuff. What Moana Jackson added to*

---

12 The WAI 262 claim to the Waitangi Tribunal was for the protection of Māori intellectual property rights to flora and fauna. The claim resulted in wide-reaching reform to laws and policies regarding Māori culture and identity. The claim also initiated a shift in the Waitangi Tribunal claims process, moving from being grievance-based to focusing on co-management of resources. Both Hori Parata and Te Warihi Hetaraka were expert witnesses in this revolutionary claim.

> *that was a clause ... and it just said 'And it depends whose culture you're talking about.' So, you don't talk about an Australian, an Australian Aborigine's culture from a Māori perspective ... if you don't understand ... enough [about the culture], well then you don't do it at all, don't touch it ... Leave it alone. There are other people looking after that.*

This links directly to an argument made in this book that one's perspective of what is right, wrong, or something in between will always be culturally dependent; it will depend on the cultural lens being used. Our thoughts then turn to the notion of becoming culturally competent, particularly for teachers of Māori students becoming competent in Māori culture against the backdrop of colonisation. I ask Hori his thoughts on the possibilities of this notion:

> *So, cultural competency ... Māoris have got it, they've got it because ... Māori are both cultures ... We understand a lot about Western culture, and we understand a lot about, well, an amount, of our own Māori culture. Whereas Pākehā, you could not expect them to be able to attain that unless they went through a certain process, and a lot of them won't because it's not part of the curriculum, I guess. So, there are other ways ... that they end up getting their Māori cultural grounding.*

Here Hori reminds us of the care that must be taken by non-Māori when seeking Māori cultural grounding, or when seeking to tell a story that is not yours to tell. He gives an example that is a very real illustration of just how problematic it can be to gain genuine cultural understanding, especially when the people whose knowledge you seek do not trust you:

> *... one of the good things about ... being academics today, Māori academics, is that we're producing thoughts and ideas ... we're, not like let's say in my parents' time, where the only avenue that they had was Elsdon Best or somebody like that ... when you get to know the Tūhoe people, where Elsdon wrote a lot of stuff, you know, from*

living with them—and their own story was that they just played with him.

We then discuss in-depth concepts such as the "civilisation" of the native, religion, cultural dominance, similarities and differences in cultural perspective, responsibilities of initial teacher educators, and agency of student teachers—all in relation to the complex notion of becoming culturally competent:

> *I think that that thing about cultural competency ... what you get is [Pākehā] who are saying, insisting that these things be ... as if they know what it is themselves ... Now, [I'm] sick of it, sick of them blimmin' talking like that about us.*

> *... even with things like cultural competency there's aspects of Māori culture, not the culture.*

> *... I'm saying once our tūpunas launched themselves onto the ocean, into the Pacific, they became a culture alone for 3,500 years. How's that!? ... So, it's a culture that's been uncontaminated ... Sure, it's still Stone Age culture, but ... at the same time it was still very ... here and now. And so that's why that whole thing about our whole cultural context ... needs to be ... understood properly ... When you got so-called superiors saying to you as a trainee school teacher, 'This, this, this, and this' and it's up to yourself to ask them the question: 'Just explain what you mean by that. We understand, certainly, we understand Māori culture to be a huge kaupapa, so what do you mean? And if you're talking about that huge kaupapa can you describe some of it yourself?' Otherwise, don't go there!*

I discuss with Hori the role that cultural competencies currently play in education, and that the Teaching Council is ultimately responsible for assessing teachers' Māori cultural competence. His response is straightforward:

> *Yeah so that cultural competence thing, you know, it needs to be said too, you know that those Pākehā need to ... got to stop doing that to us because it's just killing us ... it teaches people to believe that they*

> have cultural competence, and they still don't know how to say 'kia ora' properly ... Or they still don't know why they're saying it.

> ... that Western paradigm is such an ugly looking animal that it's got all of these other things behind it. See, so it's not a clear path, it's not just a clear pathway from here to there. It's a pathway where you do a bit of dilly-dallying here and there ... So Pākehās within the system ... they need to be told that hey, stop it, call it something else. Call it something else and help your students to understand what they're calling it.

As with most of the other participants in this project, Hori recognises that the issues we are discussing are not isolated to education, but stem directly from the agreement and relationship Māori have with the Crown:

> Now, I think that it's ensconced within ... those things that I described. Because I'm talking about that ... not in terms of education, but in terms of the behaviour of our treaty partner and its insistence of being—you, up, up like a bird, and me down like a worm. No. Kahore! ... if that happens then my mokopuna will become your slave.

> Because that's why I even say to our people 'Stop talking, and acting, and behaving like slaves! He rangatira koutou!' It's even like this whole education thing, teaching teachers how to be teachers, is like teaching them how to be a particular kind of a slave.

Our kōrero again turns back to our history, to the differences in the types of relationships Māori and Pākehā were looking for from each other when we first met. This discussion is important, as it highlights yet again the complexity of achieving cultural competence in another culture as you sit within the realms of your own cultural understanding. As Hori illustrates, the northern rangatira from whom we descend were purposefully seeking a well-informed political relationship with the Crown:

> ... I don't believe that our tūpunas saw any of those other Pākehās, you know like even Hobson, as being a rangatira, because they still subservient to somebody, and when you are subservient to somebody,

you do not have that ultimate power over life and death. Whereas to [rangatira] ... that was the power they had.

They recognised that power to be in British royalty, not in Pākehā, but in British royalty. What our tūpuna wouldn't have understood ... I've been doing a lot of research into ... British royalty too, and they turn out to be a whole lot of bloody nutters really. Madmen! But our tūpunas wouldn't have seen it like that because they would have been seeing just a pure picture: here's your ordinary Pākehās, and here's his boss over here.

I talk about that in my thesis, because I talk about my tupuna Mahanga, as being one of the first Māori to actually harirū with British royalty. And of course, certainly when he came home ... and started talking about 'Oh Pākehās have got these buildings that go all the way up to the sky, they've got these streets and that that are all made up, and it's got lights and ...' Yeah. They were: 'Ea, pōrangi!'

But those tohungas and that, they said 'Hey, you fullas better get that fulla over here.' Maumau taima him talking to those fullas cause ... they can't even get a handle on what he's talking about ... So that's when those tohungas and ... those rangatira ... they got him aside and that's when those Whakaminenga started ... to talk about Pākehā ... Clever people ... so that was them pulling Mahanga off to the side, you know 'Tell us, tell us about it' ... then they end up sending others, you know, you go and have a look too.

So, the rangatira ki te rangatira was our tūpunas seeing themselves having an agreement with their rangatira, and of course, even though at the end of the day ... that turned out to turn us inside out ...

Hori then begins to talk about the Western practice throughout history of using Christianity and whakapono as a means of imposing Western culture on Indigenous peoples. During this discussion, the exasperation experienced by Hori is clear. This frustration is important. It is fuel to continue working for justice, it is the context in which Māori are forced to face the modern world. Often, we face it alone as this is not the history taught in our schools, it is the side of the story swept under the rug:

I'm just saying that you ... Pākehās, you fullas have been really bloody mean to us. Big time, and I'm just saying it outright.

You're a pack of thieves, liars, murderers and pack rapists ... They were saying that what we were doing as soldiers in Sarawak was right ... even though the boys started dying quick from Agent Orange ...

I said they were liars, we weren't, we shouldn't have been there [in Sarawak].

I'm saying they're murderers because some of the boys got killed being there.

I said they're thieves because when I came home [from war] they were stealing the ... beach off my mother at Pātaua.

I said they're pack rapists because I'm with the Ministry for Primary Industries now on the Kauri Dieback Programme, and in their sixth year they have their sixth manager, and I said why I'm calling them pack rapists is because whenever a new manager comes on board, he pulls us backwards [disregarding all of the knowledge already shared and developed] so he can catch up, and then 12 months later he sees another career opportunity somewhere else and buggers off.

So, I'm not just calling them outright thieves, liars and murderers, I'm giving some of my own explanation for calling them that ... have we ever done that to you people? No, we haven't, we've never done anything like that to you ...

A laugh is had amidst the talk of grievance. Hori jokes that his first language is te reo kangakanga, the language that curses and swears. He confides that he does want to stop swearing, "... and I do want to change my attitude, but it ain't gonna happen any time soon!".

This admission makes me reflect on the role Hori has as a toa rangatira. It must be emotionally taxing to be always alert to the movements of governments. It must also be a largely thankless job that many would not understand. People who speak their minds are often accused of being angry and emotional. The anger is frowned upon, then ignored, with little attempt to understand what lies beneath—which is people who have lived through systemic violence, people who no longer want to carry the burden of generations of injustice, but who have little choice, because to concede is to shirk responsibility to future generations.

As we reach what we thought was the end of our kōrero, Hori reflects on his life, his lessons, and his purpose. He, like the other participants, returns to his culture, like an anchor in a storm:

> ... I've just been diagnosed with cancer too. It's made you sort of come to terms with yourself, what the hell is this really all about? What is the purpose of being here? Is there a purpose of being here on this blinking planet?
>
> I'm thankful for my Māori-ness, because our tūpunas left so many little gems and that behind to look after you. That's why I saw whakatauākī as being a very significant part, you know, if you get yourself lost or something, just try to recall a whakataukī or something that might have some similarities to it, and bang you feel it all sort of smooth out again.

I laughingly say I don't want to stop the recording in case Hori says something important as we finish our tea. Which he does. I switch the recorder back on as Hori begins to talk about Te Warihi and his role as tohunga. He talks about Te Warihi's cultural knowledge in relation to education and the notion of cultural competence:

> ... our Pākehā education processes sort of interferes, cuts right across all of that. Because a lot of [education professionals] wouldn't even know where to begin to start talking to a tohunga like [Te Warihi]... that's something that me and your dad have been talking about for some years, like how do we elevate our tauira ourselves, nē? How do we establish criteria around ok we can take this tauira now to the next level, and it don't need some bal'head's tick off. There are other tohunga and that around the country, they're the only ones who can gather around together, a ka tika.

> *Well you see where Western paradigm controls it eh, controls it with the funding.*
>
> *We're not going to fund you ... unless you do it like this. You know that's cruel and mean.*

What is evident is the mismatch between Māori ways of knowing and being, and Pākehā education systems, practices, and processes that ensure control remains firmly in the hands of Pākehā. Hori's final comment is one that calls for sense, for balance, and for reason from our treaty partners:

> *Well, that's just another one of those Pākehā things aye, they're saying well unless we can get some physical evidence of what you are talking about, we're not going there ... yet that is just so damn ridiculous. It goes back to that thing I was saying before, I do, I say to these Pākehā outright what ... are you scared of? Do you think it will take your food out of your mouth, or it'll ... do you some harm? No, you don't, so what are you scared of? You know, cut it out aye. We're sick of you ... doing us like that.*

Legislating education for Māori

The lessons gleaned from the pūkōrero of Hori Parata strongly highlight the differences between traditional mātauranga and pedagogical practices, and contemporary education. What Hori also allowed me to see was his trauma and frustration at consistently being forced to navigate systems that contradict and undermine almost everything about his identity. He often referred to the complicated Māori–Pākehā history that was the source of much of Māori social and cultural disruption. This section will analyse education lawmaking practices that have been a significant cause of the trauma faced by many Māori and highlighted in Hori's pūkōrero.

Lawmaking links strongly to Hori because he has long acted against unjust laws, policies, and practices. He has a deep understanding of the history that has contributed to the swift dismantling of Māori social and cultural structures. His words, "They have no memory. They don't have institutional memory" lay down a challenge to remember, to track the whakapapa of our systemic relationships in Aotearoa, because in remembering we reduce the risk of repeating mistakes. In remembering we raise the chances of gaining better understandings of each other and seeing the reasons for current situations. The wairua of Hori's pūkōrero also raises a question important to this study: What has contributed to such a swift and conclusive disruption of cultural understandings that have deep and previously uninterrupted roots? Hori's pūkōrero provides the opportunity to explore this question. This section will provide that analysis.

Māori and British law

In 1988, Tā Himi Henare (Henare, 2011) argued that the Treaty of Waitangi, which was not signed by rangatira on 6 February 1840, opened doors for the government "... to create laws to suppress us and to elevate them above us ..." (p. 3). Many of these laws have successfully subordinated Māori for generations. The injustices are reflected in Hori's words "... in terms of the behaviour of our treaty partner and its insistence of being you up, up like a bird, and me down like a worm. No! Kahore ... if that happens then my mokopuna will become your slave."

The Treaty also provided the policy utilised by representatives of the Crown, followed by settler Governments, to override the form of governance that already existed in Aotearoa in the form of sovereign rangatira. According to Crown interpretation, the Treaty was a legal way for them to begin governance in New Zealand over both British subjects and Māori. However, according to Māori, Te Tiriti gave the Crown the right to govern increasing numbers of Pākehā within a sovereign Māori nation. Tracking British lawmaking in Aotearoa clarifies how the Crown wrested control of New Zealand from Māori. Examining some key education laws will provide context as to how the education system came to be, and how education has arguably damaged the essence of being Māori. This whakapapa will assist in clarifying whether becoming culturally competent is an attainable or realistic "remedy" for a system that has its roots in colonisation and assimilation.

Deep into the 1900s, many Māori struggled with the concept that the laws of the British Crown could apply to us—Te Tiriti o Waitangi had clearly stipulated that Pākehā could govern Pākehā but had no rights to govern Māori. Indeed, there are still Māori today who do not acknowledge Pākehā law as binding. However, despite this, many Māori families have examples of our people being arrested and charged under Pākehā law that, according to the agreement our tūpuna signed, existed to manage Pākehā society, not Māori. The Native Exemption Ordinance 1844 acknowledges British hopes that Māori would embrace English law, but that Māori were exempt from their law. The ordinance called for involvement from rangatira to settle disputes among Māori, in what is an early attempt at blending cultural norms for societal order. It seems, however, that those who wrote and enforced the law quickly forgot this and consequently created laws to override the Native Exemption Ordinance.

Today, the whare tūpuna Kākā Porowini in Whangārei stands on the site where highly successful entrepreneur Kākā established a community centre from one of his estates. He used this estate as a refuge for Māori passing through Whangārei, and to educate Māori in the 1930s and 1940s about the Pākehā laws that were affecting many of our people. My own grandfather was one of many arrested for camping overnight on roadsides during long journeys between communities. I will never know if he came to fully understand how Pākehā law managed to disable Māori from walking freely on our own lands as we had for generations. What our people did come to understand was that if Pākehā laws were broken we would be punished.

Pākehā law and punishment had long been a focus of rangatira and Māori in general. In 1835, Yate (1835) records a Māori perspective of justice: "If a man commits a crime worthy of death, we shoot him or chop off his head; but we do not tell him first ... before the blow can be felt, he is dead" (p. 105). This is contrasted, and disparaged, against a Pākehā perspective: "But the law of England herein is merciful, that it gives time to the sinner to reflect ... to seek the way of peace with

God …" (Yate, 1835, p. 105). For Māori, the practice of gaoling was seen as far more cruel than a quick execution. It was better, from a Māori perspective, to kill swiftly rather than torture a person with a slow, soul-destroying death behind bars. It is ironic then that under Pākehā law Māori are incarcerated in this country in greater proportion than any other ethnicity (Statistics New Zealand, 2018).

The practice of gaoling that our tūpuna found to be so inhumane has become common to their uri. Once they had begun to make laws in Aotearoa, the Crown very swiftly began to enforce the most abhorrent punishment that would impose the generational trauma Hori discussed, and the impoverishment of the general Māori population—the removal of our lands, and therefore our sustenance and economy, from under our very feet. This punishment was inflicted for many reasons, a common one being insubordination to laws that the Crown had said did not apply to us.

Following the signing of Te Tiriti, in 1841 tohunga Aperahama Taonui (c. 1815–1882) travelled Te Tai Tokerau discussing issues with rangatira that they wished to be taken to Queen Victoria (1819–1901; r. 1837–1901) (Edwards, 2010). These hui were examples of rangatira enacting their side of the promise they had agreed to in Te Tiriti—that they would work in consultation with the Pākehā rangatira, who at this time was Queen Victoria. One of the points of discussion included a selection of Pākehā laws that rangatira were considering introducing in Aotearoa in order to manage Pākehā (Edwards, 2010). During this series of hui, rangatira also decided that all land matters would only be dealt with by rangatira of hapū (Edwards, 2010). This decision gives us a clear indication that rangatira had a well-defined understanding of the sovereignty they retained under the terms of the agreement they had signed the previous year. All the issues discussed by rangatira in hui were not intended to be presented as petitions to the Queen; they were intended as points for consultation between rangatira of different cultures. These decisions and actions have remained in Māori consciousness; however, the purposeful intentions of our tūpuna have all but disappeared in the dominant Pākehā history of our country.

The next section will investigate a number of key laws that have impacted on the direction of education for Māori. It must be read with an understanding that the ways in which laws play out in different communities are varied and that there are often contradictions between policy and practice. What is important to this project are the ways in which patriarchal ideas about "what is best" in education for Māori have been ratified by laws, become status quo, and have eventually led to, and provide a backdrop for, our current situation of seeing cultural competence as a "what is best" approach to Māori education. Three pieces of historical legislation will be discussed for the long-term impacts they have had on Māori: the Education Ordinance Act 1847; the Native Schools Act 1867; and the Tohunga Suppression Act 1907.

The Education Ordinance Act 1847

The Education Ordinance Act 1847 had a significant impact on schooling for Māori for a number of reasons. It was the first official involvement of the Crown into schooling for Māori, which had previously been the sole domain of missionaries. The Act was also the first iteration of British law defining the shape of Western education for Māori. It signalled a marked change in Crown–Māori interactions. This Act, and all others of the time, demonstrates the belief the Crown had in its right to govern Māori. There would be no more careful treading through the sovereign nation of Aotearoa; this was now a colony of the Empire. Using the decree of the Treaty of Waitangi, the Crown would apply its law to remove rangatiratanga from Māori. The Education Ordinance Act provides the first example of how the Crown, and later New Zealand Governments, would treat education for Māori. Without consultation, the Crown would use Pākehā law to control Māori, they would define Māori education, and they would use education as a tool for colonisation through assimilation.

Under the Education Ordinance Act, Māori church boarding schools were funded on the premise that they provide religious and industrial training to Māori through English instruction (Lee, 2008). As previously discussed, Māori had become disillusioned with missionary schooling due to the lack of instruction in English, which Māori believed would enable iwi to be economically competitive with non-Māori (Henare, 2010). By 1845, Governor George Grey (1812–1898), the representative of the Queen in New Zealand and the author of the Act, also held the view that Māori needed to be fluent in English, not to enable equal competition with Pākehā for economic growth, rather for the purpose of becoming Europeanised (Barrington & Beaglehole, 1974). Grey believed that, for Māori to become more like Europeans, we needed to be educated in isolation from our villages, which he saw as a demoralising influence on Māori children (Barrington, 1970).

To access secular, Crown-sponsored Western education, Māori had to be removed from their whānau, hapū, and iwi, an experience shared by many Indigenous communities colonised by Britain (Regan, 2010; Schissel & Wotherspoon, 2003). For economic reasons, many Māori did want to gain this type of education. Since before the arrival of Pākehā to Aotearoa, tohunga had made prophecies about the negative impact colonisation would have on Māori. Many of these are still relevant and continue to be recited amongst hapū and iwi. However, outside of tohunga and rangatira, everyday Māori of the 1800s probably could not imagine a time where the disconnection from Māori social structures and knowledge bases would be so great that it would endanger our language, culture, and identity. Therefore, Crown subsidisation of boarding schools, not of village day schools, probably did not initially cause too much suspicion or alarm for Māori. During this period, Māori lived Māori lives. The majority of our tūpuna would have thought it impossible that Pākehā education could teach our culture out of us. Many Māori would have thought that sending their tamariki to church boarding schools would add Pākehā knowledge to their Māori education, not de-culturalise them.

Grey believed Māori needed to be assimilated into British culture in order to hasten New Zealand's colonisation (Barrington, 1970). Walker (2016) argues that Grey was faced with a particular problem, the existence of "dispossessed owners of the soil" (p. 23) who continued to hamper the hasty colonisation of New Zealand. Grey's aggressive policies seem to express a perspective that if Māori became Pākehā, Māori opposition to the dispossession of lands and rangatiratanga would be eliminated. Grey essentially used British law in an attempt to turn Māori into what our tūpuna Kawiti refers to as poai Pākehā (Pākehā boys), with education being the tool. The Education Ordinance Act legally ratified Grey's assimilationist ideas by providing a restrictive education to Māori in boarding schools and removing Māori children from the influences and protection of their communities. The Act initialised a systematic and legal dismantling of Māori social structures and language through education.

The Crown's goals to assimilate Māori happened to coincide with Māori goals to attain Western education. Māori wanted the skills needed for iwi to flourish in the modern world. Schooling was still viewed by rangatira as a way for Māori to engage with settler society (Smith, 2016). The outcomes desired by Māori and the Crown were substantively different, as they were earlier between rangatira and missionaries. However, also as it was prior to 1840, the pathway both saw for achieving their differential goals was similar—Māori access to Western education. While Māori were committed to obtaining Western schooling, the Crown was committed to establishing a colony and assimilating Māori into their society through education. These conditions enabled the Crown to initiate the rule-making process over Māori education through British law, despite the fact that rangatira had agreed in Te Tiriti o Waitangi to allow the British Crown to make laws for British subjects in Aotearoa, and that rangatira would continue to govern Māori issues.

One of the attractions for Europeans to the new colony of New Zealand in the 19th century was that it was to be an egalitarian, classless society. However, the enactment of the Education Ordinance Act made it clear that Crown representatives intended to use education to prepare Māori for specific roles in the new society. The Crown would provide subsidised religious education along with industrial training in English in church boarding schools. The dream of a society free of class restrictions was being sold to prospective settlers at the same time as Māori were being prepared for a future as English-speaking labourers—a brown, disenfranchised, labouring underclass (Walker, 2016).

Collapse of the church boarding schools system

The mission schools system officially dissolved in the 1860s (Simon & Smith, 2001) and was replaced in 1867 by the Native Schools system. While missionaries had lost their hold of education for Māori by the 1860s, it is important to note that mission schools for Māori were continued in the form of Māori church schools operating outside of the state system (Lee, 2008). A number of independent schools, run by Māori using English as the language of instruction, also operated outside of the system, in many cases experiencing more success for both Māori students and teachers than state-controlled education (Lee, 2008). The Māori church schools are outside the scope of this book; however, Lee (2008) provides a comprehensive investigation of the work of Māori teachers in these schools, and the positive impact they had on Māori education during this time.

The reports of the Inspector of Native Schools, Henry Taylor (Taylor, 1863b), shed a great deal of light on tensions between Māori and Western education institutes in the early 1800s. His recommendations to the Government through his reports impacted on the decisions made in the remodelling of the Native Schools Act 1867. Most prominent in Taylor's report (Taylor, 1863b) is his regret that the Native Schools system is in demise and that "... no marked success has attended the efforts made by Government to promote education among the Natives" (p. 1). This is followed very closely by great concern for the future of the many acres of land under use by each school.

Taylor reported 16 Māori church boarding schools had partly or wholly discontinued operations, leaving 14 remaining schools, with attendance at the majority of those schools in decline (Taylor, 1863b). Taylor pointed to two key external reasons for the lack of success in the boarding schools, one being the hopeless endeavour the government faced in attempting to "... lead, by friendly counsel, men who dispute our authority to dictate in matters of importance paramount to Education" (Taylor, 1863b, p. 1). This clearly indicates Māori continued to operate under our own tikanga rather than Pākehā law and opposed the government approach to education. Taylor's choice of words here could also be read as beseeching the government to abandon the "friendly" approach and instead take "control" of the educational space for Māori.

Taylor (1863b) describes the second factor contributing to the closure of so many Māori boarding schools as "… the one grand cause which has already frustrated the many benevolent intentions of His Excellency to promote the real welfare of the Natives …" (p. 1). Taylor is referring to the impact of the Land Wars and movements such as the Kīngitanga. This is evidenced by his specific mention in a subsequent report of "… (a) The Taranaki War, (b) The King movement, (c) The demand for children's labour" (Taylor, 1863a, p. 35) as three external factors impacting negatively on the government's attempt at "… civilizing the Native Race" (Taylor, 1863a, p. 34) through schooling.

Taylor's language throughout his reports illustrates a patronising, paternal attitude that viewed the Land Wars as an outcome of Māori disobedience, implying expected subordination from Māori, who, instead of opposing their authority, should appreciate the favours of a government that supposedly wished the best for them. The positioning of Māori as orchestrators of unrest, offenders, and beneficiaries, and the government as patient, benevolent, benefactors is so rife in early laws and Parliamentary papers that it ultimately became the status quo perception across New Zealand society in relation to the "Māori" Wars (as they were still referred to until recently), to protest action, and to Māori people in general.

There were also several internal failures of the mission boarding schools system, one being the low level of education provided to Māori students, as well as the treatment of children in the system, with which Māori parents were greatly dissatisfied (May, 2003; Simon, 1998; Simon et al., 1994). Simon (1998) refers to missionaries and school inspectors noting strong opposition from Māori parents toward the practice of spending minimal time on studies, with much of the day dedicated to industrial training, which actually translated to hard labour on the land. Many Māori parents objected to their children being treated like slaves (Simon, 1998) in an institution they believed should be providing them with quality Western education, not preparing them to form the labouring class in a Pākehā society.

Māori expectations of good-quality Western education were in direct contrast to the intention of the Government who, according to Taylor's advice, did not:

> ... advocate for the Natives under present circumstances a refined education or high mental culture; it would be inconsistent, if we take into account the position they are likely to hold for many years to come in the social scale, and inappropriate if we remember that they are better calculated by nature to get their living by manual rather than by mental labour. (Taylor, 1863a, p. 38)

We need not look further than Taylor's vision for Māori education for the origins of the stereotype that Māori are kinaesthetic learners. Fuelling this stereotype served only the interests of a colonial government in need of a labouring class trained to serve. Unfortunately, the myth that Māori are kinaesthetic by nature stubbornly continues to dominate both Māori and non-Māori perspectives of Māori learners.

May (2003) highlights missionary observances of Māori child-rearing practices occasionally referred to as loving and caring, but often portrayed as grossly negligent for the complete lack of physical violence against children. According to the missionary perspective, Māori children were allowed to run riot, free from reprimand or physical discipline, which would, missionaries believed, cause them to become unrefined and unruly adults capable only of reproducing the savagery that civilisation sought to cure (May, 2003; Yate, 1835). It is little wonder then that Māori parents from the 1840s onwards were horrified at the "spare the rod, spoil the child" treatment their children were subjected to in education. In his discussion regarding the internal failures of the boarding schools, Taylor himself acknowledges that corporal and harsh punishments were responsible for driving many Māori from the schools, and that:

> A punishment, which to us would appear by no means harsh, would to a Native seem cruel and excessive. As Native parents never inflict chastisement upon an offending child, our summary mode of dealing with young delinquents must seem strange and tyrannical. (Taylor, 1863a, p. 35)

Taylor's view was that if a new iteration of the Native Schools Act was to be successful, it should take into account Māori parents' feelings toward corporal punishment by ensuring that no harsh punishments be inflicted on Māori children (Taylor, 1863a). This is reflected in both the 1867 Act and the Native Schools Code 1880. However, this is one area where the difference between policy and practice can be varied and changeable. How my heart breaks that the Victorian-Christian attitude toward children and child rearing was beaten into generations of Māori through education and religion. Our traditional practices of teaching acceptable social behaviours and ways to relate to self, others, and environments were abandoned and replaced with violence and disrespect. In this way, savagery, under the guise of English decency and civility, was a lesson well taught.

Māori dissatisfaction with a limited curriculum that prepared children to be labourers, along with the Land Wars, led to mission boarding schools being all but deserted by the mid-1860s (Simon, 1998). Taylor's concern for the thousands of acres of land occupied by mission boarding schools is evident in his 1862 report (Taylor, 1863b). Taylor worriedly points out to the government that, with school estates not being used for the purpose that the lands were given, due to "... the contumacy of the Natives ..." (Taylor, 1863b, p. 3), legislative action would need to be taken in order for the Crown to maintain possession of the lands. Much of the legislation relating to education up until the 1960s includes provisions for the taking of, or right of the government to continue to possess, lands for educational purposes. That is in addition to the countless number of Acts that legalised the removal of Māori land for any given purpose, including education.

Day schools—an opportunity missed

Before state-sponsored mission boarding schools were completely dissolved and replaced with the Native Schools system, Civil Commissioner to the Bay of Islands District, George Clarke, propositioned the government with a Native education scheme (Clarke, 1863). Clarke's scheme proposed that each district be subsidised by the government to provide village day school education to Māori children.

Doing so, Clarke believed, would make Western education accessible to thousands more Māori than the current boarding school system. Clarke's motivation for developing a village day school framework was his observation of the failure of what he calls "central" schools. According to Clarke (1863), the boarding schools were unsuccessful in educating any great number of Māori because of strong parental objection to sending children away where they could not be protected.

The framework devised by Clarke was somewhat revolutionary for the time in that he proposed schools be taught by Māori teachers who had been approved by the community in which they would teach (Clarke, 1863). Taylor opposed the proposal primarily because a Native would be incapable of training children in the ways of civilised life, therefore failing to progress colonisation (1863a). Taylor's argument against employing Māori teachers was on the basis that Māori were ingrained in the habits of their own people. He believed their "habits of filth and laziness impede civilisation" (Taylor, 1863a, p. 36). Taylor also invalidated Clarke's notion that Māori communities have the right to approve the teachers of their children by pointing out that if the government is subsidising schools they should be in control over who teaches in those schools (Taylor, 1863a). This is an early example of the government controlling education for Māori through the control of funding. The echoes of such thinking continue to be heard in current narratives opposing Māori voice in any political decision making.

Under Clarke's scheme, the government would pay, not subsidise, the salary of Māori teachers, and would also supply the basic tools necessary for children to participate at school. In order for his scheme to be successful and efficient, Clarke insisted that the day schools be taught by "… competent Teachers and Assistants, who must know more or less of the Native language and customs …" (Clarke, 1863, p. 17). It was important that school boards be given the power to remove "[i]ncompetent Teachers … and others more efficient voted to fill their place" (Clarke, 1863, p. 17). It appears Clarke had greater concern for the quality of education for Māori than many other Pākehā officials at the time. He certainly had more vision than Taylor, whose colonial agenda would include "… prizes … for the proficiency in the study of

Ko Nga Ture, the digest of English law ..." (Taylor, 1863a, p. 16) and proficiency in the English language, which was still proving to be a failed mission despite (or perhaps due to) Crown intervention.

The scheme imagined by Clarke was not adopted. Instead, the church boarding schools system was disestablished and replaced with the Native Schools system, which continued the precedent set by the boarding schools for not enhancing Māori life chances, but limiting and controlling them (Simon, 1998). The remodelled Native Schools system reflects many of Taylor's racist and limiting insights into education for Māori (Taylor, 1863a). It seems that the government took heed of Taylor's damaging perspectives of Māori as being " ... unaccustomed to mental exertion ..." (Taylor, 1863a, p. 16) and by nature suited to manual labour. This is the perspective that underpinned the Native Schools Act 1867, firmly establishing education as the tool to assimilate Māori into the lowest class of Pākehā society. It is also the racist perspective that became institutionalised in New Zealand education, without the support of any research, evidence, or logic, for over 100 years. This view forms the foundation on which education for Māori has been built.

Advancing the colonial agenda through education legislation

In 1854, Westminster extended certain rights of the Empire to the New Zealand Parliament (Wilson, 2016). This is significant for Māori in that it continued to undermine the conditions of Te Tiriti o Waitangi. Parliament, which was based in New Zealand but made up solely of British settlers, now held the self-vested power to make decisions and laws for Māori. There is no evidence to indicate that Māori were in support of the transfer of any powers from Westminster, with whom they had a sacred agreement, to a settler government in New Zealand.

However, evidence of Māori opposition to the transfer of powers exists. Te Pūtake o te Riri (The Source of the Fury, also known as the New Zealand Wars, or the Land Wars) were initiated in Tai Tokerau in 1845 when Te Ruki Kawiti and his allies raised arms in disgust that the Crown had not honoured the terms of their agreement in Te Tiriti

(Hirschfeld, 2017). These battles were still raging throughout the country by 1854. In Waikato, the Kīngitanga was established in 1858 (Papa & Meredith, 2012) only 4 years after the establishment of the settler government. These are just two examples of ways that Māori objected to and fought fiercely at the very first signs that the Crown had not honoured its agreement and would continue to oppose the removal of our lands and rangatiratanga in exchange for forced rule under a New Zealand Parliament.

The Native Schools Act 1867 formally brought education for Māori under the control of the settler government. The legislation clearly indicated that education would be the means by which the government would carry out its agenda for the assimilation of Māori (Smith, 2016). The Act has played a major role in both the physical colonisation of Māori and the colonisation of Māori minds. It has achieved this by first removing land from within every community and village throughout the country, then by providing a specific, limited, curriculum, and removing te reo Māori from education. These aspects are linked to each other and culminate in an embodiment of the aggressive policy to de-culturalise Māori through education.

Land alienation through education legislation

It could be argued that the Native Schools Act was less assimilationist in nature than the previous Education Ordinance, which forced Māori students to engage in schooling in isolation from their communities. However, the clause requiring Māori to "gift" land in exchange for education, and all other iterations of laws and clauses compelling Māori to relinquish lands, in numerous pieces of legislation (Walker, 1990), has aided the agenda of colonisation by alienating huge tracts of prime Māori land from hapū. The provision to take land in the Native Schools Act is reminiscent of the removal of Māori lands legalised by all versions of the Public Works Land Act from 1840 to 1981 (Marr, 1997). Land is needed for physical colonisation, so the specific targeting of Māori land using strategies such as purposely detouring roads to run through Māori land rather than acquisitioning Pākehā-owned land was common practice (Ministry for Culture and Heritage, 2016). The Native

Schools Act also targeted Māori land. In many cases, land was taken under this Act but not used for education—even when Māori objected, the lands were not returned (Ministry for Culture and Heritage, 2016).

Despite land being removed at alarming rates, despite Māori having abandoned hope in missionary education, despite war and disease ravaging the Māori population, many Māori were still committed to Western education, as it equated to survival in a changing world (Smith, 2016). This commitment was illustrated by the lengths many Māori went to in order to have schools established in often very remote communities (Barrington, 2008) from the late 1800s through to the 1900s. The Native Schools Act required Māori wanting Western education to make land available for a schoolhouse and, if needed, teacher accommodation. The Act stipulated that Māori communities were to pay half the costs of establishing the school. If finances could not be raised, communities could give land in lieu of money. Western education was such a priority to so many Māori that thousands of acres of land transferred from Māori to the Crown in this way.

Dual (but not equal) schooling

The Education Act 1877 centralised New Zealand education and established the state primary school education system. The Education Act, in conjunction with the Native Schools Act, established two separate education systems in New Zealand—one for Pākehā settler children, the other for Māori. Many New Zealand teachers are likely to be conversant with the Education Act 1877, as it signifies the foundation of modern primary education in New Zealand. There was never any legislation to prevent Māori students from attending public schools, nor preventing Pākehā students from attending Native Schools. Many of the Pākehā students attending Native Schools were the children of teachers (Simon et al., 1994). Given the remote locations of many of the schools, this could have been more by necessity rather than choice. All my grandparents attended public (Pākehā) schools; however, my father and his siblings all attended one of the four Native Schools in Whangaruru. All four school sites in this small and isolated community were "gifted" by our tūpuna for education.

What is not widely taught is that the Education Act was not intended to specifically provide equality of education for Māori and Pākehā. It was intended to provide educational equality to settler children—including poor settler children. The motivation was to progress egalitarian ideals for Pākehā. Education for Māori was provided for under the Native Schools Act and, as such, would remain a separate entity from the state primary school system for another 90 years (Barrington, 2008). The separate education systems illustrate the government's dual and conflicting purposes for education—a free, equitable, secular education for all settler children to progress egalitarian ideals, and ironically, a restrictive education to "civilise" Māori children into becoming the underclass of that egalitarian society.

Further attestation to this argument is the 1880 Native Schools Code, an organisational framework that would guide the function and form of Native Schools for many years (Barrington, 2008). Not surprisingly, Code I refers to the ways in which land could be acquired for new schools, and how the teacher must keep the "... land fenced in ... constantly in good order, and to make it ... the model garden of the village" (Rolleston, 1880, p. 1). Pākehā ideas of land ownership were clearly a concept the government wanted to impress upon Māori as part of their assimilationist programme. The model provided by the schoolteacher of a fenced-in property was perhaps also to help mitigate "confusion" over land ownership and rights the government was experiencing in its dealings with Māori. The Code was essentially the way in which government assimilationist education policy was translated into practice, containing the methods that would assist in the colonisation of Māori minds.

The Code required the teacher (and his wife, who could be employed as the sewing mistress) to become the instrument of colonisation and assimilation within Māori communities. Not only was he responsible for teaching the limited curriculum that would lock Māori into becoming the lower class of New Zealand society, but he was also expected to influence all the Natives in his community. As with Marsden's objectives for missionaries, this is another example of cultural competencies, only these were state-defined and to be employed by teachers, not just in schools, but throughout Māori communities.

Teachers were expected to be kind, diligent, and have probity, but were not required to have any knowledge of the Native tongue as it was only required in the junior classes to acquaint students with the English language (Barrington, 2008). In fact, he was to "... dispense with the use of Māori as soon as possible" (Rolleston, 1880, p. 1). To assist him in meeting these competencies, he was issued with a support booklet. The Native Schools Act 1867 had also included what was essentially a performance pay clause promising a special grant based on student English language proficiency assessment outcomes. The teacher would also be paid to board up to five local girls at a time on a 3-week rotation so they could do the housework as well as attend school. This would ensure that Māori girls learnt to keep house, illustrating the state's view that housekeeping would be a substantial life pathway for a Māori girl.

The most superficial of glances at the prescribed curriculum for Native Schools in the Code betrays its intention to not only assimilate, but also to ensure that Māori were restricted to fulfilling the role of second-class citizens in a country that was our own, but in a society that was not. The Code provided for education of Māori students up to Standard IV (approximately 9-10 years old); however, the curriculum can be seen as nothing but the most basic of reading, writing, and maths, which appear to be intentionally of a low academic level (Rolleston, 1880). A large focus of the curriculum was teaching the English language; however, there is also a peculiar geography curriculum area that progressed from knowing some geography of New Zealand in Standard III, to knowing the answers to questions such as "Why do white people living in India require to have all hard work done for them by the Natives?" (Rolleston, 1880, p. 2). Whist the intention behind such a question is unclear, it can be surmised that the state intended for Māori children to expect, as Natives, to become labourers for white people.

Students would be assessed in English language, singing, and drills from Standard I (approximately 5 years old), with Standards III and

IV also being assessed in elementary drawing (Rolleston, 1880). This also demonstrated the low expectations that were held for Māori futures. The government was, at the time of publishing the Code, in the process of developing a scholarship scheme that would allow students who did well in their examinations to continue their education beyond the village day schools. There was also a provision in the Code for transitioning day schools into "Board" or public schools should enough students master the basics offered in the village day schools (Rolleston, 1880). This again evidences the dual purposes for education in New Zealand based on ethnicity—a Native school could become a public school only if Māori were seen to have mastered "civility". With access to such limited education, even the brightest of scholars would be severely restricted should they be given an opportunity to advance their education. Māori scholars who did navigate and conquer the highest levels of Western education after enduring such controlled, low-level education must be seen as exceptional.

The Native Schools Act was decisive legislative action giving the newly established New Zealand government power to enforce the direction of education for Māori following the end of the Land Wars. The intention of the Act was to use education as the preferred tool for assimilation, and "to make Schools necessary in the work of civilising the Native race ..." (Taylor, 1863a, p. 34). This era of education had Māori prove their commitment to education through the provision of land, labour, and resources, and also by relinquishing language and traditional ways of knowing in exchange for a restricted Western education. The subsequent Native Schools Code provided the means through which policy became practice. Barrington (2008) describes the Code as "... an expression of beliefs about assimilation and progress towards civilisation held at the time" (p. 44). Unfortunately, for generations of Māori, those limiting thoughts and beliefs persisted for nearly a century in education, only to eventually be replaced by the deficit theories of the 1960s, which are explored in Chapter 6.

Tohunga Suppression Act 1907

By 1907, state-sponsored education for Māori was well established throughout the country. However, the sovereignty of the government continued to be strongly opposed by Māori, indicating that the intended hasty assimilation of Māori through education was not going to plan. In an attempt to halt Māori uprisings, a new piece of legislation was devised. The Tohunga Suppression Act 1907 arguably had the most damaging effect on Māori across all aspects of society, because it targeted the most learned and gifted teachers in te ao Māori. This law was written on the pretext of protecting Māori health and wellbeing from tohunga (Voyce, 1989), who were portrayed as crafty men peddling supernatural wizardry to cure disease—witch doctors and sorcerers. The imagery this Act evoked had as much a role to play in redefining the meaning of "tohunga" as the behaviours it deemed illegal.

The Act made it illegal for Māori to gather in groups, to offer traditional healing, or to disseminate traditional knowledge, described as "witchcraft". Voyce (1989) argued the Act was ineffectual, as Māori were reluctant to report tohunga for fear of violating tapu, and also because it failed to change Māori perspectives of disease and cure—Māori (who were still largely unacclimatised to the type and scale of introduced diseases) continued to believe that disease was caused by the transgression of tapu and could therefore be cured through natural remedies, karakia, or action from powerful tohunga. The prevailing connection to cultural knowledge illustrates that, while the law could be used to make our beliefs and practices illegal, it could not completely remove the understanding many Māori have of the multifaceted and intertwined relationships between physical, emotional, and spiritual energies of people and environments.

The Act was extremely effective, however, in driving further underground an ancient and complex educational structure. In 1836, Te Wakaminenga had formally adopted Christianity as whakapono tuku iho, the inherited faith (mātauranga ā iwi). This, in conjunction with the Act, saw the eradication of carved meeting houses throughout Tai Tokerau. The extermination of wharenui and marae was catastrophic in terms of the desecration of mātauranga Māori, and our ability to decode and encode the intricacies of whakairo and raranga. The effects are still felt today as Tai Tokerau is largely bereft of carved meeting houses. I have heard my father many times refer to our carved meeting houses as our universities. That the people of Te Tai Tokerau have managed to keep alive many of our knowledges and tikanga in an environment destitute of universities is a tribute to our tenacity and the intergenerational perseverance of great tohunga and rangatira.

The Tohunga Suppression Act was a law illustrating complete ignorance of, misinterpretation of, and contempt for, mātauranga Māori. The real motivation for the creation of the Act was an attempt by the government to discredit men like Rua Kēnana (1869–1937) and Tahupōtiki Ratana (1873–1939) who were using Christian belief systems to create resistance movements protesting injustices by Pākehā against Māori (Voyce, 1989). The Tohunga Suppression Act directly attacked Māori knowledge bases, healing practices, and the facilitators of our knowledge. It also removed several core social structures of Māori communities—leadership, in terms of ariki, tohunga, and rangatira, and our right to practise traditional communal living. While the clause prohibiting Māori gathering in groups may appear controlling but rather innocuous, the real-life impact for a communal people meant no longer harvesting on the land or water, no longer being able to practise burial rites, gathering for hui, or to practise ceremony. For Māori, it also meant disrupting engagement in traditional teaching and learning practices. Māori were now left with only one education option, the Native Schools system, and so had little choice but to push further underground cultural structures that were already increasingly subterraneous.

The evidence presented here is that the education system as we know it today has been carefully orchestrated by the Crown to ensure the core of Māori society was left broken, to be replaced with English civility. The Crown, through a settler government, took control of Māori education by enacting a range of racist and unjust laws that intentionally alienated Māori from our lands and from our knowledge bases. Despite this, many Māori were still committed to Western education because it was viewed as a way to engage in the new society they were now part of (Smith, 2005).

British law enabled by a version of the Treaty of Waitangi that arguably did not exist at the time of the writing of Te Tiriti (Fletcher, 2022) opened the floodgates for colonisation and Pākehā dominance over Māori. Education was seen as the best way to colonise Māori, to teach out of us the culture we had been nurturing and developing over many generations. Laws would provide the basis for the development of assimilationist policies throughout the 1900s. These policies, along with the enduring education philosophies that underpin New Zealand education, will be investigated following the pūkōrero of Te Aupouri Whautere. The 1900s would also entrench stereotypes about Māori in education that continue to persist in contemporary education. This will also be considered in the following chapter.

Chapter 6

Te amorangi

Te pūkōrero ō Te Aupouri Whautere

Te Aupouri Whautere, who is also affectionately known as Uncle Buster, holds quite a unique position in his role as kaumātua. As a young man, Te Aupouri was taken under the wing of the old kāhui kaumātua of Whangārei as their student. This group of kaumātua were politically astute; they were statesmen who were as knowledgeable in the workings of Pākehā societal structures as they were in te reo, tikanga, and mātauranga Māori. Te Aupouri was privileged to have learnt from this kāhui and at the time this project was carried out was one of the last (if not the only) remaining kaumātua to have been taught in this very specific way by this group of people. Yet, the first thing that has always defined Te Aupouri for me is humility. In this way, he embodies one of those values inherent to Māori leadership—he is humble. The strength of humility should never be underestimated.

As long as I have known Te Aupouri, he has been involved in education, and specifically Māori education in English-medium settings. He was a key force in the establishment of the bilingual unit which still operates at a local intermediate school in Whangārei, as well as the first bilingual class at one of our local high schools. Te Aupouri has championed the use of tikanga Māori in contexts that have longstanding histories of excluding Māori, especially education. I have my own personal experience of this, which has impacted my understanding of the immense work that goes into ensuring tikanga Māori is visible in traditionally Pākehā arenas.

I began intermediate school 2 weeks after school started. Mainly because I was scared. I missed the whakatau held for new students and thought I would quietly join the bilingual unit. However, Te Aupouri knew my family and knew that tikanga called for the correct process to be carried out—even just for one, scared and painfully shy little girl. So, with Te Aupouri driving the tikanga, and with the backing of only a handful of teachers in a large English-medium school, a full whakatau was held. The enactment of tikanga in this situation achieved several things from my perspective. It ensured that the school established a positive relationship with my family, which would prove to have benefits for them that stand even now, some 30 years later. It signalled to the school community that tikanga Māori would be observed on Māori terms. The key message I got as a 10-year-old was that important people like Te Aupouri were willing to challenge the status quo, to push for the visibility of our tikanga, and to be uncompromising in the pursuit of the best academic and cultural outcomes for tamariki Māori.

Service to both Māori and non-Māori in education and in the wider community is another feature I have always seen Te Aupouri display. Because of this I am interested in his perspectives about education success for Māori as Māori. When I arrive to the Shed at Hīhīaua, Te Aupouri is waiting for me. I am running late, and literally run through the door sweating and profusely apologetic for keeping him waiting. He smiles at me. Tells me it's OK—he is one of the kindest people I know, which heightens my sense of guilt. Te Aupouri recites a karakia to begin our discussion, and to whakatau te wairua. I feel a strong sense of aroha in the room that I'm sure will colour our discussion.

Te Aupouri begins by centring the needs of children and grandchildren:

Any education success ... embracing our mokopuna, to me, that becomes the future goal of any parent or grandparent for the maturing and the development of their moko ... culturally ... I believe is one of the main parts of the input there that they develop.

Like other kaumātua involved in this study, Te Aupouri is concerned with focusing on the individuality and aspirations of each child. He points out that checking in with students as they mature and as their needs change should be a key aspect of their schooling:

They are able to identify key goals that will be fostered in their development, at the time that they need … we know that things will change as they grow older and we need to revisit and ensure that they are still on track with the ultimate goal, which will be to heir benefit.

Te Aupouri goes on to define how he believes those involved with education can support students in achieving success. He points out some key strategies for educators, including knowing the child, being open to a range of approaches, and adequate resourcing:

I think the number one … [depends] on what the young one's interest is I guess. You know you've got to ensure that you have the relevant resources to make that goal happen. If it's like a verbal sort of a presentation, let it be, and to me, you know with the verbal part being there it gives them a chance to revisit and able to identify where they may have left out a key point that'll help them … to develop in that area.

As previously mentioned, Te Aupouri has been involved in education for many years in a range of roles. I am interested to know what skills he thinks teachers need to teach Māori students appropriately. His response strikes me as beautiful, and I hope that my own children have experienced a teacher with the values he describes. When asked what characteristics a teacher of Māori students should possess, the kaumātua participants in this study have almost always begun with spirituality, a strong sense of self, or love. As Te Aupouri talks, I note that I am not surprised that they have these perspectives. However, the contrast between what they have said they want for their mokopuna and what I know is taught on the initial teacher education programme I teach strikes me as being worlds apart:

Be aware of the Māori aspect, point of view, that they have a spiritual contribution, not only in … the children, but … to themselves first, the need to ensure that they're on track … I would start with the three factors, faith, hope, and love, you know and feeling confident that I'll be able to provide an ingredient that will

> help them [students] sort of grow and mature in whatever their
> interest is.

I ask Te Aupouri where teachers might go to upskill themselves in te ao Māori. His response is very simple, yet it says so much about the types of relationships we perhaps should aspire to within education. For him, knowledge sharing should come from "friendships that they may create".

He also discusses the important role non-Māori educators play in fostering reo and tikanga Māori in all students:

> ... non-Māori ... who may be conversant in te reo for instance, and
> then the student could maybe look at using that as a model, or part
> of a model.

The idea of upskilling teachers in their knowledge of te ao Māori then turns, as it has with other participants, to teachers having adequate knowledge about the history of our country. Te Aupouri stipulates that historical understanding must become part of the way we teach in Aotearoa in order for positive change to occur:

> But at the same time, of course, like for me, for instance, I need to
> give an assurance that if I'm talking about a pound of butter, that
> I'm fully conversant with the historical thing, how that pound of
> butter came to be.

In his positive and optimistic way, Te Aupouri comments on how he sees the current English-medium education system and its ability to help Māori students achieve education success as Māori:

> I think that we have an obligation to ensure that what we have in
> place would be a beginning of what we are hoping to develop and
> what we are going to provide our children, you know, so that they
> can expand in their knowledge.

From this starting point, he adds three concepts that he believes need to become part of every student's basic education:

> I think at the end of the [education programme], one of the main
> things is that referring to the hinengaro, the tinana, and the wairua,
> which are ... I believe three of the main basics, if you like to use

that term, that need be in place, that will help our children grow and develop.

Because I recognise the relationships between these concepts as belonging to a body of Māori knowledge, I ask Te Aupouri his thoughts on whether mātauranga Māori has a place in English-medium primary schools:

Definitely. If all children begin at say, right when they begin their primary school ... I believe that one of the opportunities, first one of the key opportunities will actually see that young one develop and grow in his or her knowledge [of things Māori].

From my experience in education, I am aware of the varying degrees and gaps in mātauranga Māori many English-medium teachers have. I suspect that Te Aupouri is also aware of this due to his long service in education. He offers a solution for teachers who have a drive to upskill themselves in te ao Māori. It is a solution that would require teachers to work carefully and with humility to achieve personal growth:

I think if any member of the education staff wants to move further in te reo for instance, or tikanga and all of that sort of stuff, then they need ... the assurance that they get to back track, just to double check that they have the relevant material to provide that knowledge, and the extension of that knowledge to further move on.

When I ask who teachers should check their information with, Te Aupouri chuckles and jokingly says, "Sadly, the kaumātua, kuia".

We laugh at his inclusion of the word "sadly" because this is exactly what I do when I have questions, I turn to my kaumātua and kuia, and I am fortunate to have their counsel. Te Aupouri then defines part of the role of kaumātua in education. What stands out for me is that this is perhaps one of those areas where there is a differentiation between what schools think the kaumātua role is, and what kaumātua themselves perceive. Many schools engage kaumātua because they have some idea that it is the correct thing to do in some, limited, usually ceremonial circumstances. Whereas, according to the perspective given by Te Aupouri, this relationship has the potential to be quite different, and far more productive for schools:

> *Yes ... understanding that it's a sort of an assurance to that person [the teacher] that they, whether they're on track or not you know. What we are doing is actually assuring in our advice, that it's going to be the ideal path to help you move that extra mile.*

As an educator, this is how I have always felt about my relationships with kaumātua. They offer cultural and spiritual protection; they offer their wisdom and knowledge to help me in my role as an educator. In return, as an educator I am obliged to treat their information with respect, and I am obliged to listen. I have seen kaumātua disengage from organisations when people aren't prepared to listen. Whether they are aware of it or not, without the protection and knowledge of kaumātua they then become vulnerable and many in the community can begin to mistrust them.

I ask Te Aupouri what a teacher capable of providing his mokopuna with the skills and tools they need to succeed in education as Māori might look like. Again, I smile as Te Aupouri centralises the mokopuna. His first thoughts go to the needs and aspirations of the child and the ability of the teacher to tap into that. His second concern is in the ability of the teachers to grow and develop in themselves:

> *I think firstly, one of the first things I'd identify is the assurance that they are on track, the journey they are taking is in line with what they are hoping to achieve, and then the second part will be to get an assurance that he or she is able to mature in themselves, and also enjoy the opportunity to actually share that knowledge with their student. And then look to see what the result is, or how that student is performing.*

We briefly discuss the role of the Ministry of Education in determining the cultural competence of teachers. I am keen to know who Te Aupouri thinks should be responsible for making decisions about a teacher's cultural "competence" or level of cultural knowledge and understanding. Te Aupouri discusses the important role whānau play in this. Again, his perspective here is different from the way many schools approach whānau—that is, to tell whānau what their children need to succeed at school, or to discuss behavioural issues. What Te Aupouri is proposing is a situation that engages the important adults in a child's education in order to really know what that student aspires to, how they can all come on board to help. Te Aupouri also highlights here the need for teachers to become more accountable to whānau, but not in a punitive way. Rather, accountability here is presented as seeking support, and reinforces the concept of "double checking":

> *I think, again I think there needs to be some assurance from the teaching side of it, an assurance that they are in consultation with the extended family, just to get the assurance that they are on track in what their expectation would be for the achievement of that young one of theirs ... If, for instance, a student seems to be getting frustrated, to me that's saying, it's sort of [seeking] an assurance that the advocacy that the teacher is providing is on track.*

Te Aupouri furthers this idea by discussing the importance of the relationships between teachers, students, and whānau that will support students and teachers:

> *... one of the things that I think they need to have in place is that the continual liaison between them and the extended family, or members of the extended family ... when the student first comes in, at day one actually, you wanting ... not just a little bit, if you're looking for the background history of the boy or the girl, then you're actually patient to be full page, not just a part one. And I'm sure the greater percentage of children, they love that, you know? Especially when they're first beginning school, the excitement is there, and you know, they are going to test everything ...*

Te Aupouri emphasises that listening and asking questions must become part of a teacher's role in their relationships with students and whānau:

> *I think one of the key things there is a good listening skill ... And I think it will be an ideal time for them also to ask questions, it becomes a two-way thing, I guess. As the old saying goes, it's give and take. Vice versa you know. He or she, the student, he or she will give their advice, not advice, but how they see the situation and the teacher will respond in the same way.*

Our discussion then turns back to what mokopuna might need from their education to live a successful life. Te Aupouri turns to two of the most fundamental skills a student should have from a Māori perspective—the ability to first and foremost listen, and then to draw understanding and make decisions based on how we perceive the information:

> ... an ideal listening skill, and being able to understand, of course, what's being said. I think we all know as adults, when we are talking about something we will present a response, an answer to whatever our expectation would be ... It's clear, well from your point of view, you understand the meaning of what is being said, and what may become complications if it went another way.

Te Aupouri also stresses that students must gain a sense of positive identity from their education, and in the content of what they are being taught:

> Like, a sense of pride, and also a passion, they're very passionate with what they achieve, it gives us the assurance that maybe we're on track with the beginning of the development of their knowledge ... You most probably know yourself, when you were going to school and you know there were times where you didn't feel 100%, and you knew when you were quite more at ease, more comfortable with what's being presented to you.

We reminisce about my own schooling, about the opportunities that my classmates and I were given in terms of our Māori identities and language due to the care and willingness of people such as Te Aupouri to stand up for us and for our culture. Te Aupouri encourages parents, families, and students to question schools when things are not meeting our expectations:

> I think one of the best things parents can do is have the confidence to be able to question it, the situation, from day one ... and don't be hesitant. Just question it with confidence.

It is fitting that our discussion ends on these thoughts. Te Aupouri has dedicated a lifetime to pushing, to questioning, to ensuring that te ao Māori has a genuine presence, not only in our schools, but in society in general. He is confident in who he is and is therefore fearless in his approach to protecting tikanga and te reo in contemporary contexts;

however, his approach is driven by aroha. This is a trait that makes working with him easy, but it also presented me with a challenge when analysing his pūkōrero.

Where other kaumātua participants identified particular problems in the education system, or with the positioning of Māori cultural competence, Te Aupouri concentrated almost completely on the student, and on his expectations of teachers. His care for students' physical, spiritual, emotional, and intellectual wellbeing comes through strongly in his words, without strong critique of the education system or experiences for Māori students. Te Aupouri was so clear about his aspirations for education for Māori that it appeared to me initially that there were not many nooks or crannies in his words for me to investigate further. I was challenged and was unable to immediately see what I could analyse. The use of tauparapara as an analytical tool came into play strongly here as I read, reread, and re-listened to the pūkōrero in order for the distant question I had far in the back of my mind to come more into focus.

Over and over, I could see what it was Te Aupouri wished for our children and mokopuna to experience in education. It was clear, it was straightforward. As his pūkōrero settled in my mind the key point of investigation started to become clear. Te Aupouri wanted every child to experience love, confidence, and commitment to developing strong, positive cultural identities; he hoped for teachers to have a sense of accountability first to the student, then the whānau; he wanted teachers to feel supported in their own development of cultural understandings. If these were his aspirations for education, then what was it about current education that was preventing these things from happening? I began to wonder to what extent education philosophies in New Zealand impacted on achieving these aspirations. If Te Aupouri had at the centre of his concern the wellbeing of the individual child, does the preoccupation in our current education system on the collective (for Māori learners) take away from individuals?

In many ways, Te Aupouri's concern for the individual challenged my thinking, because in many ways I have been convinced that group learning is a traditional Māori pedagogy, along with kinetic learning.

Indeed, all throughout my life I have heard this rhetoric in education. I had always felt unsettled at being Māori but not favouring those particular learning styles myself, yet somehow, I came to more or less accept these beliefs. Here I have been presented with the perspective that the desires of the individual in education are of utmost importance. All the kaumātua stated this; however, this perspective came through strongly in Te Aupouri's pūkōrero. Coming to understand how particular beliefs about Māori teaching and learning in contemporary education will be analysed to answer the questions that have arisen from the pūkōrero of Te Aupouri.

The philosophical underpinnings of modern New Zealand education

The strongest message that can be heard in the pūkōrero of Te Aupouri is that every child has the right to an education that meets their individual aspirations and that, on completion, graduates will be complete in their identity and in a position to choose their future pathway. Te Aupouri has positively focused on these outcomes, which is currently not the norm for Māori graduates of English-medium schools. Te Aupouri has spent much of his life working with others to improve experiences and outcomes for Māori within education and health. That he has dedicated his life to this work is evidence that change has been needed for a long time.

An important overarching message within Te Aupouri's pūkōrero concentrates on the individual child. Te Aupouri clearly sees value in honouring the skills, aspirations, and potential of every individual. Part of the analysis in this section will therefore investigate the origins and preoccupation modern education has with the importance of the group in relation to Māori students. The wairua of Te Aupouri's pūkōrero opens an important line of inquiry in that perhaps the focus contemporary education has on the collective is leading us away from what this kāhui kaumātua have highlighted as important to education success—the mana of the individual.

Te Aupouri has a deep understanding of the education system; he has worked in it for many years and has identified the areas of the system that pose challenges for Māori. His pūkōrero identified three philosophical beliefs that, in his perspective, are essential to education: "I would start with the three factors, faith, hope, and love …". These philosophical perspectives appear to be far removed from current education philosophies. Therefore, I have been provided with an opportunity to investigate the philosophical underpinnings of modern New Zealand education. This investigation will clarify how education has moved from a relentless torrent of laws ratifying racist assimilation policy and practice, through to the current Māori Potential Approach that has fostered the notion of Māori cultural competence. The second part of this chapter will investigate changes in education approaches to clearly define how education has arrived at aspiring for cultural competence. It will also question if changes to the structure of education still pose problems for English-medium education in delivering education success for Māori, as Māori.

The education programme of the 1800s was dominated by missionaries, and had taught, to varying degrees, the lesson of British superiority and Māori inferiority through not only the skill of literacy, but also through the meanings transmitted in the printed word (Jenkins, 1993). The political focus of this period was the colonisation of New Zealand, with missionary education being the tool to subjugate Māori culture, beliefs, and thoughts, replacing them with Western "civilisation". The effects of this agenda have been discussed previously.

By the 1900s, the political movement to be advanced by education was that of nation building. Mutch (2013) attributes the innovative, arts-based, child-centred, and comparatively radical education system in action in New Zealand since at least the early 1960s to New Zealand's egalitarian and liberal-progressive philosophy that "… permeated social, political and educational thought" (p. 2). The oneness of thought of the 1900s throughout society, politics, and education provided the conditions for an innovative New Zealand education system based on models provided by Britain and America, but also trying to find its own identity.

I will argue that, while consistent liberal-progressive messages were being transmitted across all sectors of society, this also created a

Eurocentric environment that continued to erode Māori society, politics, and education. Liberal-progressive philosophies sought to create a balance in New Zealand education between the dualities of mind and body—or knowledge and experience—created by an exclusively liberal education system. It will become apparent that these philosophies are very different from those of Te Aupouri, and the other members of the kāhui kaumātua. This chapter will very briefly provide an overview of the liberal philosophies that are fundamental to the Western education system of New Zealand, before investigating the move to liberal-progressivism and stereotypes about Māori that have become deeply ingrained in English-medium education. Finally, I will investigate how Māori resistance forced policy change from 1970 to the 2000s. These ideas will trace the whakapapa of New Zealand's educational transition from assimilation policies to the Māori Potential Approach. I will also investigate how these philosophies have constructed education for Māori, and how they have constructed Māori in education.

Classic liberal education philosophy

Liberalism, fuelled by the thinking of the Enlightenment period that drove imperialist ideology, has driven the direction of education for Western countries. Liberalism forms the foundation of all iterations of Western education in New Zealand. This section provides a brief overview of classical liberal philosophy to illustrate that liberalism has been added to over the years, rather than replaced. Classic liberal education philosophy is foundational to New Zealand's education system and is increasingly emphasised with current governmental arrangements.

General liberal education is argued by Bailey (1984) to have four key characteristics: the ability to liberate one from the present and the particular; the engagement of students in fundamental and general education; the presentation of intrinsically worthwhile education; and the development of rational minds. An ideology of liberal education is that individual freedom paired with a rational mind will benefit society.

It could be argued that there appears to be some alignment between liberal characteristics and philosophies within Māori communities. One principle of kaupapa Māori theory is the principle of socioeconomic mediation, by which the negative stresses experienced by Māori communities can be alleviated through Māori research and initiatives (Smith, 1990). This is similar to the idea of education freeing us from the present and particular. In his pūkōrero, Te Warihi argues that individuals must be educated in the things they need to know to live successful, fulfilling lives—this is essentially education that is fundamental and generally useful. Bailey (1984) argues "… in education knowledge and understanding sought for their intrinsic worthwhileness can have a general and powerful utility precisely because they are not trapped in response to the present and particular" (p. 22). I have already argued that knowledge and understandings from the kauae runga was sought for its intrinsic value—it was abstract and esoteric, it moved beyond physical realities, and connected to the workings of the universe.

The goals of liberation for individuals to make rational decisions for themselves and to live free from subordination appear to be sound goals; indeed, these are goals of the rangatiratanga movement. What proponents of liberal education do not articulate is that these philosophies are culturally located in the West. They were developed in response to Western problems (Pihama, 2016). The fundamental, general, worthwhile, and powerful knowledge they seek for all is located exclusively in the knowledge of the West. Liberal philosophies advance Eurocentric agendas by actively excluding Indigenous knowledges and languages (Battiste, 2013).

Classical liberal ideas such as individual freedom to make decisions, freedom from subordination to the state and church, self-reliant individuals and independent communities, liberation from the oppression of tradition (Siteine, 2017) must be understood in the context in which they were devised—17th century England, where society in general was forced into subordination by a powerful monarchy, a stifling class system, and an omnipotent church. In the 19th century, ideas around liberty expanded to include equality, and a free market economy in the form of laissez-faire capitalism (Mutch & Tatebe, 2017). It can be argued that all these expansions were responses to oppressive social and political structures and systems, intended to enable individuals to flourish regardless of the circumstances into which they had been born (Bailey, 1984). As such, liberal philosophies are at the core of democracy, a highly valued aspect of Western society that permeates education.

The discourse of individual liberation from cultural domination has and continues to be used to position Māori culture and traditions as oppressive and restrictive, and to justify the omission of Māori knowledges and language from education. Battiste (2013) argues that forced assimilation such as this provides the conditions for cognitive imperialism, the whitewashing of the mind. The "liberal" of liberal-progressive philosophies is the aspect that has waged an ongoing assault on mātauranga Māori from the kauae runga and attempted to discount the epistemological nature of this knowledge. From this perspective, liberal education philosophy has driven colonisation by excluding and silencing any knowledge bases that fall outside of their own ways of knowing, considering knowledge from outside of its epistemological frame to be repugnant (L. Smith, 2012).

Classical liberalism values abstract, individual, rational thought and was developed originally to liberate individuals from the constraints of tradition. Ironically, it has come to be seen as "... engendering a problematic unquestioning and uncritical respect for authority and traditional values" (McPhail, 2017, p. 83). Liberal education philosophy has become everything it was originally developed to resist, due to its dogged determination to reject knowledge from outside of its own worldview.

Liberal-progressive education philosophy

Liberal-progressive and egalitarian philosophy permeates New Zealand education. A key role of progressive education is the connection of education to society. Dewey (1916) argued that education, in its broadest sense, is the "social continuity of life" (p. 2), the means by which human beings reproduce, continue, and recreate the experiences of forebears, their "... customs, institutions, beliefs, victories and defeats, recreations and occupations" (p. 2). Dewey's definition of the purpose of education resonates with mātauranga Māori. However, I will argue that the New Zealand experience of progressive philosophy often presented Māori experiences in superficial ways and therefore neglected to reproduce them in meaningful ways.

Former New Zealand Prime Minister Peter Fraser's now famous "objective" in his 1939 Annual Report to Parliament signalled clearly that education in New Zealand in the 1920s and 1930s would move toward progressive thinking by ensuring "… that every person, whatever his level of academic ability, whether he be rich or poor, whether he live in town or country, has a right, as a citizen to a free education of the kind for which he is best fitted, and to the fullest extent of his powers" (Fraser, 1939, pp. 2–3). Fraser and Dr Clarence Beeby are often credited as being the founders of progressive education in New Zealand, first with Fraser as Director of Education and Beeby as his deputy, then with Fraser as Prime Minister and Beeby as Director of Education (Beeby, 1992).

The argument that it was "necessary to convert a school system, constructed originally on a basis of selection and privilege, to a truly democratic form where it can cater for the needs of the whole population over as long a period of their lives as is found possible and desirable" (Fraser, 1939, p. 3) was born out of international instability and the Great Depression of the 1930s. The Depression had exposed a severe lack of equal opportunities, perpetuated by the binary opposition in education of the academic and the vocational. The depressed economic state of the 1930s made it apparent to teachers that they were preparing the majority of New Zealand children for work that did not exist and therefore "… were facing a life devoid of hope" (Beeby, 1992, p. 132). World War One and the Depression that followed created a growing Pākehā underclass, which went against the objectives of New Zealand's egalitarian society. The reform of education then became focused on creating equal opportunity to stabilise the post-war economy. Progressive politics and progressive education were also viewed as vital in combatting anti-democratic impulses of the time (Mutch, 2017).

However, Māori education was excluded from the widespread social and educational changes. It seems a Pākehā underclass was contrary to egalitarian ideals; however, a Māori underclass was not seen by Pākehā society as problematic. In the same Parliamentary session of 1939 in which the pivotal transformations for New Zealand education were revealed, Inspector of Native Schools, Douglas Ball, expressed his pleasure in the progress of Native Schools in providing "facilities so indispensable to a practical and useful kind of training, and in the development, in the Native schools, of that emphasis on realistic, as contrasted with abstract, teaching which is generally conceded to be desired" (Ball, 1939, p. 1).

The Native Schools' regime of limited academic education placed a heavy emphasis on practical skills which, according to the state, Māori still needed to acquire to assimilate successfully into Pākehā society. The theory and practice underlying education for Māori had for many years been based on the assumption that Māori would "integrate" into Pākehā society to such a degree that the only difference would be skin colour (Beeby, 1992). Based on this supposition, the Native Schools system would continue to restrict Māori education through limited access to academic content and a relentless emphasis on domestic and labour training until 1969.

The history and effects of the Native Schools system has been discussed; however, of importance here are the ways progressive philosophy has constructed Māori knowledge and identities in education. Gerlich (2013) argues that Beeby's reforms, especially in the areas of physical education, arts, and crafts, caused a more balanced, child-centred, and bicultural curriculum that enabled creativity and focused on understanding. These aspects of the reforms appeared to be influenced by revered leader and Member of Parliament Tā Apirana Ngata who, in the 1920s, had initiated a training programme for teachers in Native Schools as a strategy to put into practice the objective of the Māori Arts and Crafts Act 1926 to "… encourage the Dissemination of Knowledge of Māori Arts and Crafts". Long before becoming the Director of Education, Beeby had attended this course and commended it as an excellent programme, as did Māori elders and parents, Native School teachers, and Fraser (Beeby, 1992). So, while Native Schools would be excluded from the overall social and educational reforms, the inclusion of more creative practices into "board" (now "mainstream" or English-medium) schools had been borrowed and adapted from the Native Schools programme to better engage Pākehā students and encourage creativity.

Ngata's vision of reviving Māori confidence through visual arts (Walker, 1996) was appropriated by New Zealand education to advance progressive ideals for Pākehā students by transferring the creative component without the Māori knowledge base attached to the practice. As argued previously, it was racist Western thinking, converted to education policy that started the stereotype that Māori are by nature suited to practical learning (Taylor, 1863a). However, in my experience, many Māori elders teach us that as Māori we can learn by engaging conceptually and physically with people and environments, which requires abstraction as well as practical approaches. The appropriation of Māori creativity into Western education, devoid of the accompanying Māori ways of knowing, for the benefit of Pākehā students, has perpetuated and entrenched the stereotype that Māori are practical learners as espoused by decision makers in New Zealand education.

Sentiments of the time provide insight into what Māori continued to aspire to in the early 1900s—economic equality with their Pākehā counterparts, by way of access to Pākehā social norms and language. Many Māori parents during the early 1900s encouraged the use of the English language in order for Māori to improve successful outcomes in the Pākehā "mainstream" (Peterson, 2000). Ngata stated that "[t]he most important subjects in Māori schools are first English, second English, and third English" (Beeby, 1992, p. 206). This statement is sometimes quoted out of context by politicians attempting to justify racist policy well into the new millennium. Ngata did not say this to devalue or to encourage the abandonment of te reo or te ao Māori; his insistence on making English a priority at that time was to ensure equality of opportunity for Māori (Beeby, 1992). Simon (1998) argues that many Māori communities developed a "... strong sense of ownership and commitment to what they had initiated" (p. 22) in the development of local Native Schools. For many Māori at the time, Native Schools were a valuable part of the community, as they served Māori who were still fluent speakers of te reo and still lived in relative isolation from Pākehā society (Walker, 1990). Māori at this time in our history saw no fragility in Māori culture or language and wanted to learn about Pākehā society so as to survive the Pākehā world (Simon, 2000).

Pragmatic progressive ideologies that encourage sensory and experiential engagement with the world (Matapo & Roder, 2017) along with the idea that education is child-centred and functionally useful, has links to Māori concepts of knowledge from the kauae raro. In many ways, the practical and useful ideals of progressivism can be viewed as similar to our own concepts of the kauae raro. What was removed in education for Māori was access to academic education. From a Māori perspective, kauae raro works in collaboration with kauae runga, so Western education was only half educating us. In the 1940s, many Māori were vocal about unjust differences between Māori education and that of their Pākehā counterparts (Beeby, 1992; Simon, 2000).

As English-medium education for Pākehā students embraced progressive philosophies to balance the singular liberal focus on knowledge and the mind, Māori were protesting the continued forced practical education that was excluding so many from full and equal participation in New Zealand society. The difference between Māori goals for education at the time, and the progressive goals of the state, are captured in this recollection by Beeby (1992):

> I called a meeting where [Māori] parents could air their grievances. They objected to the curriculum, and I asked what else they wanted in it. The answer was 'Typewriting and Latin!' ... On the subject of Latin I gave them an address, which Professor Percy Nunn would have applauded, on the concept of education through the use of the hands, in practical skills rather than words. As I sat down the leading elder asked, 'Did you take Latin at school, Dr Beeby?' I admitted to six years of it, and he retorted, 'And look where you got to!' Nearly half a century later, I have still not thought of an apt reply. (p. 210)

The progressive purpose of education in society that influenced both Beeby and Fraser (O'Connor, 2017) caused them to gladly view education as "... an arm of a wider policy of social reform ... that education itself could cause change in society" (Beeby, 1992, p. 133). Indeed, the impoverished state of Pākehā society caused by the Depression had been transformed through education. For Māori, prospects of social transformation through education were limited. Access to education was not providing equality of opportunity for Māori, rather "... policies and provisions could only serve to widen the gulf between Pākehā and Māori in terms of economic and political power" (Simon, 2000, p. 56).

The liberal-progressive philosophies of the Labour Government under the direction of Dr Beeby created more educational opportunities than any other administration (Simon, 2000). However, having been subjected to restrictive education for a century, Māori were still demanding a complete education that would enable access to academic learning. This contrasted with the state's progressive push toward experiential learning that would stabilise New Zealand's economy by providing opportunities for greater numbers of citizens.

Sylvia's powerful imagery

A story about Māori has formed the foundations of literacy education and progressive education globally through the work of educator Sylvia Ashton-Warner. Ashton-Warner linked her key vocabulary method to the daily lives and realities of the young Māori children she taught (Mutch, 2013). Ashton-Warner had an eccentric, non-conformist, and radical approach, not just to education, but to life, which aided her creative teaching approaches. However, her unconventionalities also caused her to experience what she perceived as persecution at the hands of New Zealanders, specifically Education Department officials (Dobson, 2007). Ashton-Warner's approach to progressivism was largely ignored during her time because she was regarded as somewhat eccentric and too radical in her thinking, which did not align well to the progressive education reform that began in the 1940s (Jones & Middleton, 2009).

However, while Ashton-Warner's work was largely ignored by policy makers of the time, "to many educators around the world, progressive education in New Zealand is synonymous with the story of Sylvia Ashton-Warner teaching Māori children in a remote village ..." (Mutch, 2013, p. 99). Her imagery has constructed both Māori and Pākehā in education in very specific ways that continue to be reflected in contemporary New Zealand education.

Ashton-Warner's love for, yet sense of superiority over, Māori students continues to colour the lens of the relationship between education and Māori. In many ways, her methods of teaching literacy to Māori students were successful, yet she herself was troubled that this would not guarantee their success in the life they faced (Ashton-Warner, 1980). I will argue that, while Ashton-Warner had the potential to seed positive progress for Māori education, instead the most superficial aspects of her work with Māori continue to be reflected in longstanding English-medium concepts of best practice for teaching Māori.

Through Ashton-Warner's work *Teacher* (Ashton-Warner, 1980) we get a glimpse, from her perspective, of an important time for education in New Zealand. Robinson (2010) argues that the way Western education has constructed knowledge, as academic and non-academic, has caused chaos and convinced many people who are brilliant that they are not. Ashton-Warner's work to push New Zealand education to think of and centre the child through innovative methods that deviated from those prescribed by the state gives a sense that perhaps she felt the same way. Her experience of New Zealand children taught her that the English, Scottish, and American models on which our education system was based (Ashton-Warner, 1980; Simon, 2000) were inappropriate within our context.

Her approach to teaching was in contrast to the rigid style of the time; intensive learning took place through discussion and was more in line with what many Māori were used to (Tawhiwhirangi, 2009). While her work is largely centred around methods for teaching Māori students, Ashton-Warner (1980) also provides her perspective of Pākehā students and society. There is such complexity in her perspectives of both cultures: many Pākehā students are presented as "victims" of their respectable parents; Māori children are the products of a primitive, highly emotional, and often abusive people that must transition into Pākehā culture. This complexity is illustrated in the description she records of a key vocabulary session:

'Mohi,' I ask a new five, an undisciplined Māori, 'what do you want?' 'Jet!' I smile and write it on a strong little card and give it to him … 'What do you want, Gay?' Gay is the classic overdisciplined, bullied victim of the respectable mother. 'House' she whispers … 'What do you want Seven?' Seven is a violent Māori. 'Bomb! Bomb! I want Bomb!' So Seven gets his word 'bomb' and challenges anyone to take it from him. (Ashton-Warner, 1980, pp. 35–36)

Violent Seven's "old Mummy" arrives at the classroom door, "humble with natural dignity, a barefooted, tattooed Māori woman" (Ashton-Warner, 1980, p. 37) desperate to see the child she has raised in the hills alone who she has returned to his "real" family so he can attend school. We learn that violent Seven has gone from a loving home to a home full of brothers who hit him. All this child wants is to return to his old Mummy. Through this interaction, Ashton-Warner gains some understanding about Seven but laments that she cannot make a "good story of it and say he is no longer violent …" (Ashton-Warner, 1980, p. 38), but she has captured Seven's key words—"old Mummy", "new Mummy", "hit", and "brothers", which she uses to engage him in literacy learning.

In the same description, Ashton-Warner admits defeat to Dennis' mother. Dennis has had a nervous breakdown at 5 and is "a victim of a respectable, money-making, well-dressed mother who thrashes him" (Ashton-Warner, 1980, p. 38). Her failure with Dennis is that she never captured his fear words as she did with Seven, because Dennis' fears were unnameable. Dennis does later reveal his fears through a picture he draws of a terrible ghost facing a red alligator on a roadway. While the other children take part in lively and engaging learning activities, Dennis busies himself tidying the classroom while Ashton-Warner predicts his future life as "another neurotic, pursued by the fear unnameable …" (Ashton-Warner, 1980, pp. 38–39).

Ashton-Warner has framed Māori and Pākehā in particular ways here. While I can only surmise whether this was conscious or unconscious, I argue that this positioning has become deeply embedded in the fabric of New Zealand education and general social thought. Mohi is undisciplined, Seven is violent. We also meet Rangi, who is a "backward Māori" (Ashton-Warner, 1980, p. 43) and Puki, who comes from a clever, but violent, family. In the examples above, all the fears and impediments of the Māori students are apparently observable and physical. Seven lives with the damage of being removed from his loving home into the hands of his violent brothers. Rangi lives in terror of the police (however, his trauma related to the police is blamed by the headmaster on the actions of Rangi's drunk father, who had "probably" threatened the children). Puki's mother and father loudly, and often physically, fight each other. Ashton-Warner does not silence these realities. Her success in initiating reading and writing with these children is in utilising the words that fall from these realities. Whereas the fears of her Pākehā students are apparently unnameable, they become another generation afraid of the unknown.

While the barefooted, humble, and tattooed mother of one culture starkly contrasted against the young, well-dressed, wealthy mother of the other culture paints a strong and lasting image, it is not to say that Ashton-Warner favoured the respectable Pākehā image over that of the rowdy, dramatic "pā" life. In justifying her use of schematic illustrations in her transitional readers, she reveals a "revulsion ... against respectability and the 'right thing' that Maoris and I find so intimidating" (Ashton-Warner, 1980, p. 72). She also points out that she often gets "the over-disciplined European five, crushed beyond recognition as an identity, by respectable parents, but never Maoris" (Ashton-Warner, 1980, p. 98).

Complexly, Ashton-Warner appears to have a level of disdain for the "respectable" Pākehā, apparently a feeling shared by Māori, yet it is this very respectability that is taken for granted as "right". Ashton-Warner criticises New Zealand (Pākehā) society as being a body of people whose inner resources have been atrophied by strong reliance on materialism and saturation in popular media (Ashton-Warner, 1980). She frames Pākehā society as being people unable to think for themselves and devoid of emotion. Yet a great focus of her work is to "transition" Māori students into this culture which she herself appears to disparage, so that they may succeed in life.

Ashton-Warner's knowledge of Māori stories is telling of her relationship with Māori students. The concept of effective relationships in education has become increasingly important in contemporary education (Education Council New Zealand, 2011). Ashton-Warner's insistence of her personal witnessing, and therefore truth, of the dramatic lives of Māori is confirmed in the students' stories she publishes (Ashton-Warner, 1980). We get a sense of her intimate, knowledgeable relationship with her Māori students and their families. However, alternative (Māori) perspectives of these relationships are provided by Penfold (2009), who believes Ashton-Warner did not learn much from the children because she was rarely with them. Tawhiwhirangi (2009) points out that parents thought she was odd and would stay at the school with their children all day, partly to keep an eye on their strange teacher.

There is also a difference in Ashton-Warner's interactions with Māori and her interactions with Pākehā families. She engages in direct conversation about Dennis' thoughts with his "young, pretty mother in her big car" (Ashton-Warner, 1980, p. 38). Whereas she only learns the source of Seven's violence, or as I would interpret it, profound sadness, by a chance visit from his broken-hearted "old Mummy". Differential interactions also continue to be a feature in contemporary education. Teachers have access to documents (Education Council New Zealand, 2011; Ministry of Education, 2013a) intended to help them facilitate interactions and relationships with Māori communities, but there appears to be no need to provide teachers with instructions for interacting with non-Māori—these interactions come naturally it would seem.

While Ashton-Warner arguably did have authentic relationships with her students, which have come to be prized by New Zealand education, these relationships were observational, and those observations were coloured by her Pākehā cultural perspective. For all her experiential knowledge of the "loud-mouthed and disintegrated pa" (Ashton-Warner, 1980, p. 86) that produced her students, we see nothing to indicate she had any perception of the "why" of the situations of these Māori families. They are presented as lively, colourful, violent people perceived only in the present in which she finds them. This is contrasted against the pretty, young, well-off Pākehā mother with whom she engages in direct conversation to better understand her student. This mother's abusive behaviour is diminished by her beauty and respectability.

Ashton-Warner's progressive education strategies are employed as a bridge between one culture and another (Ashton-Warner, 1980). The lives and realities of her Māori students, their words that are so full of life, then become valuable only as a platform by which they can access what Ashton-Warner herself describes as the dead vocabulary of New Zealand education (Ashton-Warner, 1980). Yet accessing this dead vocabulary is seen as necessary:

> The method of teaching any subject in a Māori infant room may be seen as a plank in a bridge from one culture to another, and to the extent that this bridge is strengthened may a Māori in later life succeed. This transition made by Māori children is often unsuccessful. At a tender age a wrench occurs from one culture to another, from which, either manifestly or subconsciously, not all recover. (Ashton-Warner, 1980, p. 31)

As in the time of missionary education, this is an example of an educator who knows the limitations of Western education for Māori. Ashton-Warner is aware that mediating the chasm between Western education and Māori cultural identity will devastate many Māori, and yet her only response, along with countless other educators, is to plough ahead with the necessary task of "transitioning".

While Ashton-Warner may not have influenced the direction of liberal-progressive education reform during her time, her imagery of Māori and of Pākehā have been woven into the subconscious of New Zealand education. Her students' stories, which she used to successfully motivate literacy learning, became "the" Māori story. The story of vibrant, loud, violent, and disintegrating people became the only story of Māori in education. The humble, bare-footed, primitive mother became "the" Māori mother, and she is so vividly contrasted against the pretty, young, wealthy woman who became "the" Pākehā mother. Educators can have direct learning conversations with the Pākehā mother, but with Māori, educators can form opinions based on coloured perceptions.

I don't believe Ashton-Warner intended for stereotypes to be derived from her work. Her work highlights that, while she may not have fully understood her Māori students, she did love them. She saw in them life, vitality, and a sense of identity that she believed was missing from their Pākehā counterparts. Her words betray her almost desperate need to connect with these students and their whānau. It seems she wanted to belong with them, to be claimed by them, perhaps in an attempt to quell the bitter disappointment she felt in her own culture. Sylvia's imagery is powerful, and the stereotypes derived from them remain deeply embedded in the structure of New Zealand education. What education forgot is that Sylvia's story is only one story, it is not our only story, nor is it our own story.

Continued Māori resistance and a revolving door of policy change

The social and political environment from the 1970s through to the late 1990s provided a climate for a range of public policy changes. Liberal-progressive ideals that saturated New Zealand politics, education, and society paved the way for the introduction of the policy approach of integration. Strong Māori discontent with the education system saw the Māori development of kōhanga reo and kura kaupapa Māori outside of state control.[13] Continued Māori objection to policies that marginalised Māori aspirations forced a move to the Māori Potential Approach. This whakapapa details how education has arrived at Māori cultural competence as a way to enable Māori education success as Māori. However, I will argue that many of the racist, assimilationist, paternalistic policies and practices that have formed this whakapapa remain deep in the psyche of education.

The more recent history of the 1960s onward is relatively easy to access; many people remember these times as part of their lived experiences. The period of the 1970s and 1980s have popularly become known as the time of Māori renaissance, featuring Māori resistance

---

13 Kōhanga reo are Māori language centres for early childhood education. They were developed by Māori who feared the extinction of the Māori language and could not trust the government to remedy the situation. Kura kaupapa Māori are Māori language primary schools. Whare kura are Māori language secondary schools.

to colonial injustice and resurgence in Māori culture and language. However, Walker (1990) argues that Māori resistance was a continual process since 1840 within Māori communities that were largely isolated from Pākehā communities, and that the renaissance was not a renaissance at all; it was simply that, by 1970, Māori and Pākehā were living less discrete lives so Pākehā became more conscious of Māori activity and discontent. The arguments presented throughout this book illustrate ongoing activism since 1840 that concurs with Walker (1990); however, Māori resistance and Pākehā awareness of that resistance during the 1970s and 1980s did finally force significant change for Māori in education.

The Hunn Report (1961) was, strictly speaking, a report on the Department of Māori Affairs, but had far-reaching implications for Māori social and education policy. According to Hunn, Māori were struggling to adjust socially and educationally largely due to socio-economic disparities between Māori and Pākehā (Hill, 2009) and our insistence on living rurally in multigenerational family units. The "solution" for Māori was to begin living in nuclear family units, move to urban areas, and quickly learn to live as Pākehā. It was believed by the report writer that doing so would ensure Māori equality of life outcomes with Pākehā. From the Hunn Report, the public policy of integration began.

However, the Māori Synod of the Presbyterian Church was concerned that "integration", according to Eurocentric government policy, meant that Māori needed to do all the adjusting (Hill, 2009). There was a dangerous inference that Māori lack of success in Western education was not due to racist colonial and assimilationist policies or having been deprived access to economic resources of land and sea, or to Western education philosophies and racist attitudes, but was due to the way Māori lived. Therefore, the new policy of integration came into being in the same breath as deficit theory.

The myth of the "urban drift" was also an outcome of the Hunn Report, giving the impression that Māori, by chance, drifted into urban centres, when the reality was Māori were forcibly removed from our lands into unfamiliar and often unfriendly urban living situations under the pretence of government concern for Māori wellbeing. Many claims to the Waitangi Tribunal evidence that forcible evictions in the 1960s of Māori from rural and traditional homelands resulted in further alienation from our lands. It is an understatement that this resulted in reduced wellness for Māori. It is important to remember that forced removal happened to people who are still living. I have heard people of my parents age recounting that, when they returned home from the city, fences had been erected and gates locked, and they were left to wonder who had done this on their lands without their knowledge and certainly without permission. These are recent events in our history with real-life consequences that people are still trying to overcome and redress.

Hill (2009, p. 99) summarises Māori suspicion of the underlying Crown motives for integration through three highly regarded Māori scholars. Sir Hugh Kawharu (Ngāti Whātua) argued "when the Pakeha says 'integration' he really means 'assimilation'"; Sir Hirini Mead (Ngāti Awa, Ngāti Tūwharetoa, Ngāi Tuhoe, Tūhourangi) criticised the Crown for continuing the "one people, one nation" policies, which had been so successful in "alienating us from our culture" since 1840; and Dr Patu Hohepa (Ngā Puhi) outrightly rejected all government policy around assimilation and integration. It was clear that many Māori saw little difference between integration and assimilation, and had little trust that integration would be implemented any differently than the policy approach it was to replace. Walker (2016) argues that, while the Hunn Report was in many respects useful, it failed to address the moral integrity of an education system that purposely drove Māori away from the professions and into manual labour.

Despite the suspicion with which Māori received it, there was some positive movement due to the Hunn Report. During the 1960s, 400 Māori were trained to be teachers. It was these teachers who began transforming education from the inside by utilising Māori content through the social studies curriculum. They also began pushing for further education reforms (Walker, 1984). Pressure from Māori along with an increase of liberal thinkers in government caused rapid education reform throughout the 1970s, punctuated by a reversal of cultural denial by assimilation (Walker, 1984).

In 1979, the state of te reo Māori was in such disrepair that Benton (1979) warned of its impending demise without urgent and intensive intervention. This realisation, along with state reports (Department of Education, 1962; Hunn, 1961), and "... loud Māori complaints about the inability of the state to deal with the escalating crisis of Māori underachievement in schools ..." (Kaa Jenkins & Ka'ai, 1994, p. 162) mobilised Māori to continue the work of tūpuna who insisted on Māori determining the future of our culture and language. Māori gave up waiting for the state to resolve the education crisis they had created and perpetuated. The first Māori education initiative to function outside of state control was kōhanga reo in the early childhood sector, the first opening in Wainuiōmata in 1982 (Thomson, 2015).

Continued Māori pressure throughout the 1970s and 1980s saw the increased introduction of culturally based programmes in state education, driven by Māori teachers who devised what would become "taha Māori" programmes. They led school visits to marae, and initiated school-based marae on some campuses (Walker, 2016). An appearance of biculturalism was beginning to emerge from the change in policy direction. However, much of the "integration" of Māori cultural concepts in state education was concealing the profound depth of deficit thinking. Well-meaning efforts to remedy the injustices caused by Pākehā dominance in education caused a name change but not a change in hearts and minds—Māori were now viewed as "culturally different" rather than a "problem" (Simon, 1984). Simon argued:

> ... 'culturally different' soon became merely a catch-phrase eagerly taken up by teachers making spurious claims that Māori educational needs were being recognized and catered for. Thus it served only to conceal the 'deficit' view. Within this view, Māoritanga could never be more than a mere appendage to the regular school programme and as such served to reinforce the belief that the Pakeha-oriented curriculum was the 'real' curriculum. (p. 5)

Marks (1984) also emphasised the continued inequality facing Māori students even with access to greater "bicultural" education, as well as the frustrations of being a Māori teacher trying to implement change within an unchanged education system:

> ... even where the school does have a taha Maori, it's probably merely a Maori Club or timetable[d] periods for language and arts and crafts. But the school is most unlikely to have changed its self so that it actually FEELS good to Maoris and actually works to give them an equal chance. Not an equal chance at Pakeha education only, but the same chance that Pakeha students get for their culture, for their own culture. (p. 12)

Delegates of the Māori Education Development Conference in 1984, where both these statements were made, resolved to initiate an alternative schooling system based on the philosophical underpinnings of kōhanga reo (Walker, 2016). In 1985, the first official kura kaupapa Māori was opened at Hoani Waititi Marae, Auckland, as a response to "... the lack of education programmes and equity of outcomes for Māori children" (Macfarlane, 2004, p. 13). Māori dissatisfaction with state-controlled education was so great that whānau were determined to establish an education system outside of state control, and without state funding (Walker, 1990). Kura kaupapa Māori were not initiated to compete with state education, but as a desperate and proactive drive to save te reo Māori (Kaa Jenkins & Ka'ai, 1994). The Māori instigation of kōhanga reo and kura kaupapa Māori did not, however, absolve the state of its responsibility for Māori education.

After 20 years of entrenched deficit theorising in New Zealand education, the Waitangi Tribunal (1985) charged the state education system as being a failure, and challenged the enduring use of cultural deprivation theory to explain Māori educational underachievement (Kaa Jenkins & Ka'ai, 1994). Despite this challenge from the Waitangi Tribunal, education policy underscored by deficit theorising arguably remains entrenched in the structure of education. Thirty-six years after that challenge, ongoing objection by Māori to Crown negligence of Māori education is illustrated by the 2021 urgent claim (WAI 1718) to the Waitangi Tribunal on behalf of all kura kaupapa Māori, whānau, and Te Rūnanga Nui (Perry, 2022).

In 1989, a Labour Government introduced a suite of policies that reformed the governance, management, and administration of New Zealand schools. These reforms, commonly known as "Tomorrow's Schools", were driven by neoliberal philosophies that sought to eradicate perceived socioeconomic instability caused by rising inflation, rising unemployment, and a depressed economy, by restructuring the education system through devolving the powers of decision making and choice to parents (Johnston, 1997). The Government-sponsored evidence needed to make these sweeping changes was Administering for Excellence (Department of Education, 1988), led by businessman Brian Picot.

As with all other educational reforms, Tomorrow's Schools continued to marginalise Māori culture and knowledge, as well as Māori aspirations in education (Johnston, 1997). The policy underpinning the reforms remained located in the ideologies of integration and deficit theorising. They also embraced market ideologies intended to change the nature of schools by utilising economic models. It was predicted at the time that the removal of government controls and zoning (attending the local school in a community "zone") would intensify schooling segregation based on socioeconomic status (Thrupp, 1997). Investigating the astounding outcomes of 30 years of neoliberal policy making is beyond the scope of this project. However, these predictions and many others have proven correct, whereas the theory that neoliberalism would stabilise the economy was a severely misguided notion. Māori interests and aspirations with regards to underachievement were reinterpreted to conform to non-Māori ideas about how the reformed system should be delivered (Johnston, 1997) and essentially repacked Hunn's "gaps".

Just prior to the dawn of the new millennium, the government took yet another policy approach, "Empowering Education. Te Ihi, Te Mana, Te Mātauranga", which appeared to present a promise from the state to Māori of real power and a partnership in education that would ensure mana Māori (Jenkins & Jones, 2000). Yet again, the "gaps" in education were identified, and the new policy direction aimed to reduce the gaps through a "... continuation of increasing the 'dosage' of English and Western culture" (Jenkins & Jones, 2000, p. 144). In 1999, Labour Prime Minister Helen Clark indicated her commitment to "closing the gaps" by establishing and chairing the "Closing the Gaps" committee. General (Pākehā) population criticised this commitment as elevating Māori over other groups who were also deprived (Walker, 2016). Interestingly, and somewhat ironically, pressure from non-Māori concerned that Māori were being privileged by the government attempting to redress a problem they had created caused the government narrative to change yet again and deficit "Closing the Gaps" was replaced by capacity-building in Māori communities (Walker, 2016).

It was under this rather ambiguous notion of capacity-building in Māori communities that a new policy direction, the "Māori Potential Approach", was developed by Te Puni Kōkiri in 2004 as the government approach to public policy (Ministry of Education, 2009). This approach is driven by an ideology that Māori culture is an advantage to education; it recognises Māori are inherently capable of achieving success and acknowledges the unlimited potential of Māori learners. It is this key shift in policy that saw a move toward developing the notion of Māori cultural competencies.

While the Māori Potential framework attempts to move away from policy underpinned by deficit theories, a space of 40 years between the Hunn Report and the "Māori Potential Approach" is a long time in our short history together. The damage caused by the deeply embedded theory that our culture has caused our deprivation is still strong, and very much alive in the hearts and minds of many. The effects of deficit theorising is an example of the insidious and long-lasting way "research" can be used to influence perceptions of common sense (L. Smith, 2012). In reviewing these particular policy changes and seeing how we have matured as a nation, it is almost inconceivable that the current National-led coalition Government threatens to regress social and education policy to a point even further back in our history than the dogged Hunn days. This is a very real display of the insidious nature of racist theories that have shaped political ideologies under the control of a Government intent on not knowing or owning the history of the country it is charged with serving.

Te Herenga

Liberal-progressive philosophies underpin and influence contemporary English-medium education in New Zealand (Mutch & Tatebe, 2017). The education reforms of the 1940s moved away from the exclusive classical liberal education system by establishing an equitable education system to provide relief for many Pākehā students who had become impoverished during the Depression years. However, Māori had been excluded from classical liberal education by way of racist policies that restricted our learning to the acquisition of manual labour skills. The liberal-progressive reforms that would innovate New Zealand education through experiential as well as intellectual learning (Mutch, 2017), would appropriate Māori ideas, but would continue to fail to meet the goals of Māori, which were to access a high-quality academic curriculum.

Many liberal-progressive pedagogies would entrench non-Māori stereotypes about Māori in education; for example, the colourful and sometime eccentric work of Sylvia Ashton-Warner. Progressive philosophies appear to be congruent with Māori ways of being, such as communal learning (Mutch, 2017), and experiential learning. However, as I have argued, all these concepts originate from Pākehā assertions, and, although they do correlate with the ways Māori interact, they are by no means a reflection of the ways Māori traditionally learned. With no real evidence, English-medium education has convinced itself that the liberal-progressive underpinnings of New Zealand education are an approach that suits Māori learning styles. These have become deeply ingrained stereotypes in education about Māori, they have limited opportunities for Māori to develop metacognitive skills (Ministry of Education, 2013b), and have continued to undermine Māori goals for education.

While there is potential for liberal-progressive philosophies to better foster the potential of Māori students, there is a continued lack of acknowledgement that these philosophies originated in the

West. They have been adapted to the New Zealand (Pākehā) context; however, they continue to restrict Māori education success because their philosophical foundations have a specific cultural location. This central problem continues to cause kaumātua, and others, to be concerned about the welfare of tamariki in English-medium education, as well as the ability of the system to genuinely enable education success for Māori, as Māori.

Māori education initiatives were born of continued frustration at the state's inability to address urgent educational crises for Māori. These initiatives have offered some respite to Māori; however, deficit theorising has continued to cause deep-seated stereotypical views about Māori in education, and Māori ways of life, regardless of the name of the policy they underpin. Deficit theory prevailed in public policymaking in New Zealand until 2004, when the government finally introduced the Māori Potential Approach. Viewing Māori culture and language as having the potential to positively influence education for Māori has caused a shift in education policy (Ministry of Education, 2013a), which currently is at risk of losing any ground made.

The policy shift from deficit theorising to the Māori Potential Approach essentially triggered the notion that Māori cultural competence for teachers of Māori students is a way to progress education success for Māori, as Māori. However, it must be perceived within the context of an education system that from its inception has devalued and attempted to erase Māori cultural knowledge, language, and economic strength. Cultural competencies, then, are a way for teachers and schools to help Māori "... in making a livelihood after the original forms of livelihood were reduced or taken away" (Battiste, 2013, p. 24).

A raft of policy approaches has supposedly taken New Zealand education from assimilation to integration, to empowerment, to capacity-building. I have argued that these are essentially similar policies by different names. *Tātaiako* has been developed as the result of the Māori potential policy; nevertheless, it continues to be situated in an education system that, despite numerous reforms, has, for the most part, remained unchanged. Te Aupouri's challenges to education and the professionals in it are powerful in his gentleness. He sees that engaging intelligence, physicality, and spirituality will enrich education experiences for students: "I think at the end of the [education programme], one of the main things is that referring to the hinengaro, the tinana, and the wairua, which are ... I believe three of the main basics ... that will help our children grow and develop."

Chapter 7
Te māreikura

Te pūkōrero ō Janet Hetaraka

Born to a Māori–Jewish father and a Scottish mother, Janet was raised in Te Wai Pounamu, the youngest of eight children. She grew up Protestant in a Catholic community; a Māori in Pākehā cities, a Māori with white skin. As a teenager, I struggled a lot with the racism I felt as a young Māori woman in a "mainstream" high school. Many parents of students in our intermediate school bilingual unit, including my own, and my Uncle Buster, who is also a participant in this project, fought for a bilingual unit to be established for us as we moved on to secondary school. Their victory was hard won but, as students, we quickly came to understand our value, or lack of it, to the school. We often did not have a teacher, let alone a classroom, to go to. Regularly, we were instructed by office staff to sit in the hallway for whole periods because we had not been included in the timetable. This gave our class one predominant message: that there was no place for us, that as a group of young Māori women we were not important.

I came to harbour real anger and grief, much of it stemming from what I felt were injustices against my tūpuna that continued to be manifest in very real and confronting ways in my own time. I will always remember an argument I had with Janet, my Mum, during this time. I was in trouble for constantly questioning the curriculum choices being made by the heads of department at my school—I wanted to be given the opportunity to learn about Te Tiriti o Waitangi and the New Zealand Wars before the Black Civil Rights movement and Elizabethan England. Mum was trying to encourage me to take a more subtle approach than the anger-fuelled path that had me often sitting in the principal's office. I scathingly spat that she didn't know what it was like to go through the education system as a dark-skinned Māori. She told me I didn't know what it was like to go through life as a white-skinned Māori.

At the time I dismissed her view. All I could see was that to be brown in this country meant to be at the bottom of the heap. I have thought about this standoff many times as an adult and it has taught me valuable lessons about perception, identity, expectation, and understanding. That exchange so many years ago taught me that, regardless of our perception of others, we have no right to attempt to define a person by our own external and limited measures. Our identities are complex, and our experiences of being Māori are diverse. Almost everything I know about being a Māori woman has come from my mother, a woman of Ngāi Tahu, arguably one of the most historically disenfranchised tribes in the country. A woman who, perhaps more than anybody else I know, has had to navigate two very different worlds because of her physical appearance, and has maintained her dignity in the face of racism based on her appearance and her cultural identity, from both Māori and Pākehā. Janet's perspective is important to this project as, in many ways, she has a very good understanding of Pākehā systems and how they can be used to benefit Māori. She also possesses the ability to navigate the tricky terrain of cultural identity with what appears to be great ease and confidence, a characteristic that would benefit many Māori in complex, contemporary contexts.

Our conversation takes place at the Shed at Hīhīaua on a sunny May afternoon. Janet's professionalism is the first thing that strikes me when I arrive. I can see she is in work mode and is ready for a serious conversation. Even though she is my mum she has her professional face on this afternoon, and I am humbled by the seriousness with which she approaches our discussion. I am armed with my interview questions to guide me, but it suddenly comes to me that perhaps I should have had Janet run her journalist's eye over them before I finalised them!

Janet's first comment in relation to what she considers as educational success for her mokopuna is that they have a positive experience of their schooling. She then expands on this by defining what positive looks like to her:

> *That they're engaged. That they're challenged. That they learn how to think for themselves, how to ask questions. How to challenge others. To seek information and knowledge.*

She also goes on to identify that student progression based on assessment is not necessarily how she would define education success. That education success is about being a well-rounded person, not necessarily just a person who does well in assessments:

> *It's not necessarily about them qualifying, ticking all the boxes, but in fact ... that they've been taught values, to interact with others, to care for the environment and that they will pursue further education and have a life-long desire to learn. That, to me, is success for my mokopuna.*

Janet articulates her belief that educational success is different from living as a successful Māori; that to live as Māori successfully requires access to cultural knowledge and values. While she states that education success is different from living successfully as Māori, she is also clear that access to cultural knowledge must form part of contemporary education:

> *... they also need to ... be very, very comfortable within their culture, that they have access to practise te reo. That they're grounded in our cultural values in terms of whakapapa and whanaungatanga as well, so that they ... know who they are as Māori and where they fit in this country and in the world. That adds ... to their education ... they both fit. I don't think you can have one without the other necessarily, as a young Māori person today.*

When discussing the education of her grandchildren, Janet is very certain about the aspects that will contribute to their ability to be successful and be Māori. Her views here have many implications for education:

> *... they need to be respected as learners. They need to feel that they are valued and that their learning is valuable, that they are not just*

> *going through a process to come out the other end as a sausage, that they come out as whole, rounded individuals ...*

The majority of Janet's mokopuna are girls. However, even before she had grandchildren, she and Te Warihi held particular beliefs about the importance of education for girls. These beliefs may appear to contrast with the assumptions many make about the patriarchal nature of Māori culture; however, it is very much in line with pre-colonial Māori concepts:

> *... particularly for girls, they, as the first educators of the next generation ... have to be well educated in all sorts of ways.*

Again, Janet refers to the need for education to be broader than the current focus on core curricula subjects or disciplines:

> *... though my mother had very limited education, she could fix anything, she could make anything, she was practical, and I'd wish some of that on the next generations as well. We're losing some of those things—the resourcefulness.*

Along with resourcefulness, Janet highlights the important role that building confidence in children plays in their success:

> *I think [teachers] have an increasing need to build confidence in our kids ... I see a lack of confidence as a huge handicap for a lot of people. Even if you can't do something, as long as you give it a go, you'll learn something ... you'll gain some strength ... But confidence is a very, very important aspect of young children's personality, to go that extra mile, to look deeper, to enquire, to have a go at something they've never done, to travel, to step out of their own little niche, their own little village.*

Ever the realist, Janet also points out that, while self-confidence is an internal feeling, it can be strongly impacted by external factors:

> *... on the negative side of that I think, as Māori, our kids so often have their confidence squashed, diminished, takahia-ed, by the*

devaluing of what is important to us as Māori ... right across the board.

I am interested to know at this point what the perfect teacher might look like, what values they would need to have to teach Janet's mokopuna. The very first quality Janet identifies gives me a lot to think about:

Firstly, love. They'd have to love kids, love what they are doing, love themselves.

The idea of self-love being a prerequisite for teaching is not a concept I have come across. I have often heard teachers, especially new teachers, refer to the fact they love children, they love to teach children new things, but the idea of self-love is interesting. Janet's perfect teacher is one who is motivated by love with high self-awareness:

They would have to demonstrate empathy, enthusiasm, respect. They need to be confident in themselves, they need to be constantly learning, refreshing, keeping their own personal and professional development up to date ... embracing technology to knit with the things of the past. They need to be well grounded themselves in our culture, or their culture.

The teacher imagined here has some correlations to the teacher described in *Tātaiako*; however, there are some subtle, yet very crucial differences. Janet's teacher has self-confidence, is confident in who they are as a person, the *Tātaiako* teacher presumes confidence in Māori culture. Janet's teacher is well-grounded in their own culture, the *Tātaiako* teacher is expected to progress to become a leader in Māori culture. I am interested in this point as I often hear Pākehā student teachers proclaim that they have "no culture". I pick up on the idea of why Janet believes teachers should be grounded in their own culture:

Because until you are [grounded in your culture], you cannot really be successful in relating to other people's culture. In New Zealand, all Māori teachers know how to interact with Pākehā, but not all Pākehā know how to interact with Māori. That's the imbalance.

Further disrupting the balance is that some Māori also have little knowledge of how to interact with Māori. Janet has some very practical solutions to correcting this imbalance and supporting teachers of Māori students to better meet their needs for cultural safety and respect:

> *Obviously, early on in their training, [teachers] need to know what is important to our kids. They need to be aware there are differences. They need to be challenged about their own cultural understandings.*

Janet also discusses some structural supports that could be established:

> *[Teachers] need to have some time to reflect and pick up on what they are good at, and acknowledge the things they are not good at … I think there needs to be some sort of audit and system whereby teachers can say 'well I need to learn …' I think it's regional, I don't think it necessarily needs to be too hard either.*

She also highlights the importance of encouraging more Māori into the teaching profession because of values that are inherent in te ao Māori that can be useful to teaching:

> *I also think that more Māori people need to be encouraged and facilitated into teaching. I think we naturally, some of us, are natural teachers in terms of our cultural values around sharing and manaakitanga, and whanaungatanga … we have a natural knack of drawing people in, and making them feel comfortable and welcome … within our cultural context … I think there are some brilliant, brilliant young Māori people who should be encouraged into teaching …*

Janet then turns her attention to teachers in general and to Māori teachers specifically, who are a minority in education and yet are often expected to carry the responsibility of all things Māori within their schools. Her thoughts here are important when thinking about the objectives of *Tātaiako* in that there are expectations of teachers to develop their Māori cultural understandings and capabilities; however, what goes unsaid is that the responsibility for professional development often falls to the Māori teacher(s), with no recognition or compensation:

> ... I don't think teachers across the board are valued enough. I'd love to see teachers getting paid far better and [get] more support than they get. They also need to be protected from burnout, from being expected to provide all sorts of cultural education to the non-Māori teachers, and the non-Māori staff, and doing all things Māori in a school where they are a minority. That's got to stop ... that's a big dump on Māori teachers ... I'm sure it leads to a lot of burnout and to a lot of them leaving the profession.

As a Māori teacher, I have experienced the weight of cultural labour Janet is pointing out here. I have also grappled with the problem, as I'm sure many other Māori teachers have—that if we do not take responsibility for things Māori in our schools then nobody will. My interpretation of what Janet is saying here is that non-Māori need to also be responsible for Māori language and tikanga within our schools. This makes me curious as to what Janet's thoughts are around supporting all teachers to develop their knowledge and understandings of things Māori in order to take on this responsibility. I also wonder if that responsibility should be given to non-Māori or not. Janet's response is very solutions-based:

> It is a double-edged sword and it's also a mixed bag ... it's the language we respond to, it's the personal relationships we respond to as kids. Maybe there is a need for another layer of training, that there is a hub, or a supervisory, a place for cultural supervision for teachers who say 'Look I really want to help Māori kids in my school, but I realise I'm Chinese, or South African, or a Pākehā New Zealander, and I don't know what I'm doing.' It needs to be demystified, and they need to be not afraid to say 'I don't know how to do this.' Maybe the universities, or the Ministry of Education needs to provide that.

My experience with Ministry of Education initiatives drives me to question whether Janet thinks the Ministry is the appropriate organisation to provide that type of education for teachers. Having had a lifetime of experience with various government organisations, Janet responds swiftly:

> *They could fund it for others to do it, they wouldn't be able to deliver it.*

Her thoughts about appropriate people to deliver this type of education are, to me, very logical. However, she also acknowledges the complexities of the situation:

> *Kuia and kaumātua [should deliver the education] to start with, in their own communities. Successful teachers can teach others, but then that takes them away from the kids as well, which is always my worry, that the best teachers always end up as managers.*

I am amused at this point in our conversation because our mother-daughter relationship comes to the fore as Janet finishes my sentence. I begin to say, "The first port of call is always …" and without hesitation my sentence is completed with:

> *within the community. The depth is there. Just have to ask … and resource it. Resource it properly. After all we are talking about equity here, we're not on an equal playing field. There's got to be resources put in to create equitable education for our children …*

Janet's thoughts about resourcing demonstrate, again, her very practical approach. It also makes me think about her personal experiences that have influenced her—her opinion here is not merely theoretical rhetoric, or even a belief about what she considers the right thing to do—this perspective is based on lived experience. Janet watched her father give of his cultural expertise far over and above his role as one of a very few Māori Affairs welfare officers for the entire South Island, with no resources beyond those of his own family. When Janet married Te Warihi she became the quiet pillar of support beside him, as he too shared his expertise and knowledge with organisations desperate for his input, with little or no resources to fund him. While Janet understands that these are important roles that must be fulfilled, the constant taking has been a source of great frustration. She and her family have had to sacrifice in many ways over the years because of the persistent expectation that Māori should give of their knowledge, energy, and scant resources for free, to whomever seeks it.

So far in our conversation, Janet has identified several "layers" of the education system that are, in her view, either missing or inadequate. So, I'm interested to know if she thinks the English-medium education system in its current form can achieve education success for Māori students:

Well some do succeed—increasing numbers are apparently. But with the growing young Māori population, if things aren't kept up, if we don't get better at it very quickly, exponentially, we're going to fall behind again ... My gut feeling is there is a lot of catching up to be done.

When I ask Janet what she believes has contributed to the education success of Māori, it is interesting that the majority of the indicators she identifies are influences outside of school, the first being parental aspirations:

... from my own experience within my own whānau, it's aspiration of the parents, and expectation that you can be whatever you want to be, and we will support you to do that. That's the first thing. Pull that plank away, it's really hard for anybody to aspire.

The second contributing factor Janet identifies is resourcing:

Then it's the resourcing of that, it's choosing education as a priority within the whānau, so we will spend the money on the kids going to school camp, or playing netball, to having proper exercise books rather than going to the pub, or pokies or whatever, doing drugs.

The third is whānau decision making and support of children:

It's decision making within the whānau, resourcing the kids, supporting the kids in every way that you can. It's a long hard slog, but people have to be encouraged that it's worthwhile making sacrifices, you know, it might take a long time, you may not even get there, but it's really worthwhile putting in that effort with your kids.

Janet then discusses community involvement with regards to contributors to Māori education success:

And then, it's drawing on the resources of the community ... getting stuck in and doing the fundraising to send them on the sports trip ...

all of the things that parents seem to do, and the mainstream parents seem to do, you know they work hard at it too.

Finally, Janet turns to the personal dispositions of children and the importance of putting positive energy into developing our children in order for them to succeed academically:

Then again, I think it comes down to ... the personality of the kid themselves, and again that word, that 'C' word, confidence. Really simple. It's no magical formula, it's building the child. It's things like the mothers having good nutrition during pregnancy; it is things like having warm clothes and a proper place to study, and a decent kai, and a warm bed, and knowing that you're free from violence and all of that other terrible stuff that goes on in our community that just cuts kids off at the knees, from birth.

Given that all of the features of education success discussed were external to schools and teachers, I ask Janet who she believes should be responsible for Māori student education success:

Primarily, it's the whānau, not just the parents, the whole whānau really. Secondly, it is the school. People send their kids to school to be educated, they can't maybe do it themselves. A lot of our people are not educated in a traditional, or in a school sense, you know?

She then goes onto explain that, while schools do need to be responsible, they also need to make schooling engaging and fun, and that pre-school education is a vital step in developing confidence in children:

... school has got to be an exciting place to be and then they've got to be able to transition easily through. I think pre-school education actually is most important ... in my day ... I went to one of the very first Playcentres in New Zealand, in 1958 or 59, and it was so exciting. It was so different from being at home with Mum, and yet my mother was a professional mother who taught her kids everything she knew, and yet here I was able to experiment with finger paint and water and go on magical journeys on the old tram car and meet other kids, and it was so exciting. I'm sure that for kids today it's just as exciting to get out from home and into that pre-school education. We certainly can see the benefits of that with 5-year olds, 4-year olds,

3-year olds today who are those confident little kids who can use scissors, pens, paint, draw, stick things on paper, make things. For me that's pretty important.

Because our conversation has been focusing on whānau influence, I begin to think about whānau and parental choice when it comes to education. Our discussion is taking place next to a Kura Hourua (a former charter school reclassified by the Labour Government as special character schools, and recently reverted back to charter schools). In New Zealand, we have kura kaupapa Māori, kura ā iwi bilingual units within state-funded schools, English-medium state-funded schools, private schools, and charter schools. All this choice makes me wonder if there is a place for mātauranga Māori in English-medium schools, and whether mātauranga Māori should then be available to all teachers to access and use as they wish. Janet first addresses the issue of unrestrained access to mātauranga Māori:

… I think the answer is: that's not going to happen. There will be resistance to that from both sides, from either those wanting to impart it, and those wanting to receive it, or needing to receive that mātauranga. I think that is the preserve of Māori to share with who we choose to share it with.

She then addresses the issue of parental choice:

… yes, there is always a choice, and again I think there is varying levels … the volume can be turned up or down … as a parent, I'd be grateful that there is a choice, and I'd be wanting the most holistic education for my kids. I'd be making decisions about where they should be schooled based on what the school has to offer and the preferences of the kids maybe as well, a little bit.

The idea of choosing a school that fits my values and ideals often leads me to think about "majority rules"-type approaches. I share a scenario I had come across in the week just passed where the only Māori student in a local school was described by the principal as "learning to fit in" to the school. The idea of choice according to this perspective becomes problematic to me. As a parent, should I choose a school appropriate for my Māori children? Should every school automatically be well-equipped to cater to my Māori children? Or, should I expect that, if they are a "minority", then nothing from te ao Māori will be taught, and my Māori children should learn to "fit in". I ask Janet what she thinks. She quickly and succinctly shares her view:

> *I think that's a breach of the treaty. I think every kid needs to be educated about this country, and the role of Māori as tāngata whenua, and the special place that we hold. At least. That's the bottom line. Then there's all those relationships and how it could open up for all children, [all] should have the right to be taught in te reo, I think te reo should be compulsory in this country. It should be given equal status. It's like you don't just teach sign language to the deaf. You teach it to those who want to communicate with them. It should be the same with te reo.*

I smile at Janet's way with words and her very straight-to-the-point manner. She has never been afraid to say exactly what she thinks in a way that paints a very clear picture. I then turn her attention to the idea of cultural competence. I'm interested to know how she would describe a teacher who was able to teach in the ways she has described during our conversation, from a cultural perspective. This discussion is interesting as her perspective shifts as she talks through the problem, as so often happens when people talk. She begins by describing such a teacher as being comfortable:

> *It's more about comfortableness I think, not competence. Because competence is very hard to judge. Because some people can feel competent and they're totally incompetent, they think they are competent. I might think I'm competent and I'm absolutely hopeless at something. But if I'm comfortable with my level of understanding, or if I'm uncomfortable with my level of understanding, if I'm uncomfortable and I'm expected to teach others, I'd need to feel comfortable to say 'I need to learn more. I need to be trained.'*

To challenge her I ask what of a person who knows nothing but is comfortable, and comfortable to continue knowing nothing:

> *Mmm and cruising along thinking 'I'm OK I can teach this, and this is how I teach it and if the kids don't, or can't relate to that and learn, well that's not my problem.' ... No, maybe it is not about*

Chapter 7 Te māreikura

comfort, we should be out of our comfort zone, shouldn't we to learn things we don't know?

After a little thought, Janet comes to the same conclusion about teachers who are committed to things Māori as Te Warihi did:

> ... at least have enough respect ... for it—just like respect for the English language, or respect for Pythagoras or whoever. Enough respect to give it a good shot of becoming part of your being, part of your way of life, part of your way of teaching, naturally. I think if we can start with a generation of speakers, everybody having access to te reo, compulsorily at school ... Most New Zealand kids in my generation could do a stick game, they might be able to twirl a poi and sing 'Pokarekare Ana' right? That was their level. So, if that's extended to actual simple sentences, greetings and, you know, knowing how the language works, that would be huge, humongous, huge leap forward. I can't understand the resistance to it, I really cannot understand why it hasn't happened in the past when in so many other countries in the world, the kids grow up speaking three or four languages.

As our conversation draws to a close, I ask Janet if there is anything she wants to add. Her final comments talk about the nature of education for many Māori, about how many of us have come to measure our achievement by the Pākehā qualifications we have or don't have, and about the relationship between past, present, and future:

> I'm saddened that my whole lifetime I've been hearing this same deafening silence about Māori underachievement in education, and yet all of the Māori people I know who have received and succeeded within the Pākehā education system far exceed, in my estimation, the non-Māori people who have the same qualifications. It's because they've worked twice as hard, it's because they have a whole different dimension to their personality and their brain that's allowed them, that's given them that success. It's astounding, their success is astounding, and I know from my own personal experience, because I had to do it at school, I had to work twice as hard to be seen as just the same.
>
> I didn't really succeed at that to be honest, I was only ever second best, I never won. I didn't get to go to university, and yet my parents

had a very strong education imperative on us because my dad had to leave school at 12 to get a trade during the Depression to help the family, to feed his mum and dad I guess in their old age, though they didn't live to be old. He always had huge aspiration for us educationally. Yet by the time he was 12, he was very literate, he was great, he had beautiful handwriting, he could write anything, and he could do maths and he had a great brain, and my mother too. They were so smart and such great parents to pass all that on to us.

So, I'm very grateful, despite the failure of the education system for them, I got through it to a certain level. But I've always had those aspirations for you kids and for my mokos. Because education is the way out of poverty. It's as simple as that. Āe, kia ora.

As stated at the beginning of this pūkōrero, Janet's life experience has been a journey of enhancing her own cultural identity and expressing her rangatiratanga. Her pūkōrero is also concerned with the education system's management and support of positive Māori identities. Janet does not shy away from discussing what have become negative aspects of Māori identities, nor does she assume Māori are void of ethnic and/or culturally based prejudice. Her honesty allows for open investigations of issues impacting Māori identities, which position Māori as human beings with real emotions, anger, fears, frustrations, and hopes. Part two of this chapter will investigate some of the issues surrounding Māori cultural identity, before analysing how Māori identities have become subject to legislation. The next part of this chapter will also discuss education discourse concerning Māori identity, with a particular focus on responding to what some describe as "ethnic politics".

"Mā wai e kawea taku kauae ki tāwhiti?"

It is unknown who first asked "Mā wai e kawea taku kauae ki tāwhiti?", a question immortalised in Māori tradition. It is an inherently female whakataukī that evokes feelings of loneliness and concern for cultural reproduction and survival. The question asks, "Who will carry my chin tattoo into the future?". In one sense, the whakataukī is a searching question about the suitability of an heir to continue the whakapapa represented on the chin in the form of moko kauae. On an epistemic level, this whakataukī refers to the survival of mātauranga Māori, from the kauae runga and the kauae raro, to convey Māori far into the future.

This whakataukī tells a story about mātauranga Māori from a traditional perspective, a perspective that has been perverted by forces such as colonisation, assimilation, and conversion to Christianity. I have chosen a gender-specific whakataukī to frame this discussion because it tells us, undoubtedly, that on issues of tapu, mātauranga, and wānanga, women's roles were as fundamental as those of men. In the reclassification of these aspects according to Western ideologies, women have largely been excluded from the realm of higher education and written out of our own history, creating a distorted view of our cultural identities.

Tuakiritanga: Identity

The whakatauākī of Tā Himi Henare presented at the beginning of this book proclaiming that it is preposterous for Māori to aspire to be poor Pākehā when our destiny is to become great Māori (Henare, 2010) speaks of the power of positive identity and the damaging impact the regime of colonisation has had. The whakatauākī resonates with the oath of Kawiti imploring Māori to hold fast to faith even as the threat of becoming poai Pākehā seem inevitable. Both these whakatauākī are fundamental to this work because, irrespective of the many theories that explain, highlight, minimise, clarify, and trouble identity, inheriting the sacred wisdom of Māori ancestors to innovate and navigate into the future is essentially about feeling a positive Māori identity. It is about having faith that to be Māori is to be great because greatness is our inheritance and our destiny.

The concept of defining and understanding the impact of identity on social, political, and educational spheres has been a topic of intellectual contention since Erikson began investigating the complexities of identity in the 1950s (Erikson, 1956). The ensuing discussion does not seek to provide a definition of identity, but rather to highlight that the concept of identity is problematic in the context of New Zealand education because, for the majority of our Western educational history, the role of education has been to remove our Māori identities.

Problematising the salience of Māori identity in education will emphasise that the notion of Māori cultural competence, and all issues, including "solutions" and "interventions", relating to Māori education will always be complicated, contextual, multifaceted, and dependent on whose indicators of identity are valued.

O'Malley (2012) maintains that cultural identities of Māori and Pākehā came into being only in relation to each other, perhaps as early as the 1600s. This is true when using "Māori" as a term to describe a national Indigenous New Zealand identity. Many Māori strongly, even fiercely, position themselves according to their whakapapa links to specific iwi, to the extent that some people will object to being referred to as Māori, and will insist on being identified by their tribal affiliations. Similarly, our Māori identities were defined in relation to each other. Iwi raised children who were confident in themselves because they had never experienced the paralysing confusion caused by identity loss, nor had they experienced the cultural amnesia suffered by many in New Zealand. Even in contemporary times, strong political alliances and oppositions continue to exist amongst iwi, and aspects of "Māoritanga" can only be taught within the context of each iwi (Rangihau, 2011). In this way, Māori epistemology is fundamentally different from Western worldviews, as our culture is designed for multiplicity, which troubles what Slater (2020) describes as the good white politics of certainty.

Exploring the complexity of identity, and of "as Māori", is a central feature in the terrain of this project because, as Milne (2009) contends, "... 'as Māori' are the most important words in the whole document [*Ka Hikitia*], and will be the most ignored by schools who have no understanding of what 'as Māori' might look like" (p. 15). A key principle that forms the basis of the Māori education strategy (in all its iterations since the 2013 *Ka Hikitia* document) is the identity principle, which is concerned with identity, culture, and language. It is likely that the intention of the identity principle was to ensure the mana of Māori identities were uplifted in education settings; however, rather than providing a manageable approach to multiple and diverse identities, it may in fact be more problematic both for teachers and for Māori learners. This is because it appears to leave room for external measures and assumptions to be made about Māori student identities by teachers. Penetito (2011) points out that a vast range of Māori identify as Māori, but have immensely different perspectives and backgrounds.

Tātaiako defines cultural locatedness from three progressive levels. First, mārama focuses on "… developing an understanding of one's own identity, language and culture …" (Education Council New Zealand, 2011, p. 2), and is confirmed by Janet's assertion that teachers "… need to be well grounded themselves in … their culture" in order to have confidence in themselves. The second level of cultural locatedness is mōhio, where certified teachers should know how to "validate and affirm Māori and iwi culture …" (Education Council New Zealand, 2011, p. 2). Finally, in mātau, leaders will be able to "lead and engage others in validating and affirming Māori and iwi culture" (Education Council New Zealand, 2011, p. 2). A substantial question arises around the process of development and progression between these levels. This becomes especially pointed when considering Janet's assertion that an imbalance exists amongst New Zealand education professionals: "… all Māori teachers know how to interact with Pākehā, but not all Pākehā know how to interact with Māori." Therefore, becoming a leader in the affirmation and validation of Māori culture may be problematic.

In terms of identity, *Tātaiako* appears to assume that Māori identities are not complex. In the levels of cultural locatedness outlined above, there is a sense of progression (despite no clear indication of how this progression might be achieved) from self-awareness to leadership in validating Māori identities. Missing from the progressions, and from the document as a whole, is any expectation that educational professionals examine Māori identities at a deeper level that would require an investigation of the impacts of colonisation on cultural identities. Also missing is an acknowledgement of the objectification of Māori identities through legislation, which the next section will investigate.

Legislating Māori identities

There are many complexities in defining "Māori", including unravelling the many definitions of iwi. One challenge is defining groups in contexts where resources or rewards are involved (Kukutai, 2004), which has given rise in Aotearoa to the development of a standardised version of iwi and hapū. A discussion paper presented in 1988 by then Minister of Māori Affairs, Koro Wetere, saw the re-emergence of iwi and hapū as players in Māori economic development (Smith, 1994). This was amidst the rise of neoliberal ideologies in New Zealand politics, and an increasing emphasis on devolving state responsibility, but not necessarily state power. The subsequent restructure of the Ministry for Māori Affairs (now Te Puni Kōkiri) saw the Crown focus on the role iwi could play in resource management. Amongst the mixed response from Māori to this new policy direction was a distrust of Crown motives, and concern from hapū and urban Māori that the Crown was only focusing on providers at iwi level, not local levels (Hill, 2009).

The Runanga Iwi Act 1990 recognised the importance of iwi and acknowledged iwi as an "enduring, traditional, and significant form of social, political, and economic organisation for Maori". The Act formalised prescriptive criteria that defined how iwi should be structured and administered financially—the Act essentially incorporated iwi. A key criticism of the Act was that it encroached on iwi rights to make decisions outside of the structure defined by the Act (Hill, 2009). It signalled to many Māori that the Government's new policy direction would soon pit iwi against iwi, and create complications in identifying as, and aligning with, pan-iwi, urban Māori, and non-iwi movements. It signalled to some Māori that all would be in competition for meagre Crown resources (Hill, 2009). The Act was an illustration of externally imposed measures of identity that attempted to constrain and standardise both the definition and function of iwi in order to make it easier for the Crown to control its relationship with Māori.

While the Act was repealed in 1991, the "divide and conquer" tactic that some argued underpinned the Act (Hill, 2009) was able to take hold in the ensuing redistribution of resources and the Treaty settlement process.[14] Issues of identity and standardisation initiated by the Runanga Iwi Act continue to be played out in very real, and often very painful, ways. One of the lingering ramifications embedded by the Act is that within New Zealand's political climate it is increasingly difficult for Māori to reach a consensus about how we choose to define ourselves collectively and politically. This is arguably due to the requirement for Māori to present as a singular and cohesive group according to measures that are not our own, for the purpose of satisfying Crown objectives in terms of its engagement with us. An interesting (and devastating) by-product of Crown-controlled definitions of Māori identities and legislation of tikanga is the weaponisation and manipulation of whakapapa some whānau, hapū, and iwi feel compelled to engage in to pursue and receive minimal Crown-controlled resources.

Dei (2011) argues that, in research, an indigenist approach must specify the diversity of knowledges whilst also emphasising shared aims and experiences. One of the complexities of decolonising methodologies such as kaupapa Māori, critical, and anti-racist methodologies, is that there are multiple expressions of each; there is no prescribed way to use or engage with these methodologies, just as there are many ways of identifying as and being Māori (Penetito, 2011). Continuing to specify our knowledges, our uniqueness, and whakapapa connections as hapū and iwi and our identities as Māori is a stand of resistance against the ongoing colonisation caused by the intolerance of multiplicity. Expressing our multiple and diverse identities as Māori is also a way to respond to incorrect assumptions, such as those presented in the following section.

A response to the discourse of ethnic politics

Those who espouse the theory that ethnicity and cultural political rights (referred to by such groups as cultural essentialism, cultural realism, ethnic politics, cultural fundamentalism) is the antithesis of

---

14 The Treaty of Waitangi settlement process has two pathways. Māori can seek redress for historical grievances directly with the Crown, whereby settlement is considered final and no further claims under the Treaty can be made by that iwi; alternatively, redress can be sought on a case-by-case basis with the Crown via negotiation in the Waitangi Tribunal.

a democratic society further complicate issues of Māori identity. May (1999) argues that much of the resistance to the politics of difference is found amongst "... an alliance of conservative and some liberal commentators whose principal aim is to defend orthodox liberalism ..." (p. 11). This is validated by Friedman's (2007) admission of shock at how the world has changed for anthropology and sociology researchers since the 1970s as they now find themselves "... confronted by Others who have become actors in their own right and whose voices have gotten in the way of a certain classificatory calm that once dominated our understanding of the world" (Friedman, 2007, p. xi).

There is much debate internationally about the role of ethnic politics in engendering separatism in democratic societies (Friedman, 1997; May, 1999; Miller, 2003; Rata & Openshaw, 2007b). Friedman's use of language in the quote above is somewhat ambiguous as it could either betray fear, or underscore feeling of sarcasm; not toward separatism, but to the disruption to the "sense" dominant discourses have made of the world they have conquered and now occupy. In New Zealand, opposition to ethnic politics is justified by rhetoric that allege Māori have made gains through separatist privileges based on race (Walker, 1990).

Such discourse presents the promotion of cultural identity as culturalism, cultural ideology, cultural essentialism, and elitism, all implying negative connotations to encourage moral panic and outrage at forces that supposedly seek to cause the demise of sacred democracy. Personally, the perception that "Māori elitism" is a dirty concept is a cause for confusion—do advocates of this divisive discourse want society to fear elite Māori? Are they fearful that some Māori might consider ourselves elite? Should we consider ourselves common? It is especially confusing as many of us actively teach our children that all iwi Māori are indeed elite, we descend from atua and rangatira and we carry their elite DNA. Our tamariki and mokopuna should not be made to feel ashamed of this.

In New Zealand, those who challenge the validity of ethnic politics attempt to reduce all socio-political aspects of culture to cultural essentialism. Alarmingly, there are even instances where tikanga

Māori are referred to in the same breath as acts of terrorism driven by religious fundamentalism (Rata & Openshaw, 2007a). Such perspectives have caused great debates in New Zealand popular culture—often triggered by former National Party Member of Parliament Don Brash—and tend to revolve around issues of censorship and freedom of speech. Social moral compasses are often in disarray over what constitutes freedom of speech, and what is nothing more than hate speech.

Debating perspectives is a healthy human activity. Harm is caused not by the debates, but through the abhorrently racist and incorrect discourse of those who portray ethnic politics as a threat to the rights of the majority. One strategy used by those who object to their perspectives is to silence them by refusing to address or acknowledge them, which caused a philosophical dilemma that I grappled with: to include a discussion that highlights racist perceptions, or delete it. As I was in the midst of considering this predicament, I attended the 2017 annual New Zealand Association for Research in Education (NZARE) conference at Waikato University. I was present at the keynote presentation of Associate Professor Leonie Pihama FRSNZ who, with great intelligence and integrity, responded with dignity to un-academic and racist claims about Māori ethnicity and culture in politics and education. Her courage helped me to come to a decision to include this section because simply being Māori in this country is a political act.

Whether we like it or not, we are an Indigenous group who have been colonised, which makes the very act of being, political. Objectors to ethnic politics seem to believe we have a choice in the matter, in the same vein as the illogical logic applied to "choosing" one's sexuality. A lesson I took from Associate Professor Pihama that day was that, while Māori may not have a choice as to our political status being always "on", we have, and will always have, a right to respond to the injustices and racism we face. This is as relevant now as it was in 2017 when I resolved this particular philosophical dilemma as we, as a nation, come to terms with and respond to a National-led coalition Government intent on expanding the voice, platform, and rights of those who are most closed-minded and fearful of the rights of "Others".

Rata (2012) states that the defining feature of what she calls "culturalism" is a politicised category of people based on racial ancestry; she claims Māori belong to and benefiting by belonging to that category. Rata (2012) claims that Māori political identity is mistakenly based on the Treaty of Waitangi. She goes to great lengths to attempt to discredit the Treaty as justification for a partnership between Māori and the Crown. Rata (2012) also rejects Māori eligibility to claim any rights based on that partnership. Presenting such opinions based on her interpretations expose a number of flawed suppositions and highlights her apparent ignorance of key historical facts.

Two clear misunderstandings she presents relate to the implications of He Whakaputanga 1835 and to Te Tiriti o Waitangi. As discussed previously, He Whakaputanga is a formal acknowledgement by the Crown of the sovereignty of rangatira Māori. It also formally recognises a specific, political relationship between Māori and the Crown. He Whakaputanga officially established two politicised categories of people in this country determined by ancestry—Māori and Pākehā. Pākehā immediately laid claim to the benefits presented to them on the basis of that partnership, while it has become the burden of Māori to ensure the terms of that partnership are honoured.

Research (Burns et al., 2024; Fletcher, 2022) is increasingly proving that Te Tiriti is indeed the treaty and uncovering evidence to suggest that the Treaty was non-existent when rangatira entered into a tatau pounamu with the Crown. This is where Rata's arguments no longer make sense–if she is referring to the Treaty then she is right, the Māori–Crown relationship is not embedded in the Treaty of Waitangi because rangatira didn't debate or sign it.[15] Therefore, any interpretation or argument based on the Treaty are invalid on the grounds that it is not the treaty. Her claims don't appear to be arguing for Te Tiriti to be recognised as the treaty; however, if she is in fact referring to Te Tiriti, that document literally provides a blueprint for the intended political relationship between Māori and the Crown, so her assumptions again become invalid.

---

15 Only 39 rangatira Māori signed an English language Treaty of Waitangi text, that being the only available document at the Manukau signing.

Whether established internally or externally, Māori, as a diverse group, do have a collective politicised identity. We are forced to engage with the state in terms of that group identity, regardless of cohesiveness (Elabour-Idemudia, 2011). Openshaw (2007) claimed those who promote identity politics were "Māori academics, as part of the newly emergent middle-class capitalist neo-tribal elite" (p. 23). This description mirrors Rata's "Māori re-tribalised elite" (2012, p. 99) whom she describes as benefiting by the centring of the Treaty in contemporary New Zealand politics. Their assumptions here construct identity politics and politicised ethnic identities as a relatively new social construction, born from the Māori revitalisation movement of the 1970s and 1980s, for the benefit of a small group of so-called elite Māori. Such claims attempt to impose a patronising negativity on honouring the whakapapa of Māori political identities, and they fail to acknowledge the group who had whole-heartedly and aggressively embraced identity politics long before the 1970s and 1980s in Aotearoa—Pākehā. Significantly, this ethnic group used identity politics to gain socio-political control in New Zealand and to purposefully exclude Māori in the process.

Milne (2009, 2013, 2017) advances concepts of identity politics and challenges that anything we accept as "normal" is, in fact, a reinforcement of "white spaces" whether they be in education, politics, or wider society. White spaces are those aspects of society that appear to be blank, unthreatening, "just there", and therefore can easily remain unchallenged—they are the status quo. However, Milne (2009) attests that the white spaces are in fact the rules that dictate and define "whose knowledge is important, what success looks like, what achievement matters, how the space is organised and who has the power" (p. 2). What makes them insidious is that they appear to be blank and value free. Linda Tuhiwai Smith (2012) also describes white spaces as those social aspects that appeal to one's perceptions of what constitutes common sense.

Rata (2012) presents ethnic and identity politics in Aotearoa as an issue with one participant and beneficiary, Māori. The failure to acknowledge that Pākehā are active players and recipients of privileges through ethnic politics fortifies the perception that societal and political rules are just there, neutral, in the background. Identity politics is then positioned as a Māori construct, aimed at providing unjustified social, political, educational, and physical gain for an (undeserving) ethnically defined category of people. Positioning Māori in this way fosters the unquestioned privilege of another ethnically defined category of people, Pākehā. It also insinuates that the democratic and liberal society in which the rules operate are free of any cultural biases, values, or persuasion, therefore protecting and perpetuating the white space.

For many, Māori cultural identities are closely associated with whakapapa. Whakapapa links us to specific tūpuna, hapū, and iwi, all with specific tikanga, geographic links, politics, histories, resources, and perspectives. Openshaw (2007) argues that culturalism—also referred to as cultural ideology and cultural essentialism—is a form of ethnic politics designed to silence diverse identities. He claims proponents of culturalism do not make real space for "different, diverse and hybrid identities" (Openshaw, 2007, p. 24). Openshaw (2007) presents this argument in reference specifically to kaupapa Māori ideology as a research framework. What is particularly perplexing about this argument is that it continues to attempt to homogenise Māori. It ignores one of the most fundamental rituals of Māori encounter—the introduction of our geographical place, our ancestors, and histories, which define our differences and diversities, as well as initiate or maintain connections. This tikanga is practised as a culturally appropriate way of making space and recognising diverse, hybrid identities.

In complete contrast to Openshaw's (2007) claim, Māori cultural identity is complex and problematic in contemporary contexts precisely because we have diverse identities, which we go to great lengths to express and confirm. Hohepa (2015) explains that, for Māori researchers, identifying ourselves is as much about anchoring our personal histories to our academic and research endeavours as it is about our whakapapa. Hohepa (2015) reminds us that all our identities—the hybrid, the diverse, and different—are not "hats" to put on and remove, nor are they multiple positionings; they are the many facets of being human. The salience of those identities may be fluid and changing depending on context, circumstance, perception of self, and the perceptions of others.

Battiste (2008) maintains that the unifying feature of Indigenous knowledge and research is its diversity. Māori are a very diverse group of people united by a range of similar traditions, values, beliefs, aspirations, and social structures. We are also united to each other and to other Indigenous peoples through our shared experiences of colonisation. While tikanga is diverse, specific to whānau, hapū, and iwi, kawa is unchanging throughout the country because of specific whakapapa which maps kawa to the highly spiritualised creation of the world (Edwards, 2010), reinforcing the function of wairuatanga in forming the foundations of Ngāi Māori. It is therefore wairuatanga that informs all other cultural indicators.

Openshaw (2007) challenges the reliability of kaupapa Māori as a research framework as it is derived from cultural perspectives that he describes as essentialist. This argument, therefore, serves as an attempt to denigrate kaupapa Māori theories. The contention that kaupapa Māori ideology is merely a form of cultural essentialism assumes there are ideologies located within a cultural vacuum, and that these are more valid, more rational, more reasonable, and "truer" than those that openly align to cultures. This approach has been used for centuries to ensure invisibility for many and to maintain unjustified positions of power for a few; the academy has played a considerable role in perpetuating Western intellectual superiority (L. Smith, 2012). The evidence presented in this book argues that all ideologies are culturally located and have specific cultural contexts. Some, such as those that value Māori ideologies, refuse to take part in the parody of neutrality and instead explicitly name and centre cultural perspectives. Being transparent about educational, political, and cultural commitments does not pose a problem or dilemma nor does it invalidate ideology, it is simply a fundamental aspect of a Māori approach to research (Hohepa, 2015).

As a Māori woman, I have experienced criticism of my culture from many angles: language, practices, appearances, beliefs, and Western ideals to name a few. The ideas presented by those who attempt to invalidate te ao Māori by claiming cultural essentialism/fundamentalism and so on are not new, nor are they exciting; they are simply further examples of endeavours to render Māori powerless under the pretext of "reliable" research. There is a suggestion that kaupapa Māori as theory, as ideology, and as methodology, is shielded from reflection and critique by the "Māori neo-tribal elite" intent on protecting their own interests (Rata, in Openshaw, 2007). However, kaupapa Māori in its many forms is robust, it sustains critique, and is constantly being reflected on by those who use it as a framework. According to Pihama (2015), a deterministic, closed, and exclusive approach to kaupapa Māori is the antithesis of what it proposes to be; that is, a flexible, responsive, reflexive tool that enables whānau, hapū, and iwi to respond to their ever-changing contexts and needs.

Smith (2015) argues that the potential of kaupapa Māori theory to be transformative lies in our engagement in praxis, which includes critically analysing theoretical underpinnings and the ways in which they impact on practice. According to Smith (2015), transformative praxis gives kaupapa Māori the ability to transform some of the subjugations of colonisation. bell hooks (1994) also contends that active critical reflection gives theories the potential to be liberatory. Critique of cultural ideologies from perspectives that fail to understand even the most basic values and perspectives of the culture in question are anti-intellectual. Māori, as human beings who have long been subjected to injustices that can propagate a sense of having less power, but who are not powerless, have a right to critically analyse our own cultural ideologies in order to make sense of our current situations. We also have a right to correct misinformation and assumptions others continue to make about us.

Furthermore, critique of theories from perspectives that fail to actually understand the ideologies, and therefore present misguided opinions rather than evidence, are anti-intellectual. Māori will always have a right to respond, even to unreliable arguments that attempt to quash our right to identify as Māori and demand justice based on our unique relationship with the Crown.

While many of the opinions presented by those who oppose political partnership and rights based on ethnicity can be easily countered, they nonetheless represent the views of a small but often loud sector of society. Given that it is altogether possible that some teachers may hold these views, the current approach we have to cultural competence—which is to expect teachers who perhaps hold polarising views and beliefs to work toward affirming Māori culture and taking on cultural leadership roles—seems somewhat naïve. Janet presents a perspective that moves the focus from teachers becoming the experts, to teachers becoming more educated: "... early on in their training [teachers] need to know what is important to our kids. They need to be aware there are differences. They need to be challenged about their own cultural understandings."

A very different approach will be needed to mediate the difference in perspective between those who validate and normalise Māori cultural ideologies, and those who are determined to actively interrupt any socio-political progress we make as Māori and as a country. A new approach must consider that the notion of "as Māori" is highly political, that modern Māori identities have been shaped, constructed, and in some cases completely distorted or destroyed by the process of colonisation. The kaumātua involved in this project have presented an approach that has the potential to provide solutions to the complex issues of identity and identity politics. Kaumātua involved in this project have also refuted the Ministry of Education's claim that the education system is under-performing (Ministry of Education, 2009) by arguing that the education system is doing exactly what the discriminatory laws and values underpinning it have designed it to do. Kaumātua have therefore re-imagined education in ways that consider the many issues attached to the notion of Māori cultural competence.

Chapter 8
Kaumātua re-imagine education in Aotearoa

Chapters 4 to 7 presented the individual pūkōrero of each kaumātua participant in this study, along with analyses associated directly with key messages raised by individual kaumātua. This chapter will weave together the overall messages of the kāhui. As a kāhui the kaumātua have framed some specific challenges to all involved in education, and to New Zealand society in general. In doing so the kāhui kaumātua have also identified a number of culturally appropriate solutions to meet those challenges. They require us to think differently about education, to be genuinely open to respecting difference, as well as being open to adjusting any dominant perspectives that perpetuate injustice in education.

This chapter provides a global analysis of the broad messages gleaned from kaumātua as a kāhui. The overall messages can be categorised into two sections; however, both sections are connected to each other, and in places overlap. The first section defines ways the kāhui reconsider the nature and role of several relationships in New Zealand education. These relationships encompass more than just human relationships. First, relationships between education professionals and the education system is considered. Then messages regarding the connection between mātauranga Māori and contemporary education will be presented. This is followed by the relationship kaumātua envision whānau having with education.

The beginning of this chapter presents the ways in which the kāhui have addressed a central educational issue—Māori education success, as Māori. Success as Māori is considered by the kāhui as valuing individuality in inherently Māori ways and fostering positive cultural identities. The kāhui have also reimagined the role of educators in enabling education success as Māori. Finally, a culturally appropriate model to replace the notion of cultural competence is presented. The second part of this chapter highlights ways in which the kāhui kaumātua have reimagined education in New Zealand.

Reconsidering relationships in education

The notion of whanaungatanga has become an almost fundamental concept for education generally in Aotearoa New Zealand. Many researchers have contributed to the growing understandings of whanaungatanga in education (Bishop et al., 2003; Bishop & Glynn, 1999; Lee, 2008; Macfarlane, 2003), which have come to be reflected in a suite of pedagogical strategies across the sector, including education for Māori.

The impact of the concept of whanaungatanga has been so profound in education that the Māori cultural competencies, *Tātaiako*, are intended to strengthen "... teachers' relationships and engagement with Māori learners and with their whānau and iwi" (Education Council New Zealand, 2011, p. 1). Therefore, all five competencies link back to relationships teachers have with their Māori students and whānau. Research informing the *Ka Hikitia* principle of productive partnerships (Alton-Lee, 2003) underpins the concept of whanaungatanga in *Tātaiako*. The productive partnerships principle recognises that:

> A productive partnership starts with the understanding that Māori children and students are connected to whānau and should not be viewed or treated as separate, isolated or disconnected. Parents and whānau must be involved in conversations about their children and their learning. They need accessible, evidence-based information on how to support their children's learning and success. (Ministry of Education, 2013a, p. 18)

The key objective for the behavioural indicator of whanaungatanga in *Tātaiako* is that an education professional "... actively engages in respectful working relationships with Māori learners, parents and whānau, hapū, iwi and the Māori community" (Education Council New

Zealand, 2011, p. 6). Productive partnerships and engaging in respectful working relationships with Māori whānau, hapū, iwi, and community is positive; however, kaumātua in this project have troubled these objectives by pointing out that, in practice, there are some essential elements that need to be addressed before these objectives can be met authentically. Kaumātua specifically pointed out that progress must be made to address several factors if we are to realise truly productive partnerships. These factors include:

- educational processes that interfere with, or cut across, cultural knowledge
- the deep distrust many Māori still have of the education system
- the impact of wider social challenges on genuine engagement between whānau and schools.

Kaumātua acknowledged that, while education has made some progress in terms of developing relationships with Māori, they are concerned with a lack of cultural knowledge on the part of educators, which continues to hinder the initiation and continuation of effective working relationships with whānau. Kaumātua expressed their frustration at so many within education who, through their limited knowledge, and/or limited desire to expand their perspectives, alienate many Māori students and their families. This is a phenomenon experienced and observed by kaumātua across multiple generations and perpetuates the distrust many Māori have of institutions. These, along with the adverse effects of wider societal problems disproportionately experienced by whānau Māori, hapū, and iwi are, according to the kāhui, very real obstructions to the objectives of relationship building between schools and Māori.

The barriers to developing genuine, mutually beneficial relationships between education institutions and Māori communities and individuals are brushed over by the current Māori education strategy. The Ministry of Education (2013a) and the Education Council New Zealand (2011) purport that productive partnerships are constituted by educators understanding that Māori students are connected to whānau and, as such, educators must have effective relationships with whānau. However, for Te Warihi—an iwi member who is constantly called on by various institutions for advice and Māori perspectives—this relationship has come to be characterised as a one-way process: "They come, take, and leave ... and leave me with nothing." This has been a repeated process over a long period of time with a multitude of organisations and has in recent times also become an approach perpetuated by some Māori organisations. In terms of authenticity and reciprocity, this approach doesn't constitute the type of relationship worth maintaining. While I do not have any information from organisations involved as to how they understand such relationships, that they continue to approach Te Warihi and others like him is some evidence that they are happy in the relationship, which also indicates that they stand to gain in the relationship.

Developing authentic productive partnerships will take more than knowing that students are connected to whānau groups. Giving whānau access to evidence-based information should be taken for granted. However, kaumātua challenge education professionals to be critically reflective of their practice and their perspectives of the nature of their relationships with Māori. Meeting Ministry of Education objectives for relationship-building will not strengthen the types of robust and genuine relationships required to activate education success for Māori, as Māori. Education professionals must realise that many education practices do not align with Māori cultural knowledge or values. The very idea of what constitutes a "productive partnership" could mean very different things to the different parties involved.

Perceptions kaumātua have of relationships within education can be categorised into three key themes:

- the connection between education professionals and systems and structures
- the relationship between education and cultural knowledge
- the relationship whānau have with education.

These themes reach well beyond school–home relationships and require education professionals to see relationship-building with Māori in ways that are different from the Ministry of Education prescribed processes. These themes often overlap and will be addressed below.

Relationships with education systems and structures

Throughout this book, I have argued that Māori have a specific relationship with the current education system based on our history of colonisation. The information that was shared by kaumātua included the argument that part of the process of developing more effective relationships for Māori in education actually involves developing educators' understandings of New Zealand education and the education system. This includes educating teachers about the educational and socio-political history of this country as a starting point. This constitutes a change in focus from how education can develop relationships with Māori, to greater education about issues that have long affected Māori. A change in focus has strong implications for the future of initial teacher education.

Kaumātua believe that educators should be in a position to assure whānau that they are aware of pertinent historical aspects of the education system and how these have shaped education for Māori. To achieve this, teachers must be given opportunities to develop deeper understandings of how Western education has come about in this country, that it is not neutral, that it is relatively new, and that it has quickly become one of the many unquestioned white spaces in New Zealand society (Milne, 2017).

While the Ministry of Education acknowledge that Māori experiencing education success as Māori is the joint responsibility of the Crown and iwi (2013a), *Tātaiako* places the bulk of this responsibility on teachers. Kaumātua refute the idea that individual teachers should shoulder this responsibility. Rather, they argue change must be systemic. Kaumātua point out that individuals within any system can be committed to a cause, but if change is not made at a systemic level, then individuals will struggle. Kaumātua expressed great frustration at the ongoing lack of real progress in developing more effective systems and structures, not only in education, but generally in New Zealand. The kāhui kaumātua have first-hand experience of being at the whim of Governments that hold the power to lay waste to years of work and collaboration between the Crown and hapū and iwi.

A strong perspective of kaumātua is that many systemic structures in our country, including in education, continue to cause injustice. Kaumātua identified that enabling educators to clearly and honestly define who and what the education system is, from where it stems, whose values it privileges, and whose knowledge is powerful, might initiate genuine shifts in the paradigm that they argue continues to suffocate so many. This perspective challenges educators to examine more deeply the structure and history of the education system in order to develop greater understandings of the relationship Māori have with the system. Encouraging educators to understand the education system is more profound than hoping to build effective relationships on the basis of knowing that students are attached to wider whānau and communities.

Linked to using understandings of systems and structures as a relationship-building tool, is learning what matters to Māori students, and understanding there are differences between Māori and non-Māori. The challenge clearly issued by kaumātua to education professionals was to find out what Māori students care about and understand differences unique to Māori. These differences are broad and varied. Being visible, welcoming, and accessible to Māori, and building and maintaining working relationships with Māori, are expectations for a professional leader in whanaungatanga (Education Council New Zealand, 2011). However, this is very different from understanding the differences between Māori and non-Māori in education. The official objectives do not specifically require education professionals to come to understand what is important to whānau Māori and students as part of their relationship-building process. According to kaumātua involved in this project, part of what is important to Māori is having wider New Zealand understand that many Māori relationships and histories differ from the dominant narratives and deserve to be recognised as valid and valuable.

Kaumātua insist that any education system charged with teaching Māori students has no room for people or ideas that are monocultural.

Part of this work has involved investigating the monocultural foundations of Western education in Aotearoa New Zealand. Many ideas that privilege Western culture are consciously and unconsciously entrenched in initial teacher education programmes and education in general, while teachers are provided with very few opportunities to step back to first see them, then question their origins or purpose. *Tātaiako*'s heavy focus on the student-teacher relationship provides no space for teachers to investigate and understand the monocultural underpinnings of our current education system. The *Tātaiako* Tangata Whenuatanga competency asks teachers to investigate Māori histories, tikanga, and cultural capital (Education Council New Zealand, 2011). But it does not require them to investigate or question the histories, tikanga, and cultural capital of the education system.

The education system in New Zealand has come to be a space highly contested by those who seek equitable outcomes for all students and highly protected by those who wish to persist with notions of "mainstream" status quo. Kaumātua highlight that systemic change is reliant on bridging the gulf between cultures, and that doing so can begin a process of healing for all, because, as kaumātua argue, operating at cross-purposes is destructive for everybody. In order for Māori to be successful in education as Māori, systemic change is urgently required. Kaumātua have made it clear that even if developing cultural competencies is a good idea, modifying teacher behaviour through them is not enough to cause change—the system needs to change. Hori explains systemic transformation will lead to individual change: "... it's not the hearts and minds of the teacher, it's the hearts and minds of the system that controls the teachers."

Mātauranga Māori in education—fragility and potential

Another key aspect of this work was developing an understanding of mātauranga Māori and the potential it has in English-medium education. As previously argued, it is somewhat disconcerting that a strategy to raise Māori education achievement for Māori, as Māori, avoids any specific reference to the use or relevance of mātauranga Māori beyond te reo Māori. The evidence presented throughout this book distinguishes three potential reasons for this:

- The liberal philosophies that underpin New Zealand education do not make genuine space for knowledge bases outside of the Western framework. The structure of the curriculum, therefore, continues to reflect and regenerate Eurocentric ideas.
- Mātauranga Māori is often valued in education as prior knowledge students bring with them that can be used as a foundation from which to build new (Western) knowledge, not for the knowledge itself.
- I deduce that there may be an assumption by the Ministry of Education that behavioural indicators for educators based on Māori values actually equates to utilising mātauranga Māori.

I have already stated that, as an educator who identifies positively as being Māori, I have always been proactive about incorporating mātauranga Māori, in a broad sense, into my teaching programmes. This includes both Māori ways of knowing and of being. I find strength in sharing what I know of my culture with all students, regardless of their backgrounds. As an educator in a tertiary institution, I have sometimes found this task difficult when I sense what I can only describe as fear and resistance to Māori knowledge and histories. The amount of resistance I have encountered in my years in initial teacher education has also caused me some anxiety, due to the fact that many of these students will take their resistance into New Zealand classrooms, where they are charged with enabling Māori to experience education success, as Māori.

Kaumātua identify fear as an obstruction to progressing shared visions. Many Māori have a fear that knowledge will be trampled on, misused, ridiculed. In the experience of kaumātua, it appears many Pākehā fear that being open to learning, understanding, and respecting mātauranga Māori might in some way take away from them. Kaumātua were unable to determine what exactly people fear would be lost by coming to a greater understanding of mātauranga. In fact, this was one issue that seemed to leave kaumātua at a loss. In bewilderment they asked: "What are you scared of?".

Due to the absence of any specific mention of mātauranga Māori in *Tātaiako*, a key question I posed to the kāhui kaumātua was how they envision mātauranga Māori in English-medium education. Their responses have been a source of much deep and analytical thought. Some of their responses were contrasting, others were comparative, which led me from the supposition that mātauranga Māori should be part of teachers' basic education, to the opposite conclusion that mātauranga should remain within the protection of Māori communities, to finally arriving at a realisation that the role of mātauranga Māori in English-medium education occupies a space that is not here, nor there, there is no absolute conclusion, rather it sits on a spectrum that, as Janet puts it, "... can be turned up or down".

By analysing the information over a long period of time I have been able to see what kaumātua have envisioned, this involves developing deep relationships with and understandings of Māori cultural knowledge, and a different perspective on how we in education view knowledge sharing. It also involves coming to greater understandings of differentiations in mātauranga Māori according to kauae runga and kauae raro. Kaumātua also strongly advocate that more care must be taken by education professionals when dealing with mātauranga Māori. In the intervening years from thesis to book I have come to think of mātauranga Māori as it tends to be used in education as aspects of Māori cultural knowledge that Māori have deemed appropriate to be accessed by the general public. For me, this is different from mātauranga tuku iho, which continues to be highly protected and necessarily exclusive of the education system.

While kaumātua had differing views on the place of mātauranga Māori in English-medium education, they did agree that professionals need to be reflective in their practice and proactive in seeking professional development. In its current form, *Tātaiako* gives the impression that education professionals should be progressing toward knowing in their own right how to use and engage with Māori cultural knowledge. What kaumātua highlight is that this should not be the expectation. Rather, they argue for professionals to view their engagement with Māori cultural knowledge as an ongoing, highly reflective, and honest process. Teachers should be encouraged to know that, no matter what stage of their career or cultural knowledge they are at, when they do not know something, or if they are unsure, a support system is available to them. Unfortunately, this is not currently the situation.

Kaumātua believe education needs to be a space where professionals can be honest in their reflections of their own cultural abilities and feel safe enough to ask for cultural support when they need it. In order to achieve this, new structures need to be put in place to provide the support educators may need. Again, this is proposing that teachers perceive Māori cultural knowledge, and their own abilities with it, differently from the expectations *Tātaiako* has of educators. Kaumātua instead require education professionals to personally assess what they know, and to identify their own knowledge gaps. Kaumātua argue that this approach is far more favourable compared to the *Tātaiako* approach, which expects teachers from non-Māori backgrounds to become experts in te ao Māori. In fact, this particular expectation in *Tātaiako* triggered a distinct sense of offence from these Indigenous knowledge keepers, which is discussed further below as kaumātua re-imagine the role of educators.

Of the kāhui kaumātua, Te Warihi and Hori may be viewed as more traditional in their perspective of mātauranga Māori in that, for them, maintaining Māori control over the protection and dissemination of our knowledge is of utmost importance. Interestingly, Te Warihi and Hori were also consistent with other kaumātua in highlighting that changing the relationship between education and Māori cultural knowledge relies on sharing the burden with our treaty partners. Te Warihi believes knowledge of Te Tiriti o Waitangi is fundamental in education to enable a changed and equitable relationship where all members of the entire school community are committed and proactive about kaupapa Māori within education. Kaumātua argue that education must come to know and understand Māori culture, New Zealand history, and the unique position of tāngata whenua in New Zealand. Shared responsibility for the respectful use of mātauranga Māori in education is, for this kāhui kaumātua, a matter of honouring Te Tiriti.

Kaumātua have experienced flawed knowledge-sharing practices at the hands of many institutions. They also identified ways to rectify these practices and propose a form of knowledge sharing and community engagement that requires genuine relationships beyond community engagement with the school, but challenges the school to share responsibility and power with the community. They put forward an exciting prospect of real power and knowledge sharing requiring experts within te ao Māori to work closely with experts in te ao Pākehā. The information shared by these groups would be utilised to benefit students. This model relies on the strength of Māori and education communities and requires the government to take responsibility for resourcing community engagement adequately.

Kaumātua view equitable resourcing, and control of resources as an essential aspect of developing greater understandings of Māori cultural knowledge. The kāhui kaumātua see issues of resourcing as a matter of rangatiratanga, of mana, and of basic respect. They have voiced their frustrations at constantly being controlled by funders who can take the mana out of projects by applying restrictive criteria. Kaumātua have also been demoralised by having to go "cap in hand" to funders for essentials such as education. They have also experienced being called on to consult on major projects and not be compensated with consultant fees. Their solution is that shared responsibility for growing Māori cultural knowledge in English-medium education requires equitable resourcing and trust that Māori experts know just as much as Pākehā experts about what will be beneficial to education. Resourcing initiatives that link community and education in respectful ways that recognise the mana of all participants is essential to progressing relationships between education and mātauranga Māori.

Schools engaging more deeply with mātauranga Māori is seen by kaumātua as having the potential to act as a support system for teachers, in that the very act of engaging requires a relationship with people who are culturally knowledgeable and resourcing that is culturally appropriate. In this way, teachers would be able to not just gain knowledge, but also acquire advice, support, and to be challenged. The kāhui kaumātua also pointed out that, in terms of the role of mātauranga Māori in education, being a teacher who is Māori matters.

Whānau–education relationships

The relationship between schools and the community is viewed by kaumātua as one that should be based on consultation. This will ensure teachers know what the goals of whānau are for their children and will ensure that teachers have a full and deep understanding of every child they teach. This differs from the *Ka Hikitia* and *Tātaiako* approach that positions teachers as the experts in home–school relationships. Kaumātua position education professionals as the group seeking advice to ensure they are progressing in ways the whānau and community see as appropriate.

The kāhui kaumātua have challenged the government approach to relationships and the use of Māori cultural knowledge. They have called for more genuine interactions between education professionals and mātauranga Māori. They have also defined ways of engaging that shift current education perspectives that require Māori communities to come closer to schools, and instead propose that schools move closer to communities. Kaumātua also call for education professionals to view community members, whānau, hapū, and iwi as experts. The previous sections of this chapter have defined kaumātua expectations of education; however, kaumātua have also been very clear about their expectations of Māori parents, whānau, hapū, and iwi.

While kaumātua have identified many problems in government approaches to education for Māori, they also challenged whānau Māori, especially in terms of developing positive cultural identities. Kaumātua firmly believe that the first point of education for all children is in the home. If children are given a strong foundation in knowing who they are, and where they belong, they can achieve anything and confidently find success anywhere in the world. Of course, this has implications for many whānau, Māori and non-Māori, in terms of decision making and responsibility.

Kaumātua emphasise the essential role parental expectations and support have on student success. They identify that aspirations and expectations of parents and whānau, along with their constant support, is a key component in student success. Without it, kaumātua argue, it is difficult for any student to aspire let alone succeed in those aspirations. Because of this, kaumātua put the onus on parents and whānau to prioritise education. They acknowledge the huge societal challenges and injustices many families face but encourage families to make decisions to resource children. Sometimes this requires making sacrifices; it is often a long struggle, but the benefits of prioritising the educational needs of the young are worthwhile.

The kāhui kaumātua also emphasise the central role whānau have in cultural development. Again, kaumātua acknowledge that contemporary contexts present many challenges for families in developing cultural understandings. They recognise that many meanings within our cultural contexts have changed over the years, and that many families live by very different cultural standards in contemporary society. Despite this, kaumātua see that many Māori still carry with them ancient Māori thoughts and actions—sometimes these are subconscious, but they are still present. In such cases, tikanga and cultural knowledge continue to be passed on to the next generation.

Kaumātua recognise that the many negative aspects of society, in which Māori are often overrepresented, must be addressed holistically. This is a challenge presented to everybody in society. According to arguments presented by kaumātua, aspects that are having an adverse effect on our culture, including drugs, alcohol, and violence, are the results of colonisation and forced subordination. They believe these social issues are beyond the scope of just education and will require a united approach where everybody becomes responsible for the wellbeing of the entire community. This reflects a more traditional Māori approach to society and societal issues. The kāhui kaumātua also challenge all Māori to unlearn the lessons we have learnt from colonisation and return to frameworks provided by our tūpuna.

Both *Ka Hikitia* and *Tātaiako* imply that "two-way relationships" (Ministry of Education, 2013a, p. 18) involve drawing parents and whānau into the school community. This is illustrated through phrases such as "[f]or education professionals, collaboration is about creating ways for whānau, hapū, iwi, Māori organisations and communities to contribute to what and how Māori students learn …" (p. 14) and "[t]hey need evidence-based information on how to support their children's learning and success" (p. 18). Kaumātua did not criticise these goals. They did, however, identify a varied perspective of this relationship, one that shifts the focus slightly, but to great effect. From the perspective of kaumātua, evidence of student progress should be shared with whānau, but they emphasise that education professionals should be accountable to whānau to ensure they are meeting the aspirations of individual students and whānau. From this perspective, extended family members become the experts on their children, they are the ones who are called on to give advice to teachers, and teachers become the party who should check in with whānau about their progress in educating tamariki.

The kāhui kaumātua encourage parents to have courage in their dealings with educational professionals and institutions. They have centred the aspirations of individual students and believe parents and whānau should be fearless in expecting institutions and professionals to know and support the aspirations of each student. Parents should question issues in the education of their children.

While this will not be an easy task for all families, it returns power to parents in their dealings with schools and will help to shift the persistent thinking that parents are accountable to schools. The kāhui kaumātua remind all Māori:

"Stop talking and behaving like slaves! He rangatira koutou!"

Kaumātua address "success as Māori"

The passion kaumātua have in relation to the success of their children and mokopuna is evident in their responses throughout their pūkōrero. They have provided a number of indicators of success for both students and teachers. It is important that kaumātua often specified that these indicators of success were not isolated to Māori students, or to teachers of Māori students, but applied to all students and all teachers in this country. Success, according to these kaumātua, is framed by changed relationships with education, as discussed above, and also by specific indicators for both students and teachers. The following highlights how kaumātua perceive success for students, then the indicators they have for teachers to be successful in educating Māori, as Māori will be examined. Finally, kaumātua address the role of educators in education success as Māori.

Valuing individuality

Liberal ideals of individuality and meritocracy have posed problems for Indigenous peoples in education (Augoustinos et al., 2005). The introduction of progressive philosophies along the with social constructivist theories into New Zealand education were intended to provide some respite from traditional liberalism that positioned many learners, both Māori and non-Māori, as non-academic (Beeby, 1992). Many progressive pedagogies have been seen as positive for Māori schooling as they purport to reflect Māori traditional pedagogies, such as reciprocal learning, experiential learning, a "hands-on" approach, and group learning.

These pedagogies have been useful to education and have in many ways halted the perspective that there are only two types of learners—the academic and the non-academic (Robinson, 2010). However, in Chapter 6 I progressed an argument that these pedagogies also produced deeply ingrained stereotypes about how Māori learn. The idea that practical learning is ideal for Māori students was born from racist assimilationist policies that sought to create a brown labouring class (Walker, 2016) and ignored the highly abstract practices of traditional higher learning. The stereotype that Māori are group learners was a direct observation of our living as tribal people, not an observation of our teaching and learning practices. This stereotype has been perpetuated over decades and supported by research such as that of Metge (1984) that declares for Māori "[l]earning in groups is favoured over the individual working on his or her own" (p. 6).

Perspectives shared by kaumātua about education success for Māori were in direct contrast to stereotypes of Māori in education. All kaumātua involved in this project saw Māori students being treated as individuals as an essential element to their success, as Māori, in English-medium education. Individuality in this case is from a Māori perspective and quite different from the liberal philosophy of individuality that tends to atomise students from their environment (Robinson, 2010). Kaumātua believe student success is dependent on the individual's proclivities and strengths and the ability of teachers to recognise and capitalise on these.

Kaumātua also contextualise individual success within cultural and educational frameworks. Student aspirations are their own, not those of their elders. Success is therefore personalised and measured by an individual's assessment of their own efforts. The value of their education through the current education system should not override their cultural identity and their tikanga Māori. In this way, education enriches their cultural identities and enables them to maintain cultural values, rather than forsake them in exchange for education through the system. The perspectives of kaumātua are inherently Māori perspectives that they believe have been interrupted by colonisation.

Connected to ideas of individual measures of success are kaumātua identification of traditional teaching and learning processes that have been silenced by contemporary education practices and stereotypes. Kaumātua discussed old processes of close observation of each individual in order to identify their skills, talents, and personal dispositions that were then nurtured to support individuals meeting their own personal aspirations. Kaumātua associate the demise of traditional practices in the development of individual talents and aspirations with the interruption of colonisation. Old ways were replaced when Māori took on what they saw as a Pākehā idea of being responsible for "making" each child "become" something; for instance, a doctor, a lawyer, a bus driver. This practice, according to kaumātua, interrupts and is detrimental to the development of a child's wairua.

Kaumātua saw success for mokopuna as being closely intertwined with what and how they are taught. They expect students to be challenged, and encouraged to challenge others, to be taught to seek information and knowledge. Success is not measured by assessment, but based on individuals accomplishing within their social, cultural, and environmental contexts. To achieve this, kaumātua believe students must be taught how to interact with others, to care for their environments, and to have instilled in them a desire for lifelong learning. Success by the measures identified by kaumātua are substantially different to those popular in current education settings. As well as success being measured against each individual's criteria, kaumātua also identified that for Māori to experience education success as Māori, positive cultural identities must also be fostered.

Fostering positive cultural identities

The kāhui kaumātua held a belief that building cultural identities was first the responsibility of whānau, hapū, and iwi. Second, educators have the responsibility of positively reinforcing that identity. This is an important shift in thinking, because *Tātaiako* gives responsibility of establishing positive Māori cultural identity to educators and schools who sometimes have little idea about their own identity, let alone what might constitute a positive Māori identity. The role of confirming Māori identities in education was an essential element to all kaumātua in the progress and development of our culture and our cultural values as part of our education experience.

However, this aspect is also one that is highly complex. Kaumātua do not necessarily perceive traditional Western measures of education success as success for their mokopuna. For them, being successful in life as Māori is possible, even where students are not experiencing education success as measured by Ministry of Education criteria. Kaumātua highlight the importance of cultural values and te reo Māori to the successful education of students. They insist that students must have access to te reo Māori and feel comfortable in their own cultural contexts. Student success is bound to positive cultural identity through access to whakapapa and whanaungatanga so that students build strong understandings of who they are as Māori, how they fit in our own country, and the world. Kaumātua believe that strong, positive cultural identities reinforced by education is a necessity for young Māori in contemporary society.

A perspective of cultural education presented by kaumātua can be applied to all people, regardless of background. Specifically, for Māori, our cultural identity is what differentiates us from other cultures.

Kaumātua emphasised the fundamental importance of knowing "... who you are, where you are, and why you are ..." in order to successfully navigate the wider world. A key point is enabling students to understand why they are. Coming to discover your own purpose is a very personal journey that may take years. However, giving students opportunities to investigate the history of their tūpuna, to see where they have come from, being encouraged to think deeply about what they want to contribute to the wider cultural "why" of being Māori (or Pākehā, or Chinese, and so on) is such a refreshing take on what constitutes success as a culturally confident being.

Many Māori students continue to need strategies for survival in the current education system. Kaumātua believe that positive cultural identity will support Māori students in successfully navigating system with their self-esteem intact. They also see whānau and teachers as being important in fostering and supporting students utilising their cultural identities to bolster their success in the education system. Kaumātua do not assume that Māori students come to Western education with whole and intact cultural identities, as is often implied in education documents. Kaumātua acknowledge that many Māori students are missing this aspect of themselves, and it is "our" responsibility to support them to develop their cultural identity. To help gain some perspective as to who "our" may include, Te Warihi points out:

> *The days are gone where ... we used to learn everything about our culture from the way we were brought up by our parents ... the parents of today haven't had the same upbringing ... they [students] are not getting it [cultural education] at home. The education they get is ... entirely from another culture's perspective, not necessarily ours ...*

The implication here is that responsibility for developing and reinforcing positive cultural identities belongs to parents and whānau and also to those who currently have political power. Māori did not strip away our own cultural values and identities, therefore some responsibility for rectifying our current situation must lie with the political decision makers and power holders. There is a challenge in Te Warihi's words for the education system to relinquish the hold it has over what knowledge, and whose knowledge, counts in education in order to participate in rebuilding Māori identities that have been fractured due to educational policies and procedures.

Connectedness and balance between the physical, spiritual, and intellectual is also emphasised by kaumātua as an important aspect in developing strong cultural identities and education success. From their perspective, the triangulation between mind, body, and spirit must be made more of a priority in developing Māori cultural identities for education success. Many researchers have identified the crucial role in the connectedness of our senses and environments to our overall development and wellbeing (Durie, 1994; Penehira, 2011; Pere, 1991). However, it seems that in English-medium education there continues to be a lack in deeply understanding what this means to individual and social wellbeing.

Kaumātua believe that developing positive, well-balanced, and connected cultural identities will instil in students a sense of pride and give them the drive to achieve their goals. They also believe that developing and reinforcing positive cultural identities will help to give students the message that they are respected as learners, that they are valuable, and that their learning is valuable. Kaumātua saw that whānau and educators both have responsibilities in ensuring this happens for students.

A perspective shift on role of educators in enabling success as Māori

Kaumātua in this study were explicit in their perspective that Māori experiencing education success as Māori was as much to do with the education system as it is to do with educators. However, they did specify that education professionals can contribute positively to this goal, even within the confines of an inadequate education system. The perspectives of the kāhui position teachers differently to the *Tātaiako* positioning of educators that encourages progression toward becoming an expert in Māori cultural understandings. In fact, the kaumātua vision of education professionals who have the ability to support Māori achieving education success, as Māori, had little or nothing to do with them assuming an expert position in te ao Māori. Kaumātua do not expect teachers to have an in-depth knowledge of mātauranga Māori; their expectations are not grand or imposing, but do require educators to remain open to learning and to be respectful.

The first aspects kaumātua outlined as being important for educators of Māori students can be described by the Māori term "kare ā roto". These are values that come from inside, from the heart. Both Te Aupouri and Janet specifically referred to love as being an essential element needed for teachers of Māori learners. They had an expectation that educators would treat Māori students with love, faith, and hope in order to support student growth and development. Janet also made it clear that as well as treating students with love, educators must also love their role in education, and love themselves. The idea of teachers having love for themselves, having faith in what they do, and maintaining a hopeful attitude in teaching is vastly different from the heavy focus in education on the mind, on processes, and on arbitrary assessment data.

Kaumātua also expand this idea to include wairuatanga. In education, there is some awareness that wairuatanga is important to Māori ways of knowing and being. The most prominent references to the importance of acknowledging wairuatanga in students appear in the Health and Physical Education curriculum (Ministry of Education, 2007). However, kaumātua extend this perspective to include teachers, a concept I have only ever seen raised once before by a Māori educator in a previous study I completed (Hetaraka, 2008). Teachers recognising their own spiritual contribution has the potential to be transformative. It would encourage teachers to look inwardly, to develop deeper self-awareness, and to investigate how their own wairua impacts on the wairua of their students. There is a preoccupation in education with teachers knowing their students. What kaumātua are saying here is that the education success of our students is also reliant on how well teachers know themselves.

Other kare ā roto aspects kaumātua included in their definition of an excellent teacher of Māori students include empathy, enthusiasm, and respect. Kaumātua believe educators need to be confident in themselves, to be constantly learning and developing both personally and professionally. Teachers need to be developing professionally and enjoy the knowledge-sharing process they are involved in with students. For some education professionals, the idea of seeing themselves in a knowledge-sharing process with students may be new, for others it may be difficult, but for kaumātua it is taken for granted. Their mokopuna have as much to offer the teaching and learning process as their teachers do and an excellent teacher will recognise this.

Linked to the concept of self-love and awareness of the impact a person's wairua has on others is the idea that educators must build confidence in learners. The experiences of kaumātua have led them to identify that the confidence of many Māori students has been damaged and diminished in education through the devaluing of things important to them. However, it is easy to build confidence in others when you are confident and happy in yourself, and just as easy to damage others when you are unhappy or lack confidence in yourself. In this way, self-confidence and self-love are essential in educators.

Kaumātua also draw on traditional Māori pedagogy as being important for educators. A key pedagogy identified by kaumātua was listening according to the Māori perspective of rongo (which encompasses all the senses, not just the ears, and implies peacefulness and calm). The *Tātaiako* dimension of wānanga is about communication and consultation with wider whānau. However, as I have already argued, this is in terms of talking to whānau, not necessarily listening to whānau. Listening is a key aspect of traditional wānanga. By defining wānanga as talking to whānau, the Ministry of Education and the Teaching Council continue to position educators and schools as the experts. Kaumātua remind us that listening is an essential role of educators, repositioning them as learners when it comes to aspects of education success for Māori, as Māori.

Know who you are, where you are, and why you are

An extremely important contradiction to the government approach of expecting educators to become experts in te ao Māori through the cultural competencies was raised by kaumātua. They warn against implying that non-Māori educators can be experts in Māori cultural concepts. Their expectation of educators is not that they become expert in Māori culture. The kaumātua view is that educators need to be aware that such objectives are in fact culturally dangerous for themselves, and offensive to Māori experts. They argue that Māori have been subjected to assumptions that other, non-experts, can be considered expert in our culture and in what is best of Māori for too long, and call for an end to this practice.

Instead of expecting teachers to become expert in te ao Māori, kaumātua believe it is far more valuable to enable teachers to deepen their understanding of their own cultures and our national history for them to support Māori to experience education success, as Māori. They see powerful potential in educators developing their own cultural identities as part of the healing that needs to take place in New Zealand society. Māori experiencing education success, as Māori, is dependent on teachers who have a strong and positive sense of who they are as cultural beings. Again, the focus here shifts from a preoccupation with the "problem" in education of Māori identity, and turns this back to educators, asking, No hea koe? Who are you? Where are you? Why are you? When teachers can answer those questions with a level of self-confidence in their own cultural identity, they may be better positioned to enable education success for Māori, as Māori.

The kāhui kaumātua had very high expectations of teachers who are Māori to utilise Māori cultural knowledge in education in culturally appropriate ways. Kaumātua perceive a Māori teacher as having a certain amount of responsibility regarding building positive cultural identities, as well as utilising cultural knowledge, by virtue of having exposure to both Māori and Pākehā cultures. Kaumātua encourage more Māori to pursue education as a career because of values inherent in our culture. Kaumātua expect education professionals to know who they are, know the history of the country they live in, and be committed to developing deeper understandings of mātauranga Māori. Kaumātua hope to see educators who are confident in themselves culturally, spiritually, and intellectually.

Very much aligned to the Māori worldview of time, and of the connectedness between the past and the future, kaumātua defined the importance of knowing the history of our country as fundamental to the role of educators. It is taken for granted that the history they are referring to is not the dominant narrative, but the history that reveals Māori voices. Kaumātua have defined the important role of history to educators in very simple terms. They remind us that historical awareness plays an essential role in exposing social injustices with the intention of not repeating them. The kāhui kaumātua encourage all of us to remember our histories. They argue that having memory, particularly institutional memory, in this country has largely been left to Māori, so the struggle has generally been a Māori struggle, not a shared effort at eliminating injustice. Kaumātua perceive the lack of education in the histories of this country to be an injustice to all students, as they believe all children in this country deserve to have access to our histories.

Because this kāhui kaumātua operate from Māori frameworks, it is little surprise that they see the relevance of history in our present and future. For them, time is not delineated by the separation of months and years; all of time is a connected series of events and relationships. Therefore, kaumātua expect education professionals to be fully conversant with New Zealand's history. They believe that more value must be put on knowing our history if more Māori are to experience education success. They are also clear that the foundations of who we are as New Zealanders are based on the signing of Te Tiriti o Waitangi, meaning that this history must be part of basic education in New Zealand.

The kāhui kaumātua have identified a number of ways that can contribute to Māori experiencing education success, as Māori. Their solutions are interconnected and reliant on a concerted effort across political and social sectors. Te Warihi consistently referred to the concept of the village raising a child. The village analogy does not refer to a place—for example, a rural village—but rather a time when communities were more connected. His words summarise many of the solutions presented here:

Look for example at the child being educated by the village ... being raised by the village. Every child goes through that village system ... the only way they can succeed is ... if everybody is on board with the concept. Everybody.

Chapter 9
Te Kauae Tuku Iho

Rejecting cultural competence, re-imagining education

While kaumātua have provided a range of perspectives about the role of Māori cultural knowledge in English-medium contexts, they have also provided a specific framework for how this knowledge can be utilised safely, whilst remaining protected by Indigenous knowledge holders and experts. This chapter will explore the model put forward by kaumātua.

Kaumātua rejected the notion of cultural competence as being an appropriate pathway to enabling Māori education success, as Māori. A strong basis for this view is their insistence that Māori cultural knowledges and understandings should remain within Māori control and protection. They also highlighted that much of the need to protect Māori cultural knowledge comes from a deep mistrust that continues to exist between cultural knowledge holders and those seeking the knowledge. A source of the mistrust can be found in many of the lived experiences of our people. Intellectual property has been given in trust, then our people have seen the information abused, distorted, or disrespected. The different ways that cultures value knowledge have also been a source of reluctance in releasing some mātauranga Māori. The kāhui highlighted that there are still very real trust issues between holders of Indigenous knowledge and the education system, and they rejected the notion of cultural competence as a way forward for Māori to experience education success, as Māori.

Kaumātua have problematised the concept of knowledge sharing through Ministry of Education's productive partnerships model by pointing out that ideas concerning knowledge sharing are culturally located. Māori concepts of the knowledge-sharing process are culturally different from the Ministry's ideas. The Ministry simplifies the knowledge-sharing process in ways that deter holders of Indigenous knowledge from wanting to release knowledge into Western education domains. Kaumātua identify that past relationships can also deter knowledge sharing. When nothing comes of sharing powerful cultural knowledge, or from trying to work in united ways, people become disillusioned and reluctant to participate in so called "productive partnerships".

Kaumātua advocate caution in using mātauranga Māori, in the broad sense, in English-medium education settings, even in its capacity to enable Māori students to experience education success, as Māori. They encourage education professionals to approach the use of mātauranga Māori with caution because they are concerned with Māori knowledge becoming so diluted that it is no longer recognisable or culturally relevant. Using mātauranga Māori with little understanding or respect in education is worse, they argue, than not using it at all. The kāhui kaumātua encourage the use of mātauranga Māori in education under the guidance of knowledgeable experts. They believe that New Zealand society is not at a stage in our development for open, unregulated access to mātauranga Māori in English-medium education. For this to happen, genuine trust and truly shared responsibility would need to exist in New Zealand society.

Kaumātua rejected the notion of cultural competence by insisting that education and education professionals need to think about the issues of education success for Māori, as Māori, differently. They reject the term "cultural competencies" as well as the notion of them. They argue that judging competence is difficult; individuals may feel they are competent but are actually incompetent. Kaumātua pointed out that judging education professionals' competence is currently left to the discretion of people many Māori would not consider experts in our cultural knowledge or values. According to the kāhui, this in itself invalidated the process of attaining Māori cultural competence.

While kaumātua did reject cultural competence, they offered an alternative to educational thinking in relation to te ao Māori and its role in education. Kaumātua put forward culturally appropriate terms, and they offered the potential of a culturally appropriate model. According to this model, cultural knowledge would remain in the realm of the expert Indigenous knowledge holders who would maintain the responsibility of protecting the integrity of the knowledge. The key term that emerged was "cultural understanding" as being a more appropriate than achieving the ambiguous objective of cultural competence. Kaumātua argue that developing cultural understanding in educators is essential, because from understanding comes respect. If education professionals have opportunities and support to develop respect for Māori knowledges, language, and cultural values then they stand a better chance in making aspects of te ao Māori a natural part of their way of being.

While there remains a need for Indigenous knowledge to remain under the protection of Indigenous knowledge holders, kaumātua also insist that shared responsibility for equitable outcomes must be realised. The model kaumātua indicated was one where local advisory groups of Indigenous knowledge holders are resourced appropriately by the government to liaise with schools and education professionals. Kaumātua believe the government, through the Ministry of Education, should be responsible for funding advisories, but should ensure that control of them remains with Māori experts. In this way, vital Māori knowledge remains protected and schools can access aspects of mātauranga in culturally safe ways. Kaumātua described this as potentially being an advisory of expert kaumātua, a knowledge hub providing appropriate cultural supervision for education professionals.

Utilised and managed appropriately, Māori knowledge could potentially change the way we "do" education, because experts in Māori cultural knowledge would have the opportunity to advise on what concepts to teach, and the best ways to teach them. A cultural knowledge hub would also allow Māori experts to maintain control over the flow of information. They would be involved in the analysis of aspirations for the future and critique aspects of our culture that will benefit the realisation of aspirations. Kaumātua envision that advisories for the safe exchange of information be regional and belong to communities.

Kuia and kaumātua expert in operating within Māori frameworks would provide support and professional development to educators.

The potential of developing regional hubs where educators could access support, advice, and have space to develop Māori cultural understandings in ways that are safe for both Māori and non-Māori is an exciting prospect. This model, as kaumātua have pointed out, would require resourcing and would also require the development of genuine relationships based on trust and integrity. Enabling greater Māori control of Māori concepts in education takes ambiguous and flawed notions of competence and transforms them into concepts of shared rangatiratanga and shared responsibility for education success of all students.

Te Warihi re-imagines education as a space like the one that produced outstanding New Zealand leaders. He identified people he considers to be "complete New Zealanders" because of their absolute confidence and ability to operate in a Māori frame, informed by deep Māori knowledge bases. These people were also just as comfortable and confident operating within a Pākehā frame. They were considered complete because they knew the rules, norms, language, and knowledges of both Māori and Pākehā cultures and both enriched their lives. Te Warihi and other kaumātua imagine a modern education system capable of producing complete New Zealanders. This type of education has implications for the way we educate teachers, from the policies, systems, and structures we create to guide education, through to the way we educate children. It would not position te ao Māori as an add-on to be integrated into the "normal" curriculum; rather, it would be an education that genuinely values the dual cultures, knowledges, and heritages that found our modern nation state.

The approach progressed by kaumātua in this project has the potential to extinguish the damage caused by deeply entrenched and narrow views of education success that continue to convince intelligent and successful people that they are not. We cannot afford to continue on a path that measures success for Māori, as Māori, by the attainment of accreditation from Western education institutions. Education, as re-imagined by the kāhui kaumātua, has the potential to transform education and to provide students with the same confidence Hori draws from his culture:

> *I'm thankful for my Māoriness, because our tupunas left so many little gems ... behind to look after you.*

An education strategy targeting Indigenous education

This study was initiated by my interest in the notion of teachers attaining Māori "cultural competence" and what that meant in a colonised society. It can be inferred that Māori cultural competencies in education are an attempt by government to assist teachers to develop more culturally responsive relationships, learning environments, teaching practices, and approaches for Māori learners (Education Council New Zealand, 2011). However, I argued that the intent and the reality of the policy is problematic, as Māori values and worldviews continue to be at odds with the values of the education system. The inclusion of the chosen competencies in their current form in *Tātaiako* reiterates the underlying assertion of those in positions of power that Māori cultural understandings are only valuable in education as a platform from which to build new knowledge (Education Council New Zealand, 2011).

The dimensions are currently positioned as tools to build relationships and to guide teacher dispositions. Effective relationships are a prerequisite for learning, they create an environment conducive to learning; however, they do not guarantee education success, especially when that success is measured by culturally biased norms and is carried out in a culturally biased structure. When deeper cultural meanings are not reflected in policies and initiatives, mauri and tikanga are lost, and the ability for teachers to become expert enough to lead others in affirming and validating cultural awareness (Education Council New Zealand, 2011) becomes a somewhat fanciful and seemingly impossible expectation.

Webber (2011) cites Mason Durie's assertion that Māori academic achievement should not be at the expense of cultural identity. While this should be a reality in New Zealand education, the evidence presented is that Māori cultural identity has almost always been sacrificed for academic achievement because, in current circumstances, the two exist in juxtaposition to each other. Certification for the criteria of academic achievement has been defined by the dominant culture and has been used to ensure that structural inequalities remain firmly in place (Walker, 1996).

The existence of a strategy intended to positively target Indigenous student outcomes in English-medium contexts is a positive step—we must remember that the existence of such a strategy acknowledges Crown responsibility to correct historical injustices against the Indigenous New Zealand population. However, there appears to be an expectation that *Tātaiako* will overlay our history of colonisation, as well as the marginalisation and rejection of Māori beliefs and values in education. The document *Tātaiako* does not provide space for professionals to interrogate deeper issues effecting education. Nor does it allow education professionals to investigate the ways in which these issues continue to impact on Māori experiencing education success, as Māori.

Divergent goals and purposes for Western education

In terms of the alignment of perspectives, expectations, and aspirations for the education of the children and mokopuna of kaumātua, with the English-medium education concepts of cultural competence and education success for Māori, as Māori, it would be easy to draw the conclusion that there is a gulf between the two and they therefore fail to align. However, the analyses of information developed from the pūkōrero of these holders of mātauranga Māori have revealed that the conclusion is not so straightforward. As their chapters unfold, evidence is presented that, while Western education has restricted Māori learning, subjugated Māori knowledge and impoverished Māori communities, the education goals of Māori have often been in alignment with those of Pākehā decision makers. What do not align are the perspective each culture (Māori and Pākehā) had of the processes and purposes of education.

By condensing the history of education in New Zealand, a pattern of similar goals for different purposes emerges. Since the time of the missionaries up until the 1970s, the shared Māori–Crown goal of Western education was to teach Māori the skills of English literacy and Pākehā social norms. The missionary goal of teaching literacy in English changed to teaching in Māori, to advance their mission to Christianise Māori. This was reversed by the assimilationist goals of Governor Grey who wanted to swiftly progress the process of colonisation by assimilating dispossessed Māori landowners into the Pākehā population (Walker, 2016).

While the goal of Western education for both Māori and missionaries, followed by the Crown, remained largely unchanged—to teach Western literacy and social norms in English to Māori—the purpose for missionaries and the Crown changed over the years. The purpose has been to convert Māori to Christianity, to assimilate Māori for an expedient colonisation, to "train" Māori to become a labouring underclass. However, for over a century, right up until the 1970s, Māori have maintained the same purpose for Western education in English—to strengthen iwi economic and power bases through full and equal participation in (what became) New Zealand society, and to determine our own futures within that society.

The rapid erosion of te reo Māori and culture through intensive colonisation strategies caused a shift in education goals for Māori in the 1970s. Our colonisation had been swift and rigorous, many Māori were faced with the prospect of losing our language, just as we had lost our lands—a prospect that even one generation before was unimaginable. During this time, Māori goals for education took a sharp turn to include the teaching of our language and affirmation of our identity for the same purpose we had preserved since the 1800s—to participate fully and equally in our own society.

In many ways, Māori and the Crown have had shared goals in terms of education; however, our visions for the purpose of education are vastly different. When *Tātaiako* is located within the context of an education system that has served the purpose of obstructing full, positive, and equal Māori participation in society, the notion of developing

Māori cultural competencies takes on the appearance of quasi-traditional Māori cultural values located in a Pākehā-oriented education system. Framed within our history of colonisation, *Tātaiako* appears to be a mediating structure, which Penetito (2010) defines as those "... devices and dynamics that apparently accept Māori ways of operating in education ... while co-opting those operations in the interests of maintaining power and authority" (p. 79).

Penetito (2010) warns against making assumptions that mediating structures within Pākehā-oriented institutions will help Māori to feel more included, and in turn increase Māori participation, with the ultimate intention of developing a sense of belonging and empowerment. The preoccupation in education with behaviour modifiers for educators of Māori students restricts educators from questioning the origin and purpose of the education system. This secures the power and authority of Western knowledge and ways of being to the point that they appear to be "normal", protecting the unquestioned authority of the white space (Milne, 2013).

Te Kauae Tuatahi: Systemic transformation

Alternative perspectives of education have been imagined by the kāhui kaumātua. Their vision for the future of New Zealand education is exciting and requires re-imagining the education system, re-positioning mātauranga Māori, and a shift in thinking for educators. In their words, transforming education is simple; it is nothing magical or massive, but it does require a change in the heart and mind of the education system, as well as changes in the hearts and minds of education professionals. That change, according to the information gleaned by kaumātua, must be underpinned by the kaupapa of Te Tiriti o Waitangi.

Currently, everybody in New Zealand comes under the kaupapa of the Crown; however, kaumātua argued that, in order to transform systems and people, New Zealand must come under the kaupapa of Te Tiriti, which encompasses a spirit of manaakitanga, shared responsibility, and rights of both rangatiratanga and kawanatanga (Henare, 2013). Kaumātua insisted that an essential ingredient in developing cultural respect, and identity as Māori, and as a nation, is an education that teaches the history of this country from a position that aims to deepen understandings, rather than restrict them. Another vital aspect they propose is education that centres the role and station of tāngata whenua in this country, from the perspective of tāngata whenua.

Tātaiako is, among other things, a strategy intended to encourage teachers to reflect on and modify their pedagogical practice, with the assumption that this will raise Māori education success, as Māori. This intention is beneficial and should indeed be an expectation in New Zealand schools. However, it also puts the responsibility of education success of Māori on teachers who are expected to critically examine their practice, with no expectation that the curriculum or educational systems and structures be critically examined. There is no onus on the education system or on keepers of the curriculum to question or modify their practice. Raising Māori education achievement then becomes the sole responsibility of under-resourced teachers.

The kāhui kaumātua rejected the notion that Māori cultural competencies for teachers of Māori students could enable education success for Māori, as Māori. Their first target for change was the education system, not the educators within that system. Evidence presented has been used to argue that the philosophical roots of the education system have been so detrimental to Māori education success, and to Māori cultural identity, that in its current form the education system is unable to rectify this damage. The kāhui kaumātua argue that, for Māori to experience education success, as Māori, the education system, as well as other social and political systems in this country, need to change. They argue that education success for Māori, as Māori would require transformation across systems and structures to create healthy families and communities.

In evidence to the Waitangi Tribunal WAI 262 claim, T. W. Hetaraka (2007) asserted that Pākehā systems must recognise Māori methods of healing, of teaching, and of protection. This sentiment applies to all systems and structures in New Zealand that are biased toward Western ideologies, including the education system. Kaumātua in this project argued that empowering educators to be successful required the education system to be purged of monocultural modes of operating, and enabling the validation and valuing of knowledge from diverse sources. Until this happens the education system will continue to perpetuate racism and disadvantage, a climate that cannot support educators in enabling education success for Māori, as Māori.

Te Kauae Tuarua: Relational transformation

Kaumātua also highlighted several ways in which relationships in education must be transformed for Māori to experience education success, as Māori. To facilitate changed relationships, they assert that, first, the deep mistrust Māori have of Pākehā systems and processes, caused in part by Eurocentric research practices (L. Smith, 2012), must be addressed. For this kāhui kaumātua a lack of trust has been caused by their experience of having mātauranga and tikanga Māori misused by people who have gained knowledge from them and other holders of mātauranga on the pretext that they would use the knowledge to benefit Māori communities. In many cases for this kāhui, the knowledge was taken, then misconstrued or (mis)represented in inappropriate, and sometimes damaging ways.

To begin healing wounds, kaumātua stipulate that Māori cultural knowledge must remain under the control and protection of those members of Māori communities who have been initiated to care for it. The Crown (as represented by various ministries) must share in decision making, they must trust that Māori are the experts of our culture, and as such know how to begin healing our culture. Rebuilding trust will allow for genuine, mutually beneficial relationships that consist of collaboration and respect to occur. Such relationships provide a basis for Māori and Pākehā to mobilise and work together. Kaumātua believe it will take a concerted effort by everybody, not just by Māori, to make real change in education and in society in general.

Tātaiako gives the chosen Māori dimensions superficial, decontextualised meanings that distort authentic understandings. It gives teachers a misleading sense of the work required of them, while shifting the responsibility for poor Māori education outcomes onto the individual classroom teacher. The logic of the policy collapses social relationships, educational relationships, and achievement. It seems to assume that better relationships between teachers and Māori students will deliver education success, while overlooking the fact that productive classroom relationships are a prerequisite, not a substitute, for achievement. The language of the document leaves much open to interpretation and fails to address vital issues facing Māori in the current education system, including the existence of a multitude of power relationships and the connection between culture and long-standing structural and institutional inequities (Lee, 2008). Crucially, kaumātua addressed the problematic positioning of Māori cultural knowledge in *Tātaiako*.

Te Kauae Tuatoru: Transformational knowledge

As already argued, there is no specific mention of mātauranga Māori in the *Tātaiako* document. This indicates that the purpose of *Tātaiako* is to act solely as a behavioural modifier without providing a means by which educators can incorporate mātauranga Māori into the curriculum. In this way, Western knowledge maintains its position of dominance in New Zealand education. However, the point made clear by kaumātua is that this constructs mātauranga in complex and problematic ways. This complexity can be summarised by Battiste (2008) who argues, "[s]chools cannot and should not be responsible for teaching Aboriginal knowledge in all its complexity and diversity, nor should they be solely responsible for reviving Aboriginal languages, even if they could" (p. 501). Herein lies the tension.

That *Tātaiako* makes no specific mention of mātauranga Māori perhaps supports the argument presented by Battiste (2008). However, in order to be deemed "culturally competent" you must know about the culture, and in this case, as I have already argued, Māori culture is based on Māori knowledge and language. This presents two problems: first, how can education professionals profess to be culturally competent without mātauranga Māori? Second, even if education professionals did have understandings of mātauranga Māori, is it their right to teach it?

Kaumātua addressed these contentions by presenting a culturally appropriate model. Their first solution was relatively straightforward:

the term "cultural competence" must be replaced in education with a term that reflects cultural understanding and respect. Battiste (2008) argues that "[b]ecause Eurocentric colonizers consider themselves to be the ideal model for humanity and carriers of a superior culture, they believe they can assess the competencies of others" (p. 504). This argument was reflected in the words of kaumātua who identified that, in *Tātaiako*, Māori communities or Māori knowledge holders do not assess the "competence" of teachers, it is the hierarchy within education who deems professionals "competent" or not. Kaumātua insisted that aspiring for "cultural competence" was inappropriate, as is the use of the term. They would prefer to build cultural understanding and respect and have this reflected in a new term.

Their model has implications across a wide range of public sectors and areas of education, from curriculum and pedagogy within classrooms to implications for initial teacher education. In direct contrast to the objective of *Tātaiako* in progressing teachers to become Māori cultural leaders, kaumātua have unequivocally said it is not the role of non-Māori educators to be experts in te ao Māori. Rather, they see it as essential that teachers come to know themselves as cultural and spiritual beings. Meyer (2008) argues "[k]nowing that you are unique at this basic level will bring a keen understanding of the nuances of your own subjectivity" (p. 220). This sentiment is just as relevant to teachers as it is to researchers.

The objective then becomes teachers becoming expert in their own cultural backgrounds with the purpose of providing them cultural grounding and confidence to relate to students of other cultures. Kaumātua believed that a key role of educators enabling education success for Māori, as Māori, is to build confidence in Māori students as learners. One way they saw of achieving this was by teachers knowing themselves, loving themselves, and deeply understanding how their wairua impacts on the wairua of their students. This, kaumātua believe, will begin healing the loss of identity both Māori and Pākehā have experienced through colonisation. Kaumātua do not want teachers to assume they are Māori cultural experts. They want them to have confidence and a deep connection to themselves culturally and spiritually.

Kaumātua insist that effective relationships will require Māori and Pākehā to work together for a common cause, and that appropriate education can cause the respect and understanding vital to establishing these relationships. They were very clear that effective relationships, greater understanding, and respect did not constitute an invitation to then open mātauranga Māori up to be taken, even for well-intentioned purposes, which has also been a cause of consternation for Indigenous knowledges globally (Battiste, 2008). Their model utilised tikanga for protection and safety of people and of mātauranga. They envisioned regional hubs or advisories, made up of local Māori experts who could provide support and appropriate aspects of mātauranga Māori for use by educators. They saw the government as having a responsibility to fund and resource these hubs adequately, but the control over what and how knowledge would be taught would remain in the hands of the Māori communities and experts.

He kōrero whakamutunga

The knowledge generated by kaumātua throughout this study reinforces that the diversity of Māori communities, knowledge, tikanga, and te reo means that education success for Māori, as Māori, will always be contextual and complex. Not complex in a way that deters problem solving, but complex in a way that forces education professionals to reconsider how they utilise and understand te ao Māori. The purpose of this study was never to construct a neatly packaged framework to assist educators in "becoming culturally competent". The evidence presented throughout is that this is not a goal for Māori in education. Even presenting a list succinctly summarising key points to aid the reader seems in many ways to contradict the messages kaumātua have given. They have been clear that to bring about authentic change we need to understand and interact differently.

To achieve the goal of education success for Māori, as Māori, the kāhui kaumātua have asked that education and education professionals listen. There is no package, there is no shiny new tool. That is the point. To truly listen we must work differently. Knowledge sharing through listening and interacting deeply does not come in a book—Google cannot help either. By asking us to listen, the kāhui kaumātua have proposed a model that requires human interaction and genuine connection, an inherently Māori way of developing knowledge. As Battiste (2008) argues, in order to acquire Indigenous knowledge you cannot simply read a book, or do field visits to specific Indigenous locations, "... rather, one comes to know through extended conversation and experiences with elders, peoples, and places ..." (p. 502).

Approximately 180 years ago, Ngā Puhi tohunga, Atuawera (also known as Te Papa Hurihia), prophesied that three forces would impact on te iwi Māori. The first would be the great struggle to retain our mana tuku iho. The second would be the courageous task of ensuring that the sacred oath given by Queen Victoria to rangatira through Te Tiriti o Waitangi be honoured. The third force that would embattle Māori would be the tenacity and strength of Pākehā to assert undivided control over te taiao. Atuawera predicted that the "... painful experience would be in trying to balance these ... forces that pull and push, and that will tear at the very fabric of the Māori heart and soul" (Edwards, 2010, p. 74).

The goals that holders of mātauranga Māori have for their children and mokopuna in education reflect the prophecy of Atuawera. Kaumātua have highlighted that education success for Māori, as Māori, relies on education professionals understanding three key aspects. First, they have to know and understand themselves as human beings with mana who are culturally and spiritually located. Second, they must know our history as a country so as to understand the origins of current inequalities (Murphy, 2016). Third, educators must come to know the system intimately because, as kaumātua argued, the system is killing us, it has turned us inside out. The assertions of kaumātua about the system are reflected by Jackson (2016), who argues "[t]he education system continues to fail so many of our mokopuna because that's what it was designed to do" (p. 41).

The narratives in this book illustrate the painful push and pull on the fabric of Māori hearts and souls. However, they have also evidenced the determination by which kaumātua have guarded and retained our mana tuku iho, and their unerring challenging of the Crown to honour the sacred rangatira-to-rangatira oaths. Kaumātua visions for the future of education for their mokopuna are wide reaching and require far more in-depth questioning of systems and structures than is required to merely alter behaviours. They have identified that, as a country, we are in a stage of development that requires us all to continue working toward justice:

> Kua tawhiti kē tōu haerenga mai, kia kore e haere tonu. He nui rawa ōu mahi, kia kore e mahi tonu. You have come too far not to go much further. You have done too much not to do more.
>
> Whakataukī, Tā Himi Henare

References

Absolon, K., & Willett, C. (2005). Putting ourselves forward: Location in aboriginal research. In L. Brown & S. Strega (Eds.), *Research as resistance. Critical, indigenous, & anti-oppressive approaches* (pp. 97–126). Canadian Scholars' Press/Women's Press.

Alton-Lee, A. (2003). *Quality teaching for diverse students in schooling: Best Evidence Sysnthesis*. Ministry of Education.

Ashton-Warner, S. (1980). *Teacher. The testament of an inspired teacher*. Virago.

Augoustinos, M., Tuffin, K., & Every, D. (2005). New racism, meritocracy and individualism: Constraining affirmative action in education. *Discourse & Society, 16*(3), 315–340. https://doi.org/10.1177/0957926505051168

Bailey, C. (1984). *Beyond the present and the particular (International library of the philosophy of education* (Vol. 2). Routledge.

Ball, D. G. (1939). Education of native children. In *Appendix to the Journal of the House of Representatives* (Vol. Session 1, E-03).

Barrington, J. (1970). A historical review of policies and provisions. In J. Ewing & J. Shallcrass (Eds.), *Introduction to Maori education* (pp. 27–38). New Zealand University Press.

Barrington, J. (2008). *Separate but equal? Maori schools and the Crown 1867–1969*. Victoria University Press.

Barrington, J., & Beaglehole, T. H. (1974). *Maori schools in a changing society*. New Zealand Council for Educational Research.

Battiste, M. (2008). Research ethics for protecting indigenous knowledge and heritage: Institutional and researcher responsibilities. In N. K. Denzin, Y. S. Lincoln, & L. Smith (Eds.), *Handbook of critical and indigenous methodologies* (pp. 497–510). SAGE Publications.

Battiste, M. (2013). *Decolonizing education: Nourishing the learning spirit*. Purich.

Beaglehole, T. H. (1970). The missionary schools, 1816-1840. In J. Ewing & J. Shallcrass (Eds.), *Introduction to Maori education* (pp. 21–25). New Zealand University Press.

Beeby, C. E. (1992). *The biography of an idea: Beeby on education*. New Zealand Council for Educational Research.

Benton, R. (1979). *The Māori language in the nineteen seventies*. Māori Research Unit, New Zealand Council for Educational Research.

Binney, J. (1968). *The legacy of guilt: A life of Thomas Kendall*. Caxton Press.

Binney, J. (2005). *The legacy of guilt: A life of Thomas Kendall*. Bridget Williams Books.

Bishop, R. (2003). Changing power relationships in education: Kaupapa Māori messages for 'mainstream' education in Aotearoa/New Zealand. *Comparative Education*, 39(2), 221–238. https://doi.org/10.1080/03050060302555

Bishop, R., & Berryman, M. (2006). *Culture speaks: Cultural relationships and classroom learning*. Huia Publishers.

Bishop, R., Berryman, M., Tiakiwai, S.-J., & Richardson, C. (2003). *Te kotahitanga: the experiences of year 9 and 10 Māori students in mainstream classrooms*. Ministry of Education.

Bishop, R., & Glynn, T. (1999). *Culture counts: Changing power relationships in education*. Dunmore Press.

Burns, C., Hetaraka, M., & Jones, A. (2024). Te Tiriti o Waitangi: The Treaty of Waitangi, principles and other representations. *New Zealand Journal of Education Studies*. https://doi.org/10.1007/s40841-024-00312-y

Clarke, G. (1863). Native schools. Appendix. In *Appendix to the Journals of the House of Representatives* (Vol. Session 1, E-9).

Cloher, D. (2003). *Hongi Hika warrior chief*. Penguin Books.

Cram, F. (2001). Rangahau Māori: Tona tika, tona pono—the validity and integrity of Māori research. In M. Tolich (Ed.), *Research ethics in Aotearoa New Zealand* (pp. 35–52). Pearson Education.

Dei, G. (Ed.). (2011). *Indigenous philosophies and critical education: A reader*. Peter Lang Publishing.

Denzin, N. K., Lincoln, Y. S., & Smith, L. (Eds.). (2008). *Handbook of critical and indigenous methodologies*. SAGE Publications.

Department of Education. (1962). *Report of the Commission on Education* (Currie Report). Government Printer.

Department of Education. (1988). *Administering for excellence, report of the Taskforce to Review Education Administration* (The Picot Report). Government Printer.

Dewey, J. (1916). *Democracy and education—An introduction to the philosophy of education*. Macmillan.

Dobson, E. (2007). Sylvia Ashton-Warner, 1908–1984. *Kotare*, 7(1), 163–176.

Durie, M. (1994). *Whaiora, Māori health development*. Oxford University Press.

Education Council New Zealand. (2011). *Tātaiako; Cultural competencies for teachers of Māori learners*. Ministry of Education. https://teachingcouncil.nz/assets/Files/Code-and-Standards/Tataiako-cultural-competencies-for-teachers-of-Maori-learners.pdf

Edwards, R. (2010). *Affidavit of Rima Edwards*. Te Paparahi o Te Raki Inquiry. [Unpublished manuscript]. Waitangi Tribunal.

Elabour-Idemudia, P. (2011). Identity, representation and knowledge production. In G. Dei (Ed.), *Indigenous philosophies and critical education: A reader* (pp. 142–156). Peter Lang Publishing.

Erikson, E. H. (1956). The problem of ego identity. *Journal of the American Psychoanalytic Association, 4*(1), 56–121.

Evison, H. (1997). *The long dispute; Maori land rights and European colonisation in Southern New Zealand.* Canterbury University Press.

Fletcher, N. (2022). *The English text of the Treaty of Waitangi.* Bridget Williams Books.

Fraser, P. (1939). Report of the Minister of Education. In *Appendix to the Journals of the House of Representatives* (Vol. Session 1, E-1). https://paperspast.natlib.govt.nz/parliamentary/AJHR1939-I.2.2.4.1

Friedman, J. (1997). Global crises, the struggle for cultural identity and intellectual pork-barrelling: Cosmopolitans vs locals, ethnics, and nationals in an era of de-hegemonism. In P. Werbner & T. Modood (Eds.), *Debating cultural hybridity: Multi-cultural identities and the politics of anti-racism* (pp. 70–89). Zed Books.

Friedman, J. (2007). Preface. In E. Rata & R. Openshaw (Eds.), *Public policy and ethnicity: The politics of ethnic boundary making* (pp. xi–xxv). Palgrave Macmillan.

Gerlich, R. (2013). Education: Beeby's, tomorrow's and today's. *Education Review, 4*(5), 20–21.

Gibson, R. (1986). *Critical theory and education.* Hodder and Stoughton.

Hemara, W. (2000). *Māori pedagogies: A view from the literature.* NZCER Press.

Henare, E. (2010). *Brief evidence of Johnson Erima Henare.* Te Paparahi o Te Raki Inquiry. [Unpublished manuscript]. Waitangi Tribunal.

Henare, E. (2011). *Closing submissions for Te Runanga o Ngati Hine.* Te Paparahi o Te Raki Inquiry. [Unpublished manuscript]. Waitangi Tribunal.

Henare, E. (2013). *Covering letter.* Consitutional Advisory Panel, Ministry of Justice.

Hetaraka, M. (2008). *Mai te whe-ki-rangi te tangi, mai te tangi te reo, mai te reo te kupu, ka puta te unaunahi i whakapiripiri ki te Ika-Nui-a-Māui: Using traditional Māori pedagogies to strengthen literacy development in contemporary settings.* [Unpublished Honours dissertation]. The University of Auckland.

Hetaraka, M. (2019). A kaupapa Māori analysis of *Tātaiako:* Considering Māori education policy. *MAI Journal, 8*(2), 159–171. https://doi.org/10.20507/MAIJournal.2019.8.2.5

Hetaraka, M. (2020). *Te Kauae Tuku Iho; Inheriting the Sacred Jawbone: Re-imagining Māori cultural competence in education by engaging the wisdom of indigenous knowledge keepers.* PhD thesis, The University of Auckland. https://researchspace.auckland.ac.nz/handle/2292/49954

Hetaraka, M. (2023). Tikanga Māori as research methods. In F. Meyer & K. Meissel (Eds.), *Research methods for education and the social disciplines in Aotearao New Zealand* (pp. 113–133). NZCER Press.

Hetaraka, M., Meiklejohn-Whiu, S., Webber, M., & Jesson, R. (2023). Tiritiria: Understanding Māori children as inherently and inherited-ly literate—Towards a conceptual position. *New Zealand Journal of Educational Studies*, 58, 59–72. https://doi.org/10.1007/s40841-023-00282-7

Hetaraka, T. W. (2007). *Closing submissions for Ngati Kuri, Ngati Wai and Te Rarawa. Claim to flora and fauna me o ratou taonga katoa Tribunal Inquiry.* [Unpublished manuscript]. Waitangi Tribunal. http://wai262.weebly.com/uploads/7/4/6/3/7463762/wai_262_closing_submissions_final_amended_version_5_sept_07.pdf

Hill, R. (2009). *Māori and the state: Crown–Māori relations in New Zealand/Aotearoa 1950–2000.* Victoria University Press.

Hīroa, T. R. (1982). *The coming of the Māori.* Whitcombe & Tombs.

Hirschfeld, C. (Writer) & S. Bennett & C. Bennett (Directors). (2017). NZ Wars: The stories of Ruapekapeka [Video]. In C. McRae & A. Stevanon (Producer), *NZ Wars: The stories of Ruapekapeka. Great Southern Television and RNZ.* https://www.rnz.co.nz/programmes/nz-wars/story/2018619186/nz-wars-the-stories-of-ruapekapeka

Hohepa, M. (2015). Kia mau ki te aka matua: Researching Māori development and learning. In L. Pihama, S-J Tiakiwai, and K. Southey (Eds.), *Kaupapa Rangahau: A reader* (2nd ed, pp. 115–124). Te Kotahi Research Institute, University of Waikato. https://matrix.prd.waikato.ac.nz/__data/assets/pdf_file/0009/339885/Kaupapa-Rangahau-A-Reader_2nd-Edition.pdf

hooks, bell. (1994). *Teaching to transgress. Education as the practice of freedom.* Routledge.

Hunn, J. K. (1961). *Report on the Department of Maori Affairs.* Government Printer.

Ihimaera, W. (1986). *The matriarch.* Raupo.

Jackson, M. (2016). Decolonising education. In J. Hutchings & J. Lee-Morgan (Eds.), *Decolonisation in Aotearoa: Education, research and practice.* NZCER Press.

Jenkins, K. (1993). *Becoming literate–becoming English. A research into the beginnings of English literacy within Māori society.* The University of Auckland.

Jenkins, K., & Jones, A. (2000). Maori education policy: A state promise. In J. Marshall, E. Coxon, K. Jenkins, & A. Jones (Eds.), *Politics, policy, pedagogy: Education in Aotearoa/New Zealand* (pp. 139–156). Dunmore.

Johnston, P. M. G. (1997). Tiptoeing through the puha: Policy reforms for Māori education. In M. Olssen & K. Matthews (Eds.), *Education policy in New Zealand: The 1900s and beyond* (pp. 83–106). Dunmore.

Jones, A. (1980). *Objectivity and educational research.* [Unpublished Master of Philosophy in Education]. The University of Auckland.

Jones, A., & Jenkins, K. (2011). *He kōrero—words between us: First Māori–Pākehā coversations on paper.* Huia Publishers.

Jones, A., & Kaa Jenkins, K. (2017). *Tuai a traveller in two worlds.* Bridget Williams Books.

Jones, A., & Middleton, S. (Eds.). (2009). *The kiss and the ghost; Syliva Ashton-Warner and New Zealand.* NZCER Press.

Kaa Jenkins, K., & Ka'ai, T. (1994). Maori education: A cultural experience and dilemma for the state—a new direction for Maori society. In E. Coxon, K. Jenkins, J. Marshall, & L. Massey (Eds.), *The politics of learning and teaching in Aotearoa–New Zealand* (pp. 148–179). Dunmore.

Kovach, M. (2005). Emerging from the margin: Indigenous methodologies. In L. Brown & S. Strega (Eds.), *Research as resistance. Critical, indigenous and anti-oppressive approaches* (pp. 19–36). Canadian Scholars' Press/Women's Press.

Kovach, M. (2009). *Indigenous methodologies: Characteristics, conversations and contexts*. University of Toronto Press.

Kukutai, T. (2004). The problem of defining an ethnic group for public policy: Who is meant by Māori and why does it matter? *Social Policy Journal of New Zealand, 23*, 86–108.

Lee, J. (2006). *Hokianga*. Raupo.

Lee, J. (2008). *Ako: Pūrākau of Māori teachers' work in secondary schools*. (Doctoral Thesis in Education). The University of Auckland.

McCaull, A. (2024, 17 May). *Ngāti Kahu pen letter to King Charles over Te Tiriti o Waitangi*. RNZ. https://www.rnz.co.nz/news/te-manu-korihi/516795/ngati-kahu-pen-letter-to-king-charles-over-te-tiriti-o-waitangi

Macfarlane, A. (2003). *Culturally inclusive pedagogy for Māori students experiencing learning and behaviour difficulties*. [PhD Thesis]. University of Waikato.

Macfarlane, A. (2004). *Kia hiwa ra! Listen to culture—Māori students' plea to educators*. NZCER Press.

McKenzie, D. (1985). *Oral culture, literacy and print in early New Zealand: The Treaty of Waitangi*. Victoria University Press.

McKinley, E., & Smith, L. (2019). Towards self-determination in indigenous education research: An introduction. In E. McKinley & L. Smith (Eds.), *Handbook of indigenous education* (pp. 1–15). Springer.

MacNeilage, P., Rogers, L., & Vallortigara, G. (2009). Evolutionary origins of your right and left brain. *Scientific American, 301*(1). https://doi.org/10.1038/scientificamerican0709-60

McPhail, G. (2017). Rethinking what it means to be a teacher through a mixed modality approach. In C. Mutch & J. Tatebe (Eds.), *Understanding enduring ideas in education: A response to those who 'just want to be a teacher'* (pp. 82–95). NZCER Press.

Marks, M. (1984). *The frustrations of being a Maori language teacher*. Paper presented at the Maori Education Development Conference, Turangawaewae Marae.

Marr, C. (1997). *Public Works takings of Māori land, 1840–1981*. Waitangi Tribunal. https://www.justice.govt.nz/assets/wt-theme-g-public-works-takings-of-maori-land.pdf

Marsden, M., & Royal, C. (2003). *The woven universe: Selected writings of Reverend Maori Marsden*. The Estate of Rev. Maori Marsden.

Matapo, J., & Roder, J. (2017). Weaving our whāriki: Re-imagining progressive philosophy in Aotearoa New Zealand early childhood education. In C. Mutch & J. Tatebe (Eds.), *Understanding enduring ideas in education: A response to those who 'just want to be a teacher'* (pp. 47–61). NZCER Press.

May, H. (2003). *School beginnings: A history of early years schooling. Case study one: Missionary infant schools for Maori children, 1830–40s*. Institute for Early Childhood Studies, Victoria University of Wellington.

May, S. (Ed.) (1999). *Critical multiculturalism: Rethinking multicultural and antiracist education*. Falmer Press.

Mead, H. (2012). Understanding mātauranga Māori. In D. Bean, T. Black, W. Collings, & W. Nuku (Eds.), *Conversations on mātauranga Māori* (pp. 9–14). New Zealand Qualifications Authority.

Metge, J. (1984). *Learning and teaching. He tikanga Maori*. Maori and Island Division, Department of Education.

Meyer, M. (2008). Indigenous and authentic: Hawaiian epistemology and the triangulation of meaning. In N. Denzin, Y. Lincoln, & L. Smith (Eds.), *Handbook of critical and indigenous methodologies* (pp. 217–232). SAGE Publications.

Miller, R. (2003). Self-determination in international law and the demise of democracy? *Columbia Journal of Transnational Law, 41*(2011–43), 601–651. https://ssrn.com/abstract=1973779

Milne, A. (2009). *Colouring in the white spaces: Cultural identity and learning in school: A research report prepared for the ASB/APPA Travelling Fellowship Trust following a study tour in 2009* (ASB/APPA Ed.). ASB/APPA Travelling Fellowship Trust.

Milne, A. (2013). *Colouring in the white spaces: Reclaiming cultural identity in whitestream schools*. [PhD thesis]. University of Waikato.

Milne, A. (2017). *Colouring in the white spaces: Reclaiming cultural identity in whitestream schools*. Peter Lang.

Ministry for Culture and Heritage. (2016). *Obtaining land*. http://nzhistory.govt.nz/politics/treaty/the-treaty-in-practice/obtaining-land

Ministry of Education. (2007). *The New Zeland curriculum*. Learning Media.

Ministry of Education. (2009). *Ka hikitia—managing for success: The Māori education strategy 2008–2012* (2nd ed.). https://www.education.govt.nz/assets/Documents/Ministry/Strategies-and-policies/Ka-Hikitia/KaHikitia2009PartOne.pdf.

Ministry of Education. (2013a). *Ka hikitia: Accelerating success 2013–2017*. The Māori education strategy. Te Kāwanatanga o Aotearoa.

Ministry of Education. (2013b). *Summary of ka hikitia: Accelerating success 2013–2017*. https://www.education.govt.nz/assets/Documents/Ministry/Strategies-and-policies/Ka-Hikitia/KaHikitiaSummary.pdf

Ministy of Education. (2023). *Ka hikitia—Ka hāpaitia.* https://www.education.govt.nz/our-work/overall-strategies-and-policies/ka-hikitia-ka-hapaitia/

Murphy, T. (2016). Reflections from the trenches: Decolonising hearts and minds in Aotearoa. In J. Hutchings & J. Lee-Morgan (Eds.), *Decolonisation in Aotearoa: Education, research and practice* (pp. 78–85). NZCER Press.

Mutch, C. (2013). Progressive education in New Zealand: A revered past, a contested present, and an uncertain future. *International Journal of Progressive Education, 9*(2), 98–116.

Mutch, C. (2017). Understanding progressive education and its influence on policy and pedagogy in New Zealand. In C. Mutch & J. Tatebe (Eds.), *Understanding enduring ideas in education: A response to those who 'just want to be a teacher'* (pp. 31–46). NZCER Press.

Mutch, C., & Tatebe, J. (Eds.). (2017). *Understanding enduring ideas in education: A response to those who 'just want to be a teacher'.* NZCER Press.

Ngata, A. (1943). *The price of citizenship: Ngarimu VC.* Whitcombe & Tombs.

Nicholas, J. L. (1817). *Narrative of a voyage to New Zealand, performed in the years 1814 and 1815, in company with the Reverend Samuel Marsden, Principal Chaplain of New South Wales.* James Black & Son.

O'Connor, P. (2017). Progressivism—a person reflection. In C. Mutch & J. Tatebe (Eds.), *Understanding enduring ideas in education: A response to those who 'just want to be a teacher'* (pp. 27–30). NZCER Press.

O'Malley, V. (2012). *The meeting place: Māori and Pākehā encounters,* 1642–1840. Auckland University Press.

O'Malley, V. (2015). *Haerenga: Early Māori journeys across the globe.* Bridget Williams Books.

Openshaw, R. (2007). *Evaluation of Te Kōtahitanga—Phase 3.* New Zealand Post Primary Teachers' Association.

Orange, C. (1987). *The Treaty of Waitangi.* Bridget Williams Books.

Papa, R., & Meredith, P. (2012). Kīngitanga—the Māori King movement. https://teara.govt.nz/en/kingitanga-the-maori-king-movement

Penehira, M. (2011). *Mouri tu, mouri moko, mouri ora! Moko as a wellbeing strategy.* [PhD thesis]. University of Waikato.

Penetito, W. (2009). Place-based education: Catering for curriculum, culture and community. *New Zealand Annual Review of Education, 18,* 5–29.

Penetito, W. (2010). *What's Māori about Māori education?* Victoria University Press.

Penetito, W. (2011). *Kaupapa Māori education: Research as the exposed edge.* Paper presented at Kei tua o te pae: The challenges of kaupapa Māori research in the 21st century, Pipitea Marae, Wellington.

Penfold, M. (2009). Sylvia Ashton-Warner and Māori children: "I do not think Sylvia learned much from the kids". In A. Jones & S. Middleton (Eds.), *Sylvia and the ghost; Sylvia Ashton-Warner and New Zealand.* NZCER Press.

Pere, R. R. (1991). *Te wheke: A celebration of infinite wisdom.* Ao Ako Global Learning New Zealand.

Perry, J. (2022). Kura kaupapa Māori makes its case for an urgent Waitangi Tribunal hearing. *Te Ao Māori News.* https://www.teaonews.co.nz/2022/04/07/kura-kaupapa-maori-makes-its-case-for-an-urgent-waitangi-tribunal-hearing/

Peterson, D. (2000). Te reo Māori—the Māori language. Part 1. *Background note.* New Zealand Parliamentary library. https://www.parliament.nz/resource/0000000292

Petrie, H. (2006). *Chiefs of industry; Māori tribal enterprise in early colonial New Zealand.* Auckland University Press.

Petrie, H. (2015). *Outcasts of the gods? The struggle over slavery in Māori New Zealand.* Auckland University Press.

Pihama, L. (2015). Kaupapa Māori theory: Transforming theory in Aotearoa. In L. Pihama, S-J Tiakiwai, and K. Southey (Eds.), *Kaupapa Rangahau: A reader* (2nd ed, pp. 5–16). Te Kotahi Research Institute, University of Waikato.

Pihama, L. (2016). Positioning ourselves within kaupapa Māori research. In J. Hutchings & J. Lee-Morgan (Eds.), *Decolonisation in Aotearoa. Education, research and practice* (pp. 101–113). NZCER Press.

Pihama, L., & Lee-Morgan, J. (2019). Colonization, education and indigenous peoples. In E. McKinley & L. Smith (Eds.), *Handbook of indigenous education* (pp. 19-27). Springer.

Potts, K., & Brown, L. (2005). Becoming an anti-oppressive researcher. In L. Brown & S. Strega (Eds.), *Research as resistance. Critical, indigenous, & anti-oppressive approaches* (pp. 255–286). Canadian Scholars' Press/Women's Press.

Rangihau, J. (2011). Being Māori. In M. King (Ed.), *Te ao hurihuri: Aspects of Māoritanga.* (pp. 183-190). Penguin Books.

Rata, E. (2012). *The politics of knowledge in education.* Routledge.

Rata, E., & Openshaw, R. (2007a). Introduction: Of Mohammad, murals and Maori ceremony. In E. Rata & R. Openshaw (Eds.), *Public policy and ethnicity: The politics of ethnic boundary making* (pp. 1-24). Palgrave Macmillan.

Rata, E., & Openshaw, R. (Eds.). (2007b). *Public policy and ethnicity: The politics of ethnic boundary making.* Palgrave Macmillan.

Regan, P. (2010). *Unsettling the settler within: Indian residential schools, truth telling, and reconciliation in Canada.* UBC Press.

Ritskes, E. (2011). Indigenous spirituality and decolonisation: Methodology for the classroom. In G. Dei (Ed.), *Indigenous philosophies and critical education: A reader.* Peter Lang Publishing.

Robinson, K. (2010). *Changing education paradigms*. TED. https://www.ted.com/talks/ken_robinson_changing_education_paradigms

Rolleston, W. (1880). Education: Native schools. The Native Schools Code. In *Appendix to the Journals of the House of Representatives* (Vol. Session 1, H-01f).

Royal, C., T. (2012). Politics and knowledge: Kaupapa Māori and mātauranga Māori. *New Zealand Journal of Educational Studies Te Hautaki Mātai Mātauranga o Aotearoa, 47*(2), 30–37.

Schissel, B., & Wotherspoon, T. (2003). *The legacy of school for Aboriginal people: Education, oppression, and emancipation*. Oxford University.

Select Committee of the House of Lords. (1838). *Report from the Select Committee of the House of Lords, appointed to inquire into the present state of the Islands of New Zealand, and the expediency of regulating the settlement of British subjects therein; with the minutes of evidence taken before the Committee and an index therein*. The House of Commons.

Sharma, R. (2005). Researching the spiritual: Applying soul to research practice. In G. Dei & G. Johal (Eds.), *Critical issues in anti-racist research methologies*. Peter Lang Publishing.

Shields, M., Bishop, R., & Mazawi, A. (2005). *Pathologizing practices: The impact of deficit thinking on education*. Peter Lang Publishing.

Simon, J. (1984, March 23–25). *The ideological rationale for the denial of Maoritanga*. Paper presented at the Maori Education Development Conference, Turangawaewae Marae, New Zealand.

Simon, J. (Ed.) (1998). *Ngā kura Māori; The Native Schools system 1867–1969*. Auckland University Press.

Simon, J. (2000). Education policy change: Historical perspectives. In J. Marshall, E. Coxon, K. Jenkins, & A. Jones (Eds.), *Politics, policy, pedagogy: Education in Aotearoa/New Zealand*. (pp. 25–70). Dunmore.

Simon, J., Jenkins, K., & Matthews, K. (1994). *Nga kura Maori no nga ra o mua; The Native Schools system research project progress report*. Research Unit for Māori Education, University of Auckland.

Simon, J., & Smith, L. (Eds.). (2001). *A civilising mission? Perceptions and representations of the New Zealand Native Schools system*. Auckland University Press.

Siteine, A. (2017). Daring to know: The liberal tradition and education. In C. Mutch & J. Tatebe (Eds.), *Understanding enduring ideas in education: A response to those who 'just want to be a teacher'* (pp. 67–81). NZCER Press.

Slater, L. (2020). A politics of uncertainty: Good white people, emotions and political responsibility. *Continuum, 34*(6), 816–827. https://doi.org/10.1080/10304312.2020.1842122

Smith, C. (1994). *Kimihia te maramatanga: Colonisation and iwi development*. [Master of Education thesis]. The University of Auckland.

Smith, G. (1990). *Research issues related to Māori education.* Paper presented at the NZARE Special Interest Conference, Massey University.

Smith, G. (2012). Kaupapa Māori: The dangers of domestication. *New Zealand Journal of Educational Studies. Te Hautaki Mātai Mātauranga o Aotearoa, 47*(2), 10–20.

Smith, G. (2015). The dialectic relation of theory and practice in the development of kaupapa Māori praxis. In L. Pihama, S.-J. Tiakiwai, & K. Southey (Eds.), *Kaupapa Rangahau: A reader* (2nd ed, pp. 17–28). Te Kotahi Research Institute, University of Waikato.

Smith, L. (2005). On tricky ground: Researching the native in the age of uncertainty. In N. K. Denzin & Y. S. Lincoln (Eds.), *The SAGE handbook of qualitative research* (3rd ed., pp. 85–107). SAGE Publications.

Smith, L. (2012). *Decolonizing methodologies: Research and indigenous peoples.* Zed Books.

Smith, L. (2016). Foreword: Keeping a decolonising agenda to the forefront. In J. Hutchings & J. Lee-Morgan (Eds.), *Decolonisation in Aotearoa: Education, research and practice* (pp. ix–x). NZCER Press.

Sperry, R. (1975). Left-brain, right-brain. *Saturday Review, 2*(23), 30–32.

Statistics New Zealand. (2018). *Crime and justice.* https://www.stats.govt.nz/topics/crime-and-justice

Stephenson, M. (2009). Thinking historically: Māori and settler education. In E. Rata & R. Sullivan (Eds.), *Introduction to the history of New Zealand education* (pp. 1–15). Pearson.

Tawhiwhirangi, I. (2009). Learning without teaching: Sylvia Ashton-Warner's classroom as a seed for kōhanga reo. In A. Jones & S. Middleton (Eds.), *The kiss and the ghost; Sylvia Ashton-Warner and New Zealand.* NZCER Press.

Taylor, H. (1863a). Native schools. Reports of inspectors. In Appendix to the Journals of the House of Representatives (Vol. Session 1, E-04).

Taylor, H. (1863b). Report of H. Taylor, Esq., inspector of Native Schools. In *Appendix to the Journals of the House of Representatives* (Vol. Session 1, E-9).

Te Kawariki & Network Waitangi. (2012). *Ngāpuhi speaks. He Wakaputanga o te Rangatiratanga o Nu Tireni and Te Tiriti o Waitangi: Independent report—Ngāpuhi Nui Tonu Claim.* Author.

Thiong'o, N. W. (1986). *Decolonising the mind: The politics of language in African literature.* Heinemann.

Thomson, R. (2015, 13 November). Celebrating New Zealand's first kohanga reo—150 years of news. *Dominion Post.*

Thrupp, M. (1997). School mix and the outcomes of educational quasi-markets. In M. Olssen & K. Matthews (Eds.), *Education policy in New Zealand: The 1990s and beyond* (pp. 372–390). Dunmore.

Voyce, M. (1989). Maori healers in New Zealand and the Tohunga Supression Act 1907. *Oceania*, *60*(2), 99–123.

Waitangi Tribunal. (1985). *Finding of the Waitangi Tribunal relating to Te Reo Maori and a claim by Huirangi Waikerepuru and Nga Kete Wananga*.

Walker, R. J. (1984). *Māori response to education in New Zealand*. Paper presented at the Māori Education Development Conference, Turangawaewae Marae, New Zealand.

Walker, R. J. (1990). *Ka whawhai tonu matou; Struggle without end*. Penguin Books.

Walker, R. J. (1996). *Ngā pepa a Ranginui: The Walker papers, thought-provoking views on the issues affecting Māori and Pākehā*. Penguin Books.

Walker, R. J. (2004). *Ka whawhai tonu matou: Struggle without end* (2nd ed.). Penguin Books.

Walker, R. J. (2016). Reclaiming Māori education. In J. Hutchings & J. Lee-Morgan (Eds.), *Decolonisation in Aotearoa: Education, research and practice* (pp. 19–38). NZCER Press.

Webber, M. (2011). Gifted and proud: On being exceptional and Māori. In P. Whitinui (Ed.), *Kia tangi te tītī: Permission to speak: Successful schooling for Māori students in the 21st century: Issues, challenges and alternatives* (pp. 227–241). NZCER Press.

Webber, M., & Macfarlane, A. (2019). The transformative role of iwi knowledge and genealogy in Māori student success. In E. McKinley & L. Smith (Eds.), *Handbook of indigenous education* (pp. 1049–1073). Springer.

Webber, M., McKinley, E., & Hattie, J. (2013). The importance of race and ethnicity: An exploration of New Zealand Pakeha, Maori, Samoan and Chinese adolescent identity. *New Zealand Journal of Psychology, 42*(2), pp. 17-28.

Wilson, J. (2016). *Nation and government—From colony to nation*. https://teara.govt.nz/en/document/2453/the-first-act-passed-by-parliament

Yate, R. W. (1835). *An account of New Zealand: And of the formation and progress of the Church Missionary Society's mission in the Northern Island*. R. B. Seeley and W. Burnside.

Index

28th Māori Battalion 54
    named 41

Administering for Excellence 160
Ann (ship) 77–78
appropriation of Māori concepts, creativity 102, 147
arts and crafts curriculum 146
Ashton-Warner, Sylvia 149–55
aspirations, parental 147–47, 173, 178, 203
aspirations, student 205, 207
assimilation 11, 74, 222
    through education 114–16, 123, 125, 127–28, 144, 157–58, 206
Atuawera (Te Papa Hurihia) 229

Ball, Douglas 146
Beeby, Clarence 145–46, 146, 148–49
bilingual units 131–32, 175
    limitations of 47–48, 165
Booth, Chris 43
Brash, Don 185
British law, Māori and 111–13
    see also Education Ordinance Act; justice, injustice; Native Schools Act; Tohunga Supression Act
buildings, opening rituals for 71
Busby, James 39

capacity-building in Māori communities 161
carved meeting houses, destruction of 128–29
Cavalli Islands (Motukawanui) 76
Charles III, King 35
Christianity 58, 83, 107, 222
    and cultural competence 86–88
    as whakapono tuku iho 21, 128
    see also missionaries

church boarding schools 114–20, 117–18
Church Missionary Society (CMS) 80, 83, 86
Clark, Helen 161
Clarke, George 120–22
Closing the Gaps 161
Coates, Danderson 85–86
co-governance, Proclamation of NZ as 39
colonisation 6, 32, 88, 141, 185, 220
    arguments against 85
    education and 47, 59, 61, 68, 95, 123, 125, 130, 144
    history of 196, 220–23
    impacts of 204, 207
    symbolism of 44
    Tai Tokerau perspectives of 21, 31–32
    through assimilation 114–15, 123, 129–30
confidence 138, 147, 166, 220
    as teacher attribute 169, 212–13, 227
confidence-building in learners 168, 173–74, 212
Constitutional Advisory Panel 41
corporal punishment in schools 119–20
Cruise, Richard 34
cultural competence 2–3
    assessment of 136, 176–77
    and cultural knowledge 109–10
    early definitions of 86–88, 125–26
    non-Māori and 104–06
    as unhelpful concept 163–64, 216–20, 227
    see also cultural understanding
cultural development 204–05
cultural identity 92–93, 208–10
cultural knowledge 53–54, 109–10, 167, 194, 213
    Māori control over 216–17, 225
        advisory hubs for 218–19, 228

cultural locatedness 181
cultural understanding 58-60, 218, 227

day schools (for Māori) 88, 120-22
decolonising methodologies 27, 183
deficit theory, thinking 157, 158-59, 161-62, 163
Department of Conservation (DoC) 92
Durie, Mason 220

education, politics of 61, 141-42
    and Māori resistance 155-62
education, traditional 68, 93-96, 207-08
Education Act 1877 68, 124-27
Education Council New Zealand 194
Education Department (Ministry) of 3-4, 194
    Sylvia Ashton-Warner and 149
Education Ordinance Act 1847 114-16
education success "as Māori" 2-3, 45-46, 166-68, 177-78, 191, 192-93
    kaumātua framework for 216-20
    kaumātua perceptions of 205-06, 210-12
    Māori perceptions of 219-20
    systemic responsibility for 196-98, 223-25
education systems and philosophies 86-90, 124-27, 140-49
    Māori relationships with 49-50, 196-198
Empowering Education. Te Ihi, Te Mana, Te Mātauranga 161
England, Māori trips to 34-35, 77, 80-82, 107
English print literacy 79-83, 88-89
    see also Western education
environment, care and management of 17, 55, 91-92
ethics committee, University of Auckland 15
ethnic (identity) politics 183-91
evictions, forced 157

fear as obstruction to education success 199

Fraser, Peter 145, 146

gaoling, practice of 113
generational trauma 92-93, 110, 113
George III, King 77
George IV, King 33, 35, 41
Gerlich, R 146
Gibson, R 8
Grey, George 115-6, 222

hair-cutting, ceremonial 68
hapū, roles of 35, 182
    and kāhui rangatira 29, 72, 113
He Whakaputanga 1835 32, 35-36, 38-41, 85
    and Māori-Crown relations 186
He Whakaputanga o Te Puea 103
Health and Physical Education Curriculum, wairuatanga in 211
Heke, Hone 36
Henare, Erima 5, 37, 40, 41-42, 65
Henare, Himi (James) 41, 43, 58, 66, 111, 179
Hetaraka, Janet 15, 41, 181, 191, 200, 211
    pūkōrero 25, 165-78
Hetaraka, Te Warihi 15, 67, 69, 73, 195-96, 209, 214-15, 219
    Hori Parata on 108
    pūkōrero 25, 43-59
    and WAI 262 claim 224
Hetaraka, Wiki Te Pirihi 9
Hīhīaua (Precinct) 43-44
    The Shed 43, 132, 166
Hika, Hongi 33-35, 39, 41, 79, 80
history, historical understanding 33, 134, 196, 198, 213-14, 229
    non-Māori teachers and 58, 134
Hoani Waititi Marae 159
Hohepa, Patu 30, 157
Hongi, Eruera Pare 35-36
Hongi Hika. See Hika, Hongi
Hunn Report (1961) 156-57
Hurihia, Te Papa (Atuawera) 229
Hurukokoti 76

identity, "as Māori" 93-94, 138-39, 180-83

identity politics 183–85, 187–89, 191
individuality, education and 95–96, 132–33, 139–41, 206–08
industrial training. *See* manual training
institutional memory 97–98, 111, 214
integration policies 155–57, 160
intellectual property 103, 216
    knowledge as 76–79
iwi, identity as 180, 181–82

Jackson, Moana 103–04, 229
justice, injustice 7, 92, 112–13, 129, 156, 165, 190, 214

Ka Hikitia - Ka Hāpaitia 4
Ka Hikitia - Managing for Success: The Māori Education Strategy 2008-2012 3–4, 180–81, 193, 204
Kākā Porowini, Kākā 112
kape tī, kape tā 67
karakia, meaning of 23
kare ā roto 211–12
kauae raro, kauae runga 63–65, 69–75, 148
    and mātauranga Māori 200
kaumātua, kāhui kaumātua 16, 30, 101–03
    research context 14–17
    roles of 4, 135–36
kaupapa Māori theory 142–43, 183
    as research framework 188, 189–90
Kauri Dieback Programme 108
Kawharu, Hugh 157
Kawiti, Te Ruki (The Oath of) 19–22, 123, 179
Kēnana, Rua 129
Kendall, Thomas 34, 78, 80
    and cultural competence 87
King, Philip 76
King Charles III 35
King George III 77
King George IV 33, 35, 41
Kingitanga, the 118, 123
knowledge 16–17
    as intellectual property 76–79, 103–04, 216–17
    Pākehā 34–35, 80, 83

    as tapu 62–63, 69–70
    see also mātauranga Māori
knowledge bases. *See* kauae raro, kauae runga
kōhanga reo 155, 158, 159
kōhuru, tuhi kōhuru 65–66
korae, tuhi korae 65–66
Korokoro 39, 80, 82
kura ā iwi bilingual units 175
Kura Hourua (Special Character School) 54, 175
kura kaupapa Māori 155, 159, 175

land alienation 85, 120, 123–125, 129, 157
Land Wars (New Zealand Wars) 122–23
    as "Māori Wars" 118
language conflict 92–93
liberalism and education system 142–44
liberal-progressive education philosophies 144–49, 162–64
listening 136, 137–38, 228–29
    as research tool 18–19
    as rongo 212

Mahanga (Moehanga) 33–34, 107
Mahi Ngutu 54–55
Mair, Gilbert 98
mana, mana Māori 33, 61, 140, 161, 202
mana tuku iho 229
Manaia 80
manual (industrial) training in schools 116, 118–19, 126, 146, 148
Māori, stereotyping of 119, 147, 151–52, 154–55, 162, 206
Māori Affairs, Department (Ministry) of 156, 182
Māori Arts and Crafts Act 1926 146
Māori church schools, independent 117
Māori Council 41
Māori creativity, appropriation of 147
Māori culture (kaupapa Māori) 46–48, 70, 105, 201
    see also cultural competence
Māori Education Development Conference 1984 159

Māori 'elitism' 69, 184, 187
Māori land. *See* land alienation
Māori Potential Approach 141, 155, 161, 163
Māori Synod, Presbyterian Church 156
Māori teachers. *See* teachers, Māori
Māori-Crown relationship 32, 40-42, 106-07, 111-12, 113, 122-23, 182-83, 186
  and education goals 222-23
  as rangatira-to-rangatira 33, 35-37
Māori-Pākehā relationships 6-7, 34-35, 75-77
  see also missionaries; racism
māreikura 68
Marsden, Māori 24, 73
Marsden, Samuel 34, 77-79, 80, 84, 86, 87
mātauranga Māori 70, 74-75, 129
  in education system 51-54, 61-65, 201-02, 226
  in English-medium schools 55-56, 100-03, 175-76, 198-202, 217
    see also teachers (non-Māori)
  see also knowledge
mātauranga tuku iho 16, 25, 74, 200
Māui 11, 63-64
Mead, Hirini 63, 69, 74, 157
Metge, J 206
Ministry of Education. *See* Education, Department (Ministry) of
missionaries 34, 77-82, 84-89
  mission schools 88, 117, 118, 120
Moehanga (Mahanga) 33-34
moko kauae 178-79
monoculturalism in education 88, 98-100
Motukawanui (Cavalli Islands) 76
Murihiku, early contact in 75-76
Murirangawhenua 63-64

Native Exemption Ordinance 1844 112
Native Schools Act 1867 117, 120, 122, 127
  and land alienation 123-124
Native Schools Code 1880 120, 125-27
Native Schools system 117-120, 122, 146, 147
Network Waitangi 32, 39
New Zealand Army 91

New Zealand Association for Research in Education (NZARE) 185
Ngā Hapū o Tai Tokerau 41
Ngā Puhi 11, 20, 80, 229
Ngā Puhi Nui Tonu (WAI 1040) 32
Ngāi Tahu 11, 75
Ngāi Tai 11
Ngāpuhi Speaks 32
Ngare Raumati 39, 80
Ngata, Apirana 146-47
Ngāti Hine 20
Ngāti Kuri 92
Ngāti Māmoe 11, 75
Ngāti Manaia, Manaia 43, 80
Ngāti Paoa 11
Ngāti Wai 11, 44
  Pukepoto Pā 20
Ngāti Wai Kāhui Kaumātua 92
Nicholas, John 34
non-Māori students 84, 153
non-Māori teachers. *See* teachers, non-Māori
Norfolk Island 76

Oath of Kawiti. *See* Kawiti, Te Ruki
Ōhaeawae, Battle of 20
Ōkiato 98

Pākehā, stereotyping of 151-52, 154-55
Parata, Hori 15, 30
  pūkōrero 25, 33-34, 91-110
parents, role in education 47, 49-50, 173, 203-04
  see also whānau
Parliament (NZ), power transferred to 122-23
Parramatta, Australia 80
Pātaua 91
Picot, Brian 160
Pihama, Leonie 185, 190
Place-Based Education 60
poai Pākehā 19, 21-22, 116, 179
positionality 8-12
Presbyterian Church, Māori Synod of 156
pre-school education 174-75

see also kōhanga reo
Proclamation of New Zealand 1808 39
puhi, role of 71
Pukepoto Pā (Ngāti Wai) 20
pūrākau 63–64
    pūkōrero and 17–18

Queen Victoria 37, 113, 229

racism 74, 147, 165–66, 185
    institutional 27, 122, 155, 156, 162, 206
racist academic discourse 13
rangatira Māori 5, 29–30, 34–35, 75
    Hori Parata as 108
    and Native Exemption Ordinance 1844 112
    rangatira-to-rangatira relationship. See Māori-Crown relationship
    see also Te Wakaminenga
rangatiratanga 22, 27, 32, 36, 39, 143, 202, 205, 219, 223
    and liberalism 143
Rangihoua mission school 88
Ratana, Tahupōtiki 129
relationships in education 153–54, 193–95, 225–26
    kaumātua perceptions of 195–205
relationships. See Māori-Crown relationship
research premise 2–3
researcher identity 8–9, 52–53, 185
    school experience 131–32, 165–66, 199
resourcing 173, 202
    of Indigenous knowledge holders 218–19
ritual for opening buildings 71
Ruapekapeka, Battle of 20–21
Ruatara 39, 77–79, 80, 84
Runanga Iwi Act 1990 182–83

Select Committee on the Islands of New Zealand (UK House of Lords) 85
self-confidence as teacher attribute 169, 212–13, 227
Simōn, Edna née Veitch 9

Simōn, George 9
socioeconomic mediation 143–44
Special Character School (Kura Hourua) 54
spirituality. See wairua, wairuatanga

tā moko 66–67, 81, 179
"taha Māori" programmes 158–59
Tai Tokerau 27–28, 75–76
    carved meeting houses eradicated 128–29
    and He Whakaputanga 35
    Māori-Pākeha early contact 75–76
    and poai Pākehā 21–22
    and Te Wakaminenga 38
    see also Ngāpuhi Speaks
Tainui 11
Takitimu 11
takutaku, tauparapara 19–24, 62–63
    as analysis tool 25–26, 139
Taonui, Aperahama 113
Tātaiako: Cultural Competencies for Teachers of Māori Learners 2–3, 164, 181
    analysis, criticisms of 4, 13–14, 196, 212, 220–21, 225–26
    and Māori cultural knowledge 200–01
    and reciprocal relationships 193–94, 204
    Tangata Whenuatanga competency 198
    and teacher attributes 169–70
tatau pounamu 35–36
Tawhiwhirangi, I 153
Taylor, Henry 117–18, 119–20, 121–22
Te Hāpuku 40*ft*
Te Ika Nui ā Māui (North Island) 64
Te Kawariki 32, 39
Te Pahi 77
Te Puni Kōkiri 161, 182
Te Pūtake o te Riri (The Source of the Fury) 122–23
Te Rangi Hiroa 23
te reo Māori 158–59, 176, 208
    Christianity and 86–88

removed from curriculum 123
types of 65–66
Te Rūnanga Nui and WAI 1718 160
Te Tiriti o Waitangi 5*ft*, 30, 32, 35, 41–42, 229
    and education systems 201, 214, 223–25
    and He Whakaputanga 38
    and Māori-Crown relations 20, 186
    as tatau pounamu 35–37
    and The Treaty of Waitangi 36–37, 41–42, 111–12, 130, 186
    universal kaupapa of 48–49
Te Wakaminenga 21, 35–36, 38–40, 128
    and mātauranga tuku iho 74
Te Whero Whero 40*ft*
Teacher. See Ashton-Warner, Sylvia
teachers 169–70, 203, 227–28
    of Māori students 210–12
    responsibilities of 171–72, 196, 224
teachers, Māori 76, 82, 87–88, 121–22, 157–58, 213
    responsibilities of 51, 56–58, 170–71, 172
teachers, non-Māori, and te ao Māori 104–05, 134–35, 171, 201, 212–13, 227–28
    see also Ashton-Warner, Sylvia
Teachers' Council of New Zealand (TCNZ) 3
'The Shed'. *See* Hīhīaua (Precinct)
The Source of the Fury (Te Pūtake o te Riri) 122–23
tikanga Māori 71, 131–32, 184–85, 288
    as research framework 8, 17–19, 188
Titere 80–82
tohunga 24, 62
Tohunga Suppression Act 1907 128–29
Tomorrow's Schools 160
Treaty of Waitangi 5*ft*, 36–37, 38, 40, 41, 186–87
    and British law 111–12, 114, 130
    settlement process 183*ft*
trust 50, 73
    knowledge sharing and 54, 104–05, 202, 216–17, 219, 225

Tuai 36, 79–83, 87
tuakana-teina relationship 82
tuakiritanga. *See* identity
tuhi kohuru 65–66
tuhi korae 65–66, 72
tuhi marae kura 65–66, 72
Tukitāhua 76

University of Auckland Human Participants Ethics Committee 15
urban drift 157

village as concept 50–51, 54, 55, 57, 60–61, 214–15
violence against children 119–20

wairua, wairuatanga 133, 134, 189, 211, 227
    Christianity and 83
    as research tool 19
    and secular education 59, 68–69
Waitangi Tribunal 157, 159–60, 183*ft*
    claims:
        Ngā Puhi Nui Tonu (WAI 1040) 32
        WAI 262 103–04, 224
        WAI 1718 160
Waka and Wave sculpture 44–45
wānanga, *Tātaiako* concept of 212
    see also whare wānanga
Western education 36, 88–90, 115–16
    divergent goals of 221–23
    monocultural history of 107, 197–98
Wetere, Koro 182
whakapapa 53, 69, 167, 188–89, 208
    of researcher 10–12
    weaponisation of 183
whakatauākī, whakataukī 29, 65, 109, 178–79
whānau 50–51
    in education system 136–37, 203–05
    role of 173–75
whanaungatanga 170, 193–95
Whangaruru 9, 91, 125
whare wānanga 36, 61, 62–63, 66, 67–68, 72, 80, 89
    see also wānanga

*Te Kauae Tuku Iho / Inheriting the sacred jawbone:
Indigenous knowledge holders re-imagine education*

Whautere, Te Aupouri (Uncle Buster) 15,
    164, 165, 211
    pūkōrero 25, 131–40
white spaces 187–88, 196, 223
women as educators 168, 178–79

Yate, William 85, 112–13

www.ingramcontent.com/pod-product-compliance
Lightning Source LLC
Chambersburg PA
CBHW080802300426
44114CB00020B/2800